TALKIN
AND
TESTIFYIN

TALKIN AND TESTIFYIN

The Language of Black America

Geneva Smitherman

Wayne State University Press, Detroit

Originally published by Houghton Mifflin Company, 1977. Copyright © 1977 by Wayne State University Press, Detroit, Michigan 48202. All rights are reserved. No part of this book may be reproduced without formal permission.

Waynebook 51

92   91   90   89   88   6   5   4   3   2

Library of Congress Cataloging-in-Publication Data

Smitherman, Geneva.
  Talkin and testifyin.

  (Waynebook; 51)
  Reprint. Originally published: Boston: Houghton Mifflin, 1977. With new afterword.
  Bibliography: p.
  Includes index.
  1. Black English. 2. Afro -Americans—Language. 3. English language—United States. 4. Americanisms. I. Title.
PE3102.N42S5 1985   427'.008996073   85-22615
ISBN 0-8143-1805-3

The author is grateful for permission to reprint from the following sources:
  "I Can't Get Next to You" by Norman Whitfield and Barrett Strong © 1969 Jobete Music Co., Inc. and "I'll Try Something New" by William Robinson, © 1961 by Jobete Music Co., Inc. All Rights Reserved. Reprinted by Permission • "Grammar and Goodness" in *Simple Stakes a Claim* by Langston Hughes, reprinted by permission of Harold Ober Associates, Inc. Copyright © 1957 by Langston Hughes. Copyright renewed 1985 by George Houston Bass • "Mister Toussan" by Ralph Ellison, reprinted by permission of William Morris Agency, Inc., on behalf of the author. Copyright © 1941 (renewed) by Ralph Ellison • *The Autobiography of Malcolm X* by Malcolm X with the assistance of Alex Haley, reprinted by permission of Random House, Inc., and Hutchinson Publishing Group, Ltd. Copyright © 1964 by Alex Haley and Malcolm X. Copyright © 1965 by Alex Haley and Betty Shabbaz • *Sundiata: An Epic of Old Mali* by D. T. Niane, translated by G. D. Pickett, reprinted by permission of Longman Group Limited and Humanities Press, Inc., New Jersey • *Bridge — A Cross-Culture Reading Program*, copyright © 1977 by Houghton Mifflin Company • *Black Boy* (pp. 68–71, hardbound edition) by Richard Wright, copyright 1937, 1942, 1944, 1945 by Richard Wright. By permission of Harper & Row, Publishers, Inc. • "Don't You Know I Love You" by Ahmet Ertegun, copyright © 1953 by Progressive Music Publishing Co., Inc. Copyright assigned to Unichappell Music, Inc. International Copyright Secured. ALL RIGHTS RESERVED. Used by permission.

To my family, who understood and helped me "git ovuh"; to Edna and Beverly, who loved me and kept the faith; to all those who believe in the New World, knowing that our collective Will can bring that World into being; and to Jeff

CONTENTS

CHAPTER 1

From Africa to the New World and into the Space Age   1
Introduction and History of Black English Structure

CHAPTER 2

"It Bees Dat Way Sometime"   16
Sounds and Structure of Present-Day Black English

CHAPTER 3

Black Semantics   35
Words and Concepts in Black English, Past and Present

CHAPTER 4

"How I Got Ovuh"   73
African World View and Afro-American Oral Tradition

CHAPTER 5

"The Forms of Things Unknown"   101
Black Modes of Discourse

CHAPTER 6

Where It's At   167
Black–White Language Attitudes

CHAPTER 7

Where Do We Go from Here? T.C.B.!   201
Social Policy and Educational Practice

AFTERWORD   242

APPENDIX A
Some Well-Known Black Proverbs and Sayings   245

APPENDIX B
Get Down Exercises on Black English Sounds
and Structure   247

APPENDIX C
Black Semantics — A Selected Glossary   251

Notes   261

Bibliography   265

Index   277

TALKIN
AND
TESTIFYIN

From Africa to the New World and into the Space Age

Introduction and History of Black English Structure

"WHAT IT IS! What it is!"
"That cat name Shaft is a bad mother —" "Hush yo mouf!"
"Can't nobody never do nothin in Mr. Smith class."
"Least my momma don't buy her furniture from the Good Will!"
"I come here today to testify what the Lord done did for me."
"It bees dat way sometime."
What it is! What is it? It is the voice of Black America, variously labeled Black English, Black Dialect, Black Idiom, or recently, Ebonics. Black writer Claude Brown, author of *Manchild in the Promised Land,* called it the "language of soul." White writer Norman Mailer named it the "language of hip." Some folk, like black poet Nikki Giovanni, refer to it as just plain "black talk."

Before about 1959 (when the first study was done to change black speech patterns), Black English had been primarily the interest of university academics, particularly the historical linguists and cultural anthropologists. In recent years, though, the issue has become a very hot controversy, and there have been articles on Black Dialect in the national press as well as in the educational research literature. We have had pronouncements on black speech from the NAACP and the Black Panthers, from highly publicized scholars of the Arthur Jensen–William Shockley bent, from executives of national corporations such as Greyhound, and from housewives and community folk. I mean, really, it seem like everybody and they momma done had something to say on the subject!

Now, concern over the speech of blacks and educational programs to bring about dialect change have been generated by two major forces. The first major force was the social change movements (or upheavals — depending on where you comin from) of the sixties, spearheaded by the 1954 Supreme Court school desegregation decision, followed by the 1955 refusal of black Rosa Parks to move to the back of the bus, and the emergence of Martin Luther King, Jr., and the civil rights thrust, followed by black power and the black cultural consciousness movement. The second major force was embodied in White America's attempt to deal with this newly released black energy by the implementation of poverty programs, educational and linguistic remediation projects, sociolinguistic research programs, and various other up-from-the-ghetto and "Great Society" efforts. As we all know, these two forces have not acted in concert. While blacks were shouting "I'm black and I'm proud," Anglos were admonishing them to "be like us" and enter the mainstream. While you had black orators, creative artists, and yes, even scholars rappin in the Black Thang, educators (some of them black, to be sure) were preaching the Gospel that Black English speakers must learn to talk like White English speakers in order to "make it."

Much that you hear nowadays about Black Dialect tends to be general and to focus on global concerns over social policy and political matters, with insufficient attention to elements of the language itself and the historical background and sociocultural development of that language (aside from the special academics mentioned earlier). That has been unfortunate because we need much more knowledge about the language and the way it functions in the communication system of blacks. Therefore, let us get off this global trip and get down to the nitty-gritty of answering the questions, just what *is* Black English, where did it come from and what are the implications for black-white interaction and teaching black children?

In a nutshell: Black Dialect is an Africanized form of English reflecting Black America's linguistic-cultural African heritage and the conditions of servitude, oppression and life in America. Black Language is Euro-American speech with an Afro-American meaning, nuance, tone, and gesture. The Black Idiom is used by 80 to 90 percent of American blacks, at least some of the time. It has allowed blacks to create a culture of survival in an alien land, and as a by-product has served to enrich the language of all Americans.

Think of black speech as having two dimensions: language and style. Though we will separate the two for purposes of analysis, they are often overlapping. This is an important point, frequently overlooked in discussions of Black English. Consider two examples. Nina Simone sing: "It bees dat way sometime." Here the language aspect is the use of the verb *be* to indicate a recurring event or habitual condition, rather than a one-time-only occurrence. But the total expression — "It bees dat way sometime" — also reflects Black English style, for the statement suggests a point of view, a way of looking at life, and a method of adapting to life's realities. To live by the philosophy of "It bees dat way sometime" is to come to grips with the changes that life bees puttin us through, and to accept the changes and bad times as a constant, ever-present reality.

Reverend Jesse Jackson preach: "Africa would if Africa could. America could if America would. But Africa cain't and America ain't." Now here Reverend Jesse is using the language of Black Dialect when he says "ain't" and when he pronounces *can't* as "cain't." But the total expression, using black rhythmic speech, is the more powerful because the Reb has plugged into the style of Black Dialect. The statement thus depends for full communication on what black poet Eugene Redmond calls "songified" pattern and on an Afro-American cultural belief set. That belief holds that White America has always failed blacks and will continue to do so; and that going back to Africa or getting any help from African countries is neither feasible nor realistic because newly emerging African nations must grapple first with problems of independence (economic and otherwise) inherited from centuries of European colonization.

These two very eloquent examples of Black English illustrate that the beauty and power of the idiom lies in its succinctness: saying the same thing in standard written English has taken more than ten times as many words. Black English, then, is a language mixture, adapted to the conditions of slavery and discrimination, a combination of language and style interwoven with and inextricable from Afro-American culture.

Where did this black language and style come from? To an-

swer this question, we have to begin at least as far back as 1619 when a Dutch vessel landed in Jamestown with a cargo of twenty Africans. The arrival of this slaveship marked the beginning of slavery in Colonial America. What kind of language did these and immediately succeeding generations of slaves speak? Was it Ibo, Yoruba, Hausa, some other West African language, Pidgin English? We know that these "new Negroes" (as they were often described in Colonial America) did not jump fresh off the boat doing the Bump and speaking White English! Yet we don't have any tape or phono recordings, nor any other actual direct speech samples of early Black American English. Thus we have to rely on reconstructions of black talk based on indirect evidence, such as representations of Black Dialect in White and Black American literature, written reproductions of the dialect in journals, letters, and diaries by whites, and generalized commentary about slave speech, usually also from whites. Another important source of evidence is based on analogies of Black American speech characteristics with those of other English-based pidgins and creoles found in the Caribbean and in parts of Africa. Language systems such as Jamaican Creole or Nigerian Pidgin English are still in active use today and provide a kind of linguistic mirror image of Black American (Pidgin and Creole) English in its early stages of development.

What this image suggests is as follows. African slaves in America initially developed a pidgin, a language of transaction, that was used in communication between themselves and whites. Over the years, the pidgin gradually became widespread among slaves and evolved into a creole. Developed without benefit of any formal instruction (not even a language lab!), this lingo involved the substitution of English for West African words, but within the same basic structure and idiom that characterized West African language patterns. For example, West African languages allow for the construction of sentences without a form of the verb *to be*. Thus we get a typical African-English Pidgin sentence such as "He tell me he God," used by Tituba, a slave from the island of Barbados in the British West Indies, and recorded by Justice Hathorne at the Salem witch trial in 1692. In Tituba's *he God* statement, the words are English, but the grammar or structure is West African. Such sentence patterns, without any form of the verb *be*, can frequently be heard in virtually any modern-day black community.

Now, as anyone learning a foreign tongue knows, the vocabularly of the new language is fairly easy to master; to some extent, sounds are also. But syntactical structure and idiomatic rules require considerable time and practice to master. Moreover, the one item of a language that remains relatively rigid and fixed over time is its structure. The formation of this Black American English Pidgin demonstrates, then, simply what any learner of a new language does. They* attempt to fit the words and sounds of the new language into the basic idiomatic mold and structure of their native tongue. For example, when I used to teach English to foreign students at the university, I once had a German student render Patrick Henry's famous motto as "Give me the liberty or the death." He was generalizing from the German rule which dictates that definite articles must accompany nouns. Similarly, when I used to teach high school Latin, I'd get native English speakers (whites) who would insist on using the apostrophe rather than the proper case ending to indicate possession, producing, for instance, *agricola's filia* (or sometimes even worse, *agricolae's filia*) for *the farmer's daughter*. And then there is the typical error of the English speaker learning French who forms the compound *paille-chapeau* on the model of *straw hat*.

Below are a few of the West African language rules that were grafted onto early Black English, and which still operate in Black English today.

Grammar and Structure Rule in West African Languages	Black English
Repetition of noun subject with pronoun	My father, he work there.

---

*In traditional usage, this sentence would have begun with the masculine pronoun "he," since it refers to "any learner," which is singular. However, due to the public's increased awareness of sexist uses of the English language, plural pronouns have now become acceptable substitutes for the masculine singular. I will continue to follow this procedure throughout, along with using "his or her." For an excellent set of guidelines for avoiding sexist language use, see "Guideline for Nonsexist Use of Language in NCTE Publications," National Council of Teachers of English.

Question patterns without *do*	What it come to?
Same form of noun for singular and plural	one boy; five boy
No tense indicated in verb; emphasis on manner or character of action	I know it good when he ask me
Same verb form for all subjects	I know; you know; he know; we know; they know

SOUND RULE IN WEST AFRICAN LANGUAGES	BLACK ENGLISH
No consonant pairs	*jus* (for *just*); *men* (for *mend*)
Few long vowels or two-part vowels (diphthongs)	*rat* or *raht* (for *right*); *tahm* (for *time*)
No /r/ sound	*mow* (for *more*)
No /th/ sound	Black English speaker substitutes /d/ or /t/ for /th/; thus *souf* (for *south*) and *dis* (for *this*)

The slave's application of his or her intuitive knowledge of West African rules to English helped bridge the communications gap between slave and master. However, the slaves also had the problem of communicating with each other. It was the practice of slavers to mix up Africans from different tribes, so in any slave community there would be various tribal languages such as Ibo, Yoruba, Hausa. Even though these African language systems shared general structural commonalities, still they differed in vocabulary. Thus the same English-African language mixture that was used between slave and master had also to be used between slave and slave. All this notwithstanding, it is only logical to assume that the newly arrived Africans were, for a time at least, bilingual, having command of both their native African tongue and the English pidgin as well. However, there was no opportunity to speak and thus reinforce their native language, and as new generations of slaves were born in the New World, the native African speech was heard and used less and less, and the English pidgin and creole varieties more and more. Needless to say, didn't nobody sit down and decide, consciously and deliberately, that this was the way it was gon be — languages, pidgins, creoles, dialects was all like Topsy: they jes grew.

Unfortunately, we have little empirical record of this growth in what we may call its incubation period, that is, for the period from the arrival of the first slaves in 1619 up until the Revolutionary War in 1776. In point of fact, not until 1771 do we get an actual recorded sample of Black American speech *from a black*. (Slightly before this time, there are a few recorded instances of *whites* trying to speak "Negro" in addressing both slaves and Indians.) In the comedy *Trial of Atticus Before Justice Beau, for a Rape,* written in 1771, a Massachusetts Negro named Caesar is given a bit part in the play — two short lines — in which he says:

> Yesa, Master, he tell me that Atticus he went to bus [kiss] 'em one day, and a shilde [child] cry, and so he let 'em alone . . . Cause, Master, I bus him myself.

Though scant, this speech sample is striking for its parallel to modern-day black speech forms. For example, note the lack of *-s* on the verb in *he tell* and the repetition of the subject in *Atticus he*. Contemporary Black English examples are found in sentences like "The teacher, he say I can't go" and "My brother, he know how to fix it."

As mentioned, if we broaden our scope to encompass African slaves in English-speaking communities outside the United States, we can pick up some additional cogent examples of early Black Dialect that parallel the structure of many sentences heard in contemporary Black America. For instance, there is the seventeenth-century statement of Tituba, "He tell me he God," which was alluded to earlier, and there is a 1718 representation of black speech from the colony of Surinam in South America: "Me bella well" (I am very well). Both sentences parallel contemporary Black English structures like *My momma do that all the time* (no-*s* on verb *do*), and *They rowdy* (no form of verb *to be* in the sentence). Toby, a Barbadian slave in 1715, used plural forms like "There

lives white mans, white womans, negree mans, negree womans
. . ." These forms are similar to today's Black English plurals in
phrases like *five womens* and *these mens*. A possible explanation for
the derivation of this kind of plural is the process of "hypercorrection." That is, in trying to appropriate White English without the
aid of specified grammatical rules (or teachers to teach the rules),
the African speaker took the initiative and made some rather
sensible deductions and analogies about English speech forms.
Thus, if in English an *-s* is used to indicate the plural, then
logically you should put an *-s* on all words in the plural — we have
one boy, two boys, and *one book, two books*, so why not *one man, two
mans* (or *two mens*), and *one child, two childrens*? Another kind of
hypercorrection is in the use of *-s* in certain verb forms. Not being
exactly sure where the *-s* goes, the speaker chooses the *-s* with
many subject-verb combinations (just to make sure!). Since English requires us to say *he does*, why not *I does*? (And is it *he do* and
they does, or *he does*, and *they do*?)

Though hypercorrection accounts for a small number of
Black Dialect patterns, Black English's main structural components are, of course, the adaptations based on African language
rules. The historical development we are reconstructing here is
the continuity of Africanisms in Black English throughout time
and space. We can possibly get a firmer grasp of the total historic
picture by considering just one aspect of Black English structure
from the early days to the present and from within as well as outside of the United States. Note, then, the following summary illustration of "zero copula" in Black English (that is, sentence patterns with no form of the verb *to be*).

He tell me he God. *Barbados, 1692*
Me bella well (I am very well.) *Surinam, 1718*
Me massa name Cunney Tomsee. (My master's name is Colonel
    Thompson.) *U.S., 1776*
Me den very grad. (I am then very glad.) *U.S., 1784*
You da deble. (You are the devil.) *U.S., 1792*
He worse than ebber now. *U.S., 1821*
What dis in heah? (What is this in here?) *U.S., 1859*
But what de matter with Jasper? (But what is the matter with Jas-
    per?) *U.S., 1882*

Don't kere, he somethin' t'other wif dis here Draftin' Bo'd. (I don't
   care, he is something or other [signifying person of authority]
   with this Draft Board.)   *U.S.*, 1926
'E mean tid' dat. (He is mean to do that.)   *Gullah Creole, from the
   Sea Islands, U.S.*, 1949
Di kaafi kuol. (The coffee is cold.)   *Jamaica*, 1966
They some rowdy kids.   *U.S.*, 1968
A siki. (He sick.)   *Surinam*, 1972
This my mother. *U.S.*, 1975

It is true that a number of early Black American English forms
have survived until the present day, but it is also true that the
distance between contemporary Black and White American English is not as great as it once was. And certainly it is not as great
as the distance between, say, contemporary Jamaican Creole English and the English of White America and Britain. How have
time and circumstance affected the African element in Black
American English? The answer to this question lies in the impact
of mainstream American language and culture on Black
America, and in the sheer fact of the smaller ratio of blacks to
whites in this country (as compared to overwhelmingly huge
black populations in the Caribbean and in Africa). With such
close linguistic-cultural contact, the influence of the majority culture and language on its minorities is powerful indeed, and
there is great pressure on the minorities to assimilate and adopt
the culture and language of the majority.

In the early period of American history, the African experience was very immediate and real to the slaves and many
yearned to escape back to Africa. As time progressed, though,
the African slave became rather firmly entrenched in the New
World, and hopes of returning to the motherland began to seem
more like unattainable fantasies. Having thus resigned themselves to a future in the New World, many slaves began to take
on what Langston Hughes has termed the "ways of white folks"
— their religion, culture, customs, and, of course, language. At
the same time, though, there were strong resistance movements
against enslavement and the oppressive ways of white folks.
Thus, from the very beginning, we have the "push-pull" syndrome in Black America, that is, *pushing* toward White American

culture while simultaneously *pulling* away from it. (W. E. B. DuBois used the term "double consciousness" to refer to this ambivalence among blacks.) A striking example of the phenomenon is the case of the ex-slave Absalom Jones, founder of one of the first separate black church movements within white Protestant denominations. Jones took on the white man's religion, and proceeded to practice it. (The "push.") Yet when he attempted to pray in a white church in Philadelphia in 1787, an usher pulled him from his knees and ousted him from the church. Thereupon, Jones, along with another ex-slave, Richard Allen, established the African Methodist Episcopal Church. (The "pull.")

The "push-pull" momentum is evidenced in the historical development of Black English in the push toward Americanization of Black English counterbalanced by the pull of retaining its Africanization. We may use the term "de-creolization" to refer to the push toward Americanizing of the language. As slaves became more American and less African, the Black English Creole also became less Africanized. It began to be leveled out in the direction of White English and to lose its distinctive African structural features — that is, the Black English Creole became de-creolized. This process was undoubtedly quite intense and extensive during the Abolitionist period and certainly following Emancipation. It was a primary tactic of Abolitionists (and, traditionally, all fighters for the black cause) to prove blacks equal to whites and therefore worthy of freedom and equality. How could blacks claim American equality if they were not speaking American lingo? Ay, but here we come to the rub or the pull. For blacks have never really been viewed or treated as equals, thus their rejection of White American culture and English — and hence today the process of de-creolization remains unfinished (not to mention various undercurrent and sporadic efforts at re-creolization, such as that among writers, artists, and black intellectuals of the 1960s, who deliberately wrote and rapped in the Black Idiom and sought to preserve its distinctiveness in the literature of the period).

The dynamics of push-pull can help to illuminate the complex sociolinguistic situation that continues to exist in Black America.

That is, while some blacks speak very Black English, there are others who speak very White English, and still others who are competent in both linguistic systems. Historically, black speech has been demanded of those who wish to retain close affinities with the black community, and intrusions of White English are likely to be frowned upon and any black users thereof promptly ostracized by the group. Talkin proper (trying to sound white) just ain considered cool. On the other hand, White America has insisted upon White English as the price of admission into its economic and social mainstream. Moreover, there is a psychological factor operating here: people tend to feel more comfortable when they can relax and rap within the linguistic framework that has been the dialect of their nurture, childhood, identity, and style. Hence, even when there is no compelling social pressure to use Black English, there may be an inner compulsion to "talk black."

Let us return to history for a minute to gain a broader understanding of these dynamics. Slaves continued to be imported into America at least up to 1808 when the African slave trade was outlawed by federal legislation. In a sense, we can extend the date even further since the Slave Trade Act was not rigidly enforced. (As late as 1858, just three years before the Civil War, over 400 slaves were brought direct from Africa to Georgia.) This constant influx of slaves made the black community one where there were always numbers of slaves who could speak no English at all. Some idea of the linguistic situation in Black America can be gleaned from newspaper advertisements about runaway slaves. These ads generally cited the slave's degree of competence in English as a method of identification. Judging from the advertisements, there were, linguistically speaking, three groups of African slaves in Colonial times.

The recent arrivals ("new" Negroes) knew practically no English at all. An ad in the *New York Evening Post* in 1774 read: "Ran away . . . a new Negro Fellow named Prince, he can't scarce speak a Word of English."

Then there were slaves who were not born in the U.S. but had been here some time and were still in the process of learning English; some of these were referred to as speakers of either "bad" English or only "tolerable" English. In 1760 the *North-Carolina Gazette* ran this ad: "Ran away from the Subscriber, living near Salisbury, North Carolina . . . a negro fellow named JACK, African born . . . came from Pennsylvania about two years since . . . He is about 30 years of age, and about 5 feet high, speaks bad English."

Those slaves who had successfully mastered English, most of whom, according to the ads, had been born and brought up in America, were referred to as speakers of "good" or "exceptional" English. In 1734 this ad appeared in the Philadelphia *American Weekly Mercury*: "Run away . . . a Negro Man named *Jo Cuffy*, about 20 Years of age . . .; he's *Pennsylvania* born and speaks good *English*."

Recall that not all blacks in early America were slaves; many either were freed by their masters or bought themselves out of servitude. An important mark of the free person of color, and thus a survival necessity for runaway slaves, was linguistic competence in White English. Moreover, early black writers such as Phillis Wheatley, Jupiter Hammon, Frederick Douglass, and others wrote in the current White English dialect of their respective times. Clearly, from these very early years, there seemed to be one variety of English prevalent among unlettered blacks and those still bound to the plantation way of life, and another variety, quite like that of whites, used and acquired by those few blacks who were literate and free, as well as by those who were more closely associated with Ole Massa. Furthermore, it is highly probable that the black speakers of White English, because of proximity and necessity, commanded the Black English Creole as well. In Beverly Tucker's 1836 novel, *The Partisan Leader*, this white Southerner distinguished two types of slave speech: field and house. Tucker asserted that the dialect of the house slave was highly similar to that of Ole Massa. Moreover, in the novel, the house slave Tom switches from the dialect acquired from his master to field speech to mislead Yankee invaders.

In short, there was a social pattern in early Black America where status — and even survival as a freeman — depended to a great extent on competence in White English (the "push"). Yet, then as now, the linguistic situation was complicated by other forces — the oppression and slavery associated with White English speakers, and the simple fact that there were more black speakers of Black English than black speakers of White English. Hence, both circumstance and psychology would propel blacks toward Black English (the "pull") and require that any black speaker of White English be fluent in Black English as well ("push" and "pull").

Our look at the history of Black English would be incomplete without attention to the special case of Gullah Creole. This dialect, also known as Geechee speech, is spoken by rural and urban blacks who live in the areas along the Atlantic coastal region of South Carolina and Georgia. While some Geechees inhabit the Sea Islands along the coast, many also live around Charleston and Beaufort. Most of the ancestors of these blacks were brought direct from Nigeria, Liberia, Gambia, Sierra Leone, and other places in West Africa where Ibo, Yoruba, Mandingo, Wolof, and other West African languages were and still are spoken. Today, Gullah people form a special Black American community because they have retained considerable African language and cultural patterns. Even the names Gullah and Geechee are African in origin — they refer to languages and tribes in Liberia. For decades, these people have lived in physical and cultural isolation from both mainstream Black and White America, and they bear living witness to the language and way of life that other American blacks have long since lost. (However, the African purity of the Geechee community has recently been threatened by the advent of American tourism attempting to capitalize on the "exotic, Old World charm" of the folk. Hotels, night spots, and other modern-day conveniences and tourist attractions are being constructed on the Sea Islands, thereby uprooting large numbers of blacks and disrupting their traditional African way of life.)

Despite a twentieth-century white writer's reference to Gullah speech as a "slovenly" approximation of English, issuing forth from "clumsy, jungle tongues and thick lips," anybody knowledgeable about African-English language mixtures can readily discern the systematic African element in Gullah Creole. In black linguist Lorenzo Turner's fifteen-year study of this dialect, he found not only fundamental African survivals in sound and syntax, but nearly 6,000 West African words used in personal names and nicknames, in songs and stories, as well as in everyday conversation. It is important for our understanding of Black English to recognize that black speech outside of Geechee areas was undoubtedly once highly similar to Gullah and is now simply at a later stage in the de-creolization process. For example, both Gullah and non-Gullah blacks still use the West African pattern of introducing the subject and repeating it with a personal pronoun. Thus, the Gullah speaker says, "De man an his wif hang to de tree, they lik to pieces." (The man and his wife hanging to the tree, they were licked to pieces.) The non-Gullah speaker handles the subject in the same way: "Yesterday, the whole family, they move to the West Side." On the other hand, only Gullah blacks still use the West African pattern of placing the adjective after the noun: "day clean broad." Other speakers of Black English follow the same pattern as White English speakers: "broad daylight."

We can say, then, that contemporary Black English looks back to an African linguistic tradition which was modified on American soil. While historical records and documents reveal a good deal about the development and change of this Africanized English, there is much that the records don't tell us. As a former slave said, "Everything I tells you am the truth, but they's plenty I can't tell you."

2

"It Bees Dat Way Sometime"

Sounds and Structure of Present-Day Black English

NOW THAT YOU KNOW about the "usta be," we will look at the elements of Black Language that have survived today. As stated in Chapter One, Black Dialect consists of both language and style. In using the term "language" we are referring to sounds and grammatical structure. "Style" refers to the way speakers put sounds and grammatical structure together to communicate meaning in a larger context. Put another way, language is the words, style is what you do with the words.

Let's look first at the language of Black English. As we do so, it is important to keep in mind two facts. One is that, if blacks continue to be accepted into the American mainstream, many of the Africanized features of Black English may be sifted out of the language. Thus we are describing a form of speech which could, in, say, the twenty-first century, be in danger of extinction. (About all I will guarantee is that the patterns I'm describing were in regular and systematic use in the black community at the time of this writing!) Again, because of the process of de-creolization, you should not expect Black English of today to be like that of the seventeenth century. All languages change over time; thus Black English of the twentieth century differs from early Black English just as White English of today is not identical to that of the founding fathers. The main linguistic differences between Black English and White English are cited below. In most other respects, the sounds and structure of the two dialects are generally the same.

◆

The pronunciation system of Black English employs the same number of sounds as White English (approximately 45 sounds counting English intonation patterns) but these sounds exist in a few different patterns of distribution. Of course, the real distinctiveness — and beauty — in the black sound system lies in those features which do not so readily lend themselves to concrete documentation — its speech rhythms, voice inflections, and tonal patterns. However, here we shall concern ourselves with those features of sound which are concrete and easily identified. For example, the *th* sounds in *then* and *with* are pronounced in black dialect as *den* and *wif*; that is, *th* may be pronounced as *d* or *f*, depending on position. (Of course it would be inaccurate to say that black language has no *th* sound simply because it's realized differently.) In linguistic environments where the initial *th* sound is voiceless, it is pronounced the same way as in white speech, as in *thought*, which is always *thought* (not *dought*), or *thing*, which is *thing*, or more usually *thang* (not *ding* or *dang*). Many times, Black Dialect sounds tend to be generally similar to those of white speakers of any given region of the country. That is, some black speakers in Boston say *pahk the cah* (deleting *r*'s) in the same way as white speakers of that area, and Southern Black Speech sounds pretty much the same as Southern White Speech. As a matter of fact, when you talk about pronunciation, there is no national standard even among white speakers, since the different regional dialects of the country all have their own individual standards. The following list indicates the few different pronunciations in Black English that are used by large numbers of black speakers:

Initial /th/ = /d/
  them = dem; then = den
Final /th/ = /f/
  south = souf; mouth = mouf
Deletion of middle and final /r/
  during = doing; more = mow; Paris = pass; star = stah
Deletion of middle and final /l/
  help = hep; will = wi
    When the contracted form of *will* is used (/'ll/), you get a kind of /ah/ sound, as : *Iah be there in a minute* (for *I'll be there in a minute*).
Deletion of most final consonants
  hood = hoo; bed = be

test = *tes; wasp* = *was*
Pluralized forms ending in such double consonants add /es/,
thus: *tests* = *tesses; wasps* = *wasses.* (One important exception to
this rule involves words ending in /s/, such as the proper name
Wes. Here the /s/ is *not* deleted.)
Vowel plus /ng/ in *thing, ring, sing* rendered as /ang/
thing = *thang; ring* = *rang; sing* = *sang*
Contraction of *going to* rendered as *gon.* Here the *to* is omitted altogether, and the nasal sound at the end is shortened, producing a
sound that is somewhat like an abbreviated form of *gone.*
He was gon tell his momma good-by.
Primary stress on first syllable and front shifting
police = *PO-lice; Detroit* = *DEE-troit*
Simple vowels
nice = *nahc*
boy = *boah*

◆

While digging on the sights and sounds of the black community, here are some things you are likely to hear:*

"Dem dudes alway be doin day thang." (*Those dudes are always doing
their thing* . . . Eighth grade student)
"Hur' up, the bell ranging." (*Hurry up, the bell is ringing* . . . Fourth
grade student)
"Sang good, now y'all." (*Sing good* . . . Female adult in Baptist
church)
"Doin the civil right crisis, we work hard." (*During the civil rights
crisis, we worked hard* . . . College student)
"We are aware of the antagonism between the PO-lice and the
black community." (Big city mayor)

◆

Linguistically speaking, the greatest differences between contemporary Black and White English are on the level of grammatical structure. Grammar is the most rigid and fixed aspect of
speech, that part of *any* language which is least likely to change
over time. Couple this linguistic fact with the historical reality
that only in recent years have there been concerted and intense

*See Appendix B for an exercise on Black Dialect sounds.

pressures on the black masses to conform to the language standards of White America. Thus it is logical that the grammatical patterns of Black English have been the last component of Black Dialect to change in the direction of White English.

Black Idiom speakers throughout the United States have certain grammatical structures in common — despite the region of the country, and in some instances despite the social class level. Middle-class blacks from Detroit, for example, were found to delete *-ed* in verbs more frequently than middle-class whites from Detroit.

◆

The most distinctive differences in the structure of Black Dialect are patterns using *be* (sometimes written and pronounced as *bees* or *be's*). These forms are mainly used to indicate a condition that occurs habitually. *Be* is omitted if the condition or event is not one that is repeated or recurring. For example, *The coffee bees cold* means *Every day the coffee's cold,* which is different from *The coffee cold* which means *Today the coffee's cold.* In other words if you the cook and *The coffee cold,* you might only just get talked about that day, but if *The coffee bees cold,* pretty soon you ain't gon have no job! The *be/non-be* rule operates with systematic regularity in the Black-English-speaking community.

Consider another example, this time from a young black Detroiter commenting on her father: *My father, he work at Ford. He be tired. So he can't never help us with our homework.* The *He be tired* here means *Every day my father is tired.* If the speaker had wanted to indicate that that fact applied to one day only, she would have left the *be* out of the sentence; thus, *My father, he work at Ford. He tired,* indicating that although he is tired today, this is generally not the case. (An unlikely situation, however, because if your father work at Ford Motor Company, on that Detroit assembly line where the Brothers bees humpin, he be tired all the time, believe me!) Here are a few other examples of *be* used to indicate habitual aspect:

They be slow all the time.
She be late every day.

I see her when I bees on my way to school.
By the time I go get my momma, it be dark.
The kid alway be messing up and everything.

Be is also used in combination with *do* to convey habitual conditions expressed in question form and for emphasis: *Do they be playing all day?* (in White English, *Do they play all day?*) and *Yeah, the boys do be messing around a lot* (in White English, *Yeah, the boys do mess around a lot*).

In addition to the use of *be* for habitual events, there is another important function of *be* that should be noted here. The Black English speaker can use *be* to convey a sense of future time, as in *The boy be here soon* and *They family be gone Friday*. Now keep in mind that these subtle distinctions in the meaning and use of *be* depend heavily on context. Thus the listener has got to heed the contextual cues in order to decode the speaker's meaning properly. For instance:

She be there later. (future *be*)
She be there everyday. (habitual *be*)
I be going home tomorrow. (future *be*)
I be going home all the time. (habitual *be*)

Future *be* may appear in combination with the contracted form of *will* ('ll). (Remember that due to the Black English sound rule of /l/ deletion, we get a kind of /ah/ sound for the letters /'ll/.) Thus you will hear: *He be looking for you next week,* as well as *He-ah be looking for you next week.* The explanation for both forms being used can be found in the process of language change described in Chapter One. That is, the transition from a more Africanized Black English to a more Americanized Black English. In the early stages of Black English, probably only *be* by itself was used to denote future time. Then, with the change in time and the collapsing of Black English structures toward those of White English, speakers of Black English began to indicate future time also with the use of *will* (pronounced, of course, according to rules for Black English sounds). However, since the process of language change is still incomplete, we find both ways of expressing future time in the black community and, indeed, within the speech of any one individual speaker of Black English.

Interestingly enough, forms of *be* (but not *be* itself) appear in places where they are needed for meaning, as in the past tense and in questions tacked on to sentences, so-called "tag" questions. For example, *He was my English teacher last year* rather than something ambiguous like *He my English teacher last year.* And *You ain't sick, is you?* rather than the unintelligible form, *You ain't sick, you?*

When the forms of *be* are used, they are simplified so that *is* and *was* usually serve for all subjects of sentences, whether the subjects are singular or plural, or refer to *I, you, we,* or whatever. For example, as above, we have *You ain't sick, is you?* as well as *She ain't home, is she?* And *He was my English teacher last year,* as above, as well as *They was acting up and going on.* The contracted form (*'s*) may also be used, as: *We's doing our book work and everythang when she start callin on us.*

As mentioned earlier, the Black English speaker omits *be* when referring to conditions that are fixed in time and to events or realities that do not repeat themselves. Applying the *non-be* rule, you get an absence of *be* before nouns: *He a hippie now;* before adjectives: *He too tall for me;* before adverbs: *They shoes right there;* before prepositional phrases: *My momma in the hospital;* and in auxiliary constructions: *They talking about school now.* Here are some additional examples of the absence of *be* to indicate a non-recurring event or a fixed, static condition*:

He sick today.
This my mother.
That man too tall for her little short self.
They daddy in the house.
The mens playing baseball and the womens cooking today.
Man, your ride really bad.

♦

Black English speakers use *been* to express past action that has recently been completed. "Recently" here depends much more on the particular words in the sentence that express the time,

---

*See Appendix B for some exercises on *be/non-be* and other features of Black English structure.

rather than the actual amount of time itself. For example, it is correct Black English to say: *She been tardy twice this semester* (which might have been several weeks or months ago as long as it's what would be called "this semester"). But it is *not* correct Black English to say: *She been tardy twice last semester* (although "last semester" might have just ended at the time the speaker is stating the fact). In order to express the idea of two tardinesses "last semester," the correct Black English statement would be: *She was tardy twice last semester.* If this sounds confusing, remember that White English has similar constraints upon the speaker's expression. Thus White English speakers can say: *I have been to New York this year,* but they *cannot* say: *I have been to New York last year.* As a rule of thumb, you can say that generally where Black English speakers use *been,* White English speakers would use *have, has,* or *had* plus *been.*

> Black English: He been there before.
> White English: He has been there before.
>
> Black English: They been there before.
> White English: They have been there before.
>
> Black English: She been there and left before I even got there.
> White English: She had been there and left before I even got there.

Note that Black English uses only the verb form *been,* regardless of the form of the subject or whether *have* is present or past tense.

Been is also used in combination with other verb forms to indicate past action, which might be recently completed, or more distantly completed action (although again, it is structural expression that counts, not the actual semantic reality). For example: *He been gone a year,* but also: *He been gone a day.* The White English equivalents would be a form of *have* plus *been* plus the verb, thus:

> Black English: He been gone a year.
> White English: He has been gone a year.
>
> Black English: They been gone a year.
> White English: They have been gone a year.

| Black English: | She been gone a year before anybody know it. |
| White English: | She had been gone a year before anybody knew it. |

As mentioned, it is not the time itself that governs the verb choice, but the way the time is expressed. Keeping this in mind will help us distinguish between use of *been* plus the verb and the past tense of *be* plus the verb. Thus, *Tony been seen at her house today,* but not *Tony been seen at her house yesterday.* Instead, this latter statement would be rendered in correct Black English as *Tony was seen at her house yesterday.*

Now just when you think you got that all straight, I'm gon throw a tricky one in here because sometimes *been* is used to show emphasis, regardless of the time that has elapsed since an action took place. *She BEEN there,* uttered with stress on *BEEN,* means that the speaker wants to emphasize the fact that the individual has been wherever she is for a long enough period of time that it's an established fact. Now, she mighta just got there, or maybe she even been there for days, but the point here is not the amount of time but the intensity and validity of the fact. In other words, she been there long enough for me to be certain bout it, so ain no point in keepin on askin questions bout it!

In similar fashion, *been* patterns with other verb forms to suggest emphatic assertion. *He BEEN gone,* meaning I'm certain of the fact of his leaving (it might have taken place long ago, or the leaving might have just occurred; at any rate, the speaker is not concerned with the precise amount of time, just the real fact of the departure). Note that in both patterns of emphasis, *been* appears in the sentence without any other kind of qualifying expressions of time or emphasis. Thus while correct Black English would be *He BEEN gone,* if you added the words *a long time,* it would be incorrect Black English. If there is another word or words that convey the intensity or duration of time in the sentence, then the Black English speaker would not put any special stress on the *been.* Thus we would have simply *He been gone a long time,* not *He BEEN gone a long time.*

◆

Done used by itself indicates past action, either recently completed or completed in the distant past. *I done my homework today* and *I done my homework yesterday* are both correct Black English statements. White English equivalents would be *I did my homework today* and *I did my homework yesterday*. When used in combination with another verb, *done* usually indicates only recently completed action (again "recently" depending on how it's expressed in the sentence). It is correct Black English to say *I done finish my work today,* but it is *not* correct Black English to say *I done finish my work yesterday.* The correct Black English here would be *I finish my work yesterday*. As explained earlier, White English has similar linguistic constraints. Thus White English speakers can say *I have finished my work today,* but they cannot say *I have finished my work yesterday.* The correct White English statement would be *I finished my work yesterday*.

What is important to keep in mind here is the distinction between *done* used by itself and *done* used in combination with other verbs. A Black English statement containing only *done* can usually be understood to mean the White English *did*. However, when it is used with another verb, you cannot substitute the White English form *did*. Instead, the White English equivalent is a form of *have* (*have, has,* or *had*). The Black English *James done seen the show* is NOT White English *James did seen the show,* NOR *James did see the show,* BUT *James has seen the show*. Similarly, the Black English *I done did my hair* is not the White English *I did my hair,* but *I have done my hair,* as in *I have done my hair five times this week*. Note here that the Black English *did* actually translates into the White English *done*. But there are Black English uses of *did*. For example, if the Black English speaker wanted to express emphasis, he or she would use *did* in the same way as White English speakers, thus:

Black English: I DID do my hair five time this week!
White English: I DID do my hair five times this week!

Done can be found in Black English in combination with *been*. In such statements, *done* still functions like White English *have*. *He done been gone all night* (White English: *He has been gone all night*) and *They done been sitting there a hour* (White English: *They have been sitting there an hour*). Sentences like these can also be used without *done* and still be correct Black English. Just as the White English speaker has many different ways of expressing the same thing, so the Black English speaker has many linguistic options. Thus, the speaker of Black English could say any of the following:

> He done been gone all night *or* He been gone all night.
> They done been sitting there a hour *or* They been sitting there a hour.
> She done been tardy twice this semester *or* She been tardy twice this semester.

Now here's a tricky one for you. This Black English use of *done* makes possible a tense that has pretty much gone out of white mainstream usage — that is, the future perfect, also referred to as past future. In White English, you used to get this kind of verb usage in sentences like the following:

> He will have left by the time we get there.
> I shall have finished before anyone arrives.

If those two expressions sound kinda stuffy, they should. Nowadays, you would more likely hear the following from White English speakers:

> He will be gone by the time we get there.
> I will be finished before anyone arrives.

Here's how Black English speakers render this future perfect: *be* plus *done* plus verb.

> He be done left by the time we get there.
> I be done finish before anyone arrive.

This usage is still very popular among Black English speakers and is found in the much-used Black Idiom expression "I be done _____ before you know it." Hip users of this Black English expression simply fill in whatever verb they want to use, according to context. Here are some examples of this use of future perfect from Black English speakers (for White English equivalents, simply substitute *will have* plus verb):

> "I *be done did* this lil' spot a hair fo' you know it."
> (middle age beautician)
> "If you mess wif me, *I be done did* you in fo' you know it."
> (young male about to git it on)
> "The Lord *be done call* me Home fo' you know it."
> (young church deacon)
> "If you ain mighty particular, yo' luck *be done run* out fo' you know
> it." (senior citizen to young black on the wild)
> "Look out, now! Fo' you know it, I *be done caught* you out there
> bluffin." (doctor at poker game)

◆

Black Dialect relies on either the context of the immediate sentence or the context of an entire conversation to signal conditions of time. There is no *-ed* in either past tense or past participle constructions (*I look for him last night* and *This guy I know name Junior* . . .). Using context to signal time, the same verb form serves for both present and past tense, as: *The bus pass me up last week,* but also: *The bus pass me up every day.* The words *last week* and *every day* signal the time of these statements rather than a change in the verb form. Similarly, in the following statement from a black sermon, the preacher has already established the fact that he's talking about the past since he's talking about the life and sacrifice of Christ: "The man Jesus, He come here, He die to save you from your sins! He walk the earth, He go among the thieves and try to save the unrighteous. The Master say whosoever will, let him come!"

◆

Most Black English verbs are not marked for person. The same verb form serves for all subjects, whether singular or plural. The subject and number of the verb are marked by the context of the sentence or by some word in the sentence. Thus, *She have us say it.* Here the singular subject is indicated by *she,* with no change in the verb *have.* Another example: *He do the same*

thang they do. In this sentence, there is no need to alter the verb *do* because the subjects *he* and *they* in the context convey the meaning and notion of two different subjects.

◆

Black Dialect obviously has the concepts of plurality and possession, but they are not indicated by the addition of -*s* or apostrophes with -*s*. *Two boy just left, two* indicates that *boy* is plural. *That was Mr. Johnson store got burn down,* the position of the noun, *Mr. Johnson,* signals who owns the store.

◆

As a result of trying to conform Africanized patterns to Americanized ones, and doing so without the benefit of formal language instruction, blacks created in Black English a number of overly correct or hypercorrect forms, such as the addition of -*s* to already pluralized forms, as in *It's three childrens in my family* and *The peoples shouldn't do that.* We also find forms such as *they does.* Such hypercorrections are due to insufficient knowledge and instruction in the erratic rules of White English. For example, in White English, an *s* is added to a singular verb form (as in *He does*) but not to a plural form (as in *They do*). In learning the language without systematic formal instruction, the traditional Africanized English speaker tries to reconcile this paradox and may end up adding an *s* to a lot of forms, so we not only get attempts to be correct producing *They does* but such attempts also produce *I does.*

◆

Black English speakers place stress on the subjects of sentences. In White English, this might be labeled the "double subject." Rather than being a duplicate subject as such, the repetition of the subject in some other form is used in Black English for emphasis. Two examples: *My son, he have a new car* and *The boy who left, he my friend.* Note that the emphasis is indicated without pronouncing the words in any emphatic way since this is accomplished by the "double subject." This feature of Black English is not a mandatory one, so you may hear it sometimes, other times not at all. As with White English speakers, there are many options open to the speaker of Black English. The repetition of subject is simply another such option.

The personal pronoun system of Black English is not as highly differentiated as that of White English. Thus, for example, with the third person plural pronoun, *they,* the same form serves for subject, possessive and so-called reflexive as in *The expressway bought they house* and *They should do it theyselves.* In the case of the third person singular pronoun, *he,* we will hear both *He gone* and *Him cool,* and in the reflexive, *He did it all by hisself.* At an earlier stage in the development of Black English, forms like *he book* (for *his book*) and *she house* (for *her house*) were prominent, but these have gradually disappeared. You may hear them in very young preschool children. With many pronouns in White English, you have a somewhat similar rule that allows the same form to be used for subjects, objects, and possessives. Thus, White English speakers say *James hit her* as well as *This is her book.* At one time in the early history of British-American English, there were different forms for all personal pronouns, but as the language changed, the English pronoun system was simplified to a reduced number of forms.

The pronoun *it* is used to refer to things and objects ("itsy" things) as in White English, but Black English adds an additional function for the pronoun. *It* can be used to introduce statements, and as such, has no real meaning. For example, *It's four boy and two girl in the family* and *It was a man had died.* The patterns of English sentences are such that they may require a "filler" word in some statements, even though the "filler" itself is empty in a semantic sense. Typically, American English uses the word *there* in such sentences. Thus, (White English) *There are four boys and two girls in the family* and *There was a man who had died.* Black English may also use the introductory *it* in question form.

Is it a Longfellow street in this city? (White English: Is there a Longfellow street in this city?)
Is it anybody home? (White English: Is there anybody home?)

◆

As an adverbial demonstrative, *Here* or *There* plus *go* is used instead of *here/there* plus *is/are*. For example, *There go my brother in the first row* and *Here go my momma right here*. The speaker also has the option of expressing these two statements with *it* as explained above. Thus, *It's my brother in the first row* and *It's my momma right there*.

As with the deletion of final consonants in many Black English sounds, the dialect omits the final *-s* in adverbs, for example, *Sometime they do that* and *He alway be here*.

◆

Whereas the old double negative goes back to Shakespeare and is in abundant use among whites today, triple and quadruple negatives are the sole province of Africanized English. Thus, *Don't nobody never help me do my work, Can't nobody do nothin in Mr. Smith class,* and *Don't nobody pay no attention to no nigguh that ain crazy*! Note that these are statements, not questions, despite the reverse word order. Now the rule for forming negatives in Black English is just a little bit tricky, so check it out closely. If the negative statement is composed of only *one* sentence, then *every* negatable item in the statement *must* be negated. Therefore, *Don't nobody never help me do my work*, which consists of only one sentence, has a negative in every possible place in the sentence. The White English translation is: *No one ever helps me do my work*. If, however, the negative statement involves *two* or more sentences combined together as one, a different rule operates. If every negatable item in the statement is negated, the White English translation would be a statement in the "positive." If, however, the statement contains all negatives plus one positive, the White English translation would be a statement in the "negative." Take the example mentioned above, the line from Lonne Elder's play, *Ceremonies in Dark Old Men*: *Don't nobody pay no attention to no nigguh that ain crazy*! Here, there are two sentences combined into one statement, and every item in the statement is negated, rendering the White English translation: *If you are a crazy nigger, you will get attention*. Now, suppose you wanted to convey the opposite meaning, that is, the White English, *If you are a crazy nigger, you will not get any attention*. The correct Black English would be expressed as all negatives plus one positive, thus: *Don't nobody pay no attention to no nigguh that's crazy!* (Keep in mind that this rule only applies to statements in which there are two or more sentences combined into one.)

To state the Black English negation rule more succinctly: if the statement consists of only *one* sentence, negate every item; if the statement consists of *two or more* sentences combined as one, all negatives indicate "positives," and all negatives, *plus one positive* indicate "negatives." Here are some other examples:

> *It ain nobody I can trust* (White English: *I can trust no one.*)
> *It ain nobody I can't trust.* (White English: *I can trust everyone.*)
>
> *Wasn't no girls could go with us.* (White English: *None of the girls could go with us.*)
> *Wasn't no girls couldn't go with us.* (White English: *All the girls could go with us.*)
>
> *Ain't none these dudes can beat me.* (White English: *None of these dudes can beat me.*)
> *Ain't none of these dudes can't beat me* (White English: *All these dudes can beat me.*)

Another distinctive Black Dialect negation pattern occurs in statements which are only partly negative. These statements pattern with *but,* as in *Don't but one person go out at a time* and *Don't nobody but God know when that day gon be.*

The foregoing discussion of Black Dialect sound and structure patterns should prove useful to teachers and others who wish to understand black lingo so as to really dig where such speakers are comin from. Obviously this kind of understanding can help bridge the linguistic and cultural gap between blacks and whites and thus facilitate communication. However, certain cautions should be observed. First, do not expect *all* Black English speakers to use *all* these patterns *all* the time. The list is intended to be exhaustive of the range of patterns you might encounter in a given situation, but some Black Dialect speakers may be more bi-dialectal than others, preferring to use White English around whites, Black English around blacks. (For example, among school-age blacks, one would find a greater degree of bi-dialectalism among older adolescents than among younger black children, for adolescents have begun to get hip to the social sensitivities associated with different kinds of languages and dialects.) Second, no speaker of any hue uses the range of patterns in their language one hundred percent of the time. This caution is the more to be exercised in the face of the transition of Africanized English towards the direction of Americanized English. Thus, one may find in any Black English speaker both *he do* and *he does* although the *he do*'s will predominate. You will also find uses of *-ed* in some past tense forms and other features of White English. Again, this is due to dialect mixture and the transition of Black English to White English as discussed in Chapter One. However, the Black English forms will prevail most of the time.

And with that, I'm going to close with a statement about "grammar and goodness" from my man, Langston Hughes, who often speaks through his folk hero, Jesse B. Simple — that beer-drinkin, rappin, profound thinkin Harlemite that Hughes first created for the pages of the well-known black newspaper, the *Chicago Defender*.

"I have writ a poem," said Simple.

"Again?" I exclaimed. "The last time you showed me a poem of yours, it was too long, also not too good."

"This one is better," said Simple. "Joyce had a hand in it, also my friend, Boyd, who is colleged. So I want you to hear it."

"I know you are determined to read it to me, so go ahead."

"It is about that minister down in Montgomery who committed a miracle."

"What miracle?" I asked.

"Getting Negroes to stick together," declared Simple.

"I presume you are speaking of Rev. King," I said.

"I am," said Simple. "He is the man, and this is my poem. Listen fluently now! This poem is writ like a letter. It is addressed to the White Citizens Councilors of Alabama and all their members, and this is how it goes:

Dear Citizens Councilors:
In line of what my folks
Say in Montgomery,
In line of what they
Teaching about love,
When I reach out my hand,

White folks, will you take it?
Or will you cut it off
And make a nub?
Since God put it in
My heart to love you,
If I love you
Like I really could,
If I say, 'Brother,
I forgive you,'
I wonder, would it
Do you any good?
Since slavery-time, long gone,
You been calling me
All kinds of names,
Pushing me down.
I been swimming with my
Head deep under water —
And you wished I would
Stay under till I drowned
Well, I did not!
I'm still swimming!
Now you mad because
I won't ride in the
Back end of your bus.
When I answer, 'Anyhow,
I'm gonna love you,'
Still and yet, today
You want to make a fuss.

Now, listen, white folks:
In line with Rev. King
Down in Montgomery —
Also because the Bible
Says I must —
In spite of bombs and buses,
I'm gonna love you.
I say, I'm gonna *LOVE you* —
White folks, OR bust!"

"You never wrote a poem that logical all by yourself in life," I said.

"I know I didn't," admitted Simple. "But I am getting ready to

write another one now. This time I am going to write a poem about
Jim Crow up North, and it is going to start something like this:

> In the North
> The Jim Crow line
> Ain't clear —
> But it's here!
> From New York to Chicago,
> Points past and
> In between,
> Jim Crow is mean!
> Even though integrated,
> With Democracy
> Jim Crow is *not* mated.
> Up North Jim Crow
> Wears an angel's grin —
> But still he sin.
> I swear he do!
> Don't you?

"I agree that the sentiment of your poem is correct," I said. "But
I cannot vouch for the grammar."

"If I get the sense right," answered Simple, "the grammar can
take care of itself. There are plenty of Jim Crowers who speak
grammar, but do evil. I have not had enough schooling to put
words together right — but I know some white folks who have
went to school forty years and do not do right. I figure it is better to
do right than to write right, is it not?"

"You have something there," I said. "So keep on making up your
poems, if you want to. At least, they rhyme."

"They make sense, too, don't they?" asked Simple.

"I think they do," I answered.

"They does," said Simple.

"They do," I corrected.

"They sure does," said Simple.

3

Black Semantics

Words and Concepts in Black English, Past and Present

> like,
> if he had da called me
> black seven years ago,
> I wd've —
>> broke his right eye out,
>> jumped into his chest,
>> talked about his momma,
>> lied on his sister
>> & dared him to say it again

> — Haki Madhubuti, "In a Period of Growth"

THE SUMMER OF 1966 marked the beginning of the nationwide shift from "Negro" to "black" as a term of racial identification for Black Americans. Expressing their annoyance at the serious insistence upon "black," people of both races were moved to the flippant response: "So what? What's in a name?" Now, of course, over a decade later, the term "black" has achieved widespread usage and acceptance by both blacks and whites. Yet terms of racial designation have posed a semantic dilemma to black people from the very beginning. The history of this racial labeling process must be viewed in the context of social, political, and cultural forces. A brief look at that history can hip us to where Black Semantics is comin from.

Toward the end of the fourteenth century, Portugal made its entry into the African slave trade and became the first European country to do so. The Portuguese chose to call their newfound property *negro,* which is Portuguese for "black." Spanish traders followed right on the heels of the Portuguese and they too used the name *negro* (Spanish for "black") to refer to their African captives. One is quickly led to speculate that the black-hued African skin must have been a striking phenomenon to what psychiatrist Frances Welsing has termed the "color deficient" Europeans, so much so in fact that the blackness, rather than the African-ness, became paramount in the European mind set. Then too, there were (and are) non-black Africans — Egyptians, for instance — and perhaps it was felt that some distinction had to be made between black and non-black African people. At any rate, for whatever reason, "negro" stuck and was picked up by the British and Americans who came into the human chattel business at a later date.

In Colonial America, whites characteristically referred to blacks as "negroes," "slaves," or "niggers." The three terms became nearly synonymous. "Negro" and "nigger" were used interchangeably and without any apparent distinction, especially by whites in the Southern United States. It was not until the twentieth century that whites began to semantically distinguish "negro" and "nigger," with the latter term becoming a racial epithet. From this perspective, nineteenth-century writer Mark Twain was simply following the naming tradition of his time when he chose to call Huckleberry Finn's black companion "Nigger Jim." In those early days, whites tended not to capitalize "negro," (or "nigger," for that matter). While at first glance, this might be deemed white racism, the fact of the matter is that in its original Portuguese and Spanish form, *negro* was an adjective, not a proper noun, and in English, adjectives are not capitalized.

Among the slaves in Colonial America, the term "African" was more common. The first black church was named the African Episcopal Church (1794); the first formally organized black self-help group was deemed the Free African Society (1787); the first black Masonic Lodge was called African Lodge No. 459 (1787); and Gustavus Vassa, writer of one of the first slave narratives (1789), referred to himself as "Gustavus Vassa, the African." This early preference for "African" was logical since the African experience was still very immediate for many blacks, and the tantalizing possibility of returning there haunted them constantly.

By the nineteenth century, however, the back-to-Africa yearning had become more a dream than a reality — at least for the majority of blacks. The cultural gap between Africa and America, and the firmly entrenched kinship ties in Black America, as well as the huge black population (well over one million by 1800) made wholesale emigration of blacks to Africa an impractical, if not impossible, move. However, right up to the Civil War, colonization societies and movements persisted among a minority of blacks and a great number of whites as well. Literally from the beginning of slavery in America, whites had pushed for the deportation of free blacks to Africa because their presence endangered the discipline and continued enslavement of slave blacks. Moreover, even if the slaves were emancipated, many whites felt that the two races could never live in America harmoniously. In 1815, Paul Cuffe, an economically successful black shipping merchant, took, at his own expense, thirty-eight blacks to settle in Sierra Leone on the West Coast of Africa. Two years later, prominent whites Henry Clay and John Randolph helped found the American Colonization Society, which paid for the transporting of nearly 2,000 free and emancipated blacks to establish the colony of Liberia in West Africa. Its capital, Monrovia, was named after President Monroe. And as late as 1862, President Lincoln convened a group of black leaders at the White House to enlist their support for the emigration of freed slaves out of America. He principally had in mind Liberia and the island of Haiti in the Caribbean.

For their part, though, the majority of blacks resisted these colonization efforts, on the argument that America was the country of their birth, one which they had helped to build through more than two hundred years of free labor. So, on the one hand, there was the internal pressure of the cultural distance between Africa and nineteenth-century Afro-America. On the other, there was the external political pressure of a white-dominated deportation effort which would, in effect, disinherit blacks from their share of the American pie whose ingredients included their blood, sweat, and tears. The two forces combined to make the racial designation "African" lose its significance in the nineteenth-century black community.

by Charles R. Johnson. Reprinted by permission of Ebony Book Division, copyright, 1970 by Johnson Publishing Company, Incorporated.

At this point, some blacks began to adopt the white man's term "negro" as their racial referent. Yet an uneasiness about this label, which was, after all, not their own, must have plagued many black people of that time. And so the term "colored" (which had been used to some extent in the earlier days) resurfaced into greater prominence in the nineteenth century. In 1818, a group of free blacks formed the Pennsylvania Augustine Society "for the education of people of colour." David Walker's radical document urging his fellow slaves to armed rebellion was titled "An Appeal, in Four Articles; together with a Preamble, to the Coloured Citizens of the World, but in Particular and very Expressly to Those of the United States of America" (1829). Abolitionist leader Frederick Douglass used both "negro" and "colored" in his speeches and writings of the nineteenth century. Even into the early twentieth century, "colored" seemed to be the preferred racial label. The Niagara Movement, organized by then radical blacks, became the forerunner of the oldest civil rights organization; the name these "militant" blacks chose was the National Association for the Advancement of Colored People, founded in New York in 1909.

Black people began the "pull" away from the term "colored" coincident with the aggressive twentieth-century "push" for full integration into White American society. These "push" efforts were extensively accelerated on all fronts during the years of the Great Wars to "make the world safe for democracy." As black soldiers, albeit in segregated regiments, proved their patriotism by shedding blood for America, black people all over the country began to shout "I, too, sing America." But it was not a song of their own composing. Black entry into the full swing of American life was on the white man's terms as integration in actuality translated into acting, talking, and thinking white. The integrationist "push," especially pronounced among national "negro" leadership in the years roughly from 1920 to 1955, must be seen as primarily responsible for black people's capitulation to White America's term for them. Apparently assuming that whites had become so accustomed to "negro" that they could not (or would not) change to "colored" or some other black culture–derived label, black leaders assented to the racial designation "negro." Even the radical and often nationalistic black scholar, W. E. B. DuBois, argued for the acceptance of the term, as can be witnessed by his many editorial "Postscripts" in the early issues of *The Crisis* (the national journal of the NAACP), founded and edited by Dr. DuBois.

Black leaders and spokesmen of the 1920s began to push for the capitalization of their adopted racial name in order to give this Portuguese slavery-time adjective the dignity and respect of a racial name for Black Americans. The NAACP launched a national campaign in this effort and sent out over 700 letters to white publishers and editors. The argument for capitalization of "negro" was perhaps most eloquently stated by Roscoe Conklin Bruce, editor of a biweekly newsletter published by the Paul Laurence Dunbar Apartments: "the colored people of the United States desire to have the word Negro capitalized, and their wishes ought to be respected." Finally, the white press capitulated: on March 7, 1930, the editorial section of *The New York Times* carried the following: "In our Style Book, Negro is now added to the list of words to be capitalized. It is not merely a typographical change, it is an act in recognition of racial self-respect for those who have been for generations in the 'lower case.' " By May of that year, according to Dr. DuBois, only the United States Government Printing Office and *Forum* magazine continued to represent Negroes in the "lower case."

Despite black leaders' vigorous campaign for "Negro," on the grass roots level, among the masses of black folk, distrust and suspicion of white folks persisted, and there was a general reluctance to plunge headlong into a mainstream that seemed to want no part of them. Among the folk, then, the term "colored" continued to be used as a counterbalancing semantic corrective to "Negro." And even DuBois himself balanced "Negro" with another term: black. Note, for instance, the title of many of his books: *The Souls of Black Folk; The Gift of Black Folk: Negroes in the Making of America; Black Reconstruction in America, 1860–1880; Black Folk, Then and Now: An Essay in the History and Sociology of the Negro Race.*

Today, many older blacks still prefer "colored" to "Negro." Can it be their "remembrance of things past" — that is, to another time when "Negro" was the white folks' word? Or is it that "Negro" sounds too close to "nigger," especially in Southern white dialect where those vowels are not differentiated? One wonders, since historically "negro" and "nigger" were semantically interchangeable, particularly among Southern whites.

The crucial fact here is that "Negro" has *never* been totally acceptable nor universally used by blacks themselves. Thus it should have come as no surprise when, in 1966, the label was repudiated by Stokely Carmichael's cry for "black power." In opting for "black," as opposed to "Negro," the black power movement consciously and deliberately chose a semantic label that had previously been denigrated by blacks and whites alike. To be sure, there is some historical evidence of blacks occasionally using the term as merely an inoffensive descriptive adjective. For instance, in Martin Delaney's 1861 novel *Blake,* Uncle Jerry talks about the whites hunting for runaway slaves: "Yes, chile, de patrolas da all de time out an' gwine in de quahtehs an' huntin' up black folks wid der 'nigga-dogs' as da call 'em." By and large, though, "black" has traditionally been a name-calling word. Particularly in the years from the Civil War to 1966, black skin color was viewed very negatively. Whites tended to favor lighter-skinned blacks for jobs and appointments to positions of prominence. Possibly this favoritism was due to the rampant miscegenation between master and slave which made many white and blacks "brothers under the skin." At any rate, in Black America, to be integrated was to be culturally and, if at all possible, genetically washed white as snow. "If you white, you all right / If you brown, stick around / If you black, stay back": the familiar childhood rhyme appears as an undercurrent theme in Black American history. Today, even with "black" so readily accepted, there are still some blacks, especially older ones, who do a double flinch at being called "black." You see, they remember when black was not so beautiful, and high-yellow (light skin) was the prime prerequisite for gittin ovuh in White America.

The black consciousness movement of the 1960s was thus not playing a Scrabble word game but asserting the right of Black America to define itself, including the right to select its own name. In a grand sweep to eradicate the old negative "whiteness" from black minds, leaders of this era deliberately chose a racial label that required blacks to purify themselves of white ideas and values, for to accept the "black" of blackness amounted to the ultimate recognition that white skin and white values were no longer important. Given the conflictive dynamics of "push-pull" in Black America, black, not Negro, becomes the appropriate antonym for white. *Black* calls to mind power, black magic, even evil, whereas, ironically, *Negro* suggests no such associations, especially to a generation of whites who had long since forgotten — if they ever knew — that *Negro* means "black" anyway. A black man, as opposed to a Negro man, is someone to be feared, reckoned with, and thus respected. Black . . . a logical choice. Besides, there has always been a kind of exotic fascination for the purity of the race, as the more black in skin color, the more indigenously African in thought and culture, and by association the more emotional, down-to-earth, sensual, and sexual. "The blacker the berry, the sweeter the juice."

The semantic designations "Afro-American" and "African-

American" accompanied the 1966 rise of "black" but have yet to achieve its widespread general usage in the black community. Perhaps it is their reference to Black America's link with Africa which many contemporary blacks simply cannot fathom — the differences and the distance are just too great. Yet the two terms denote the reality of the double consciousness and dual cultural heritage of black folk: part Africa, part America. Perhaps the more frequent use of Afro-American and African-American awaits the complete healing of the psychic wounds of the black past. Though both terms are, in a sense, more linguistically logical racial designations, neither is as semantically appropriate as "black." For the concept of "black" connotes the psychological weight of the contradictory impulses toward skin color in America. "Black" functions as a metaphorical reminder of the historical pendulum movement of denial and affirmation of black skin in White America.

What's in a name, then? Everything, as we acknowledge that names are not merely words but concepts which suggest implications, values, history, and consequences beyond the word or "mere" name itself. Words fit into a total symbolic and cultural system and can only be decoded within the context of that system. Much of black-white communication interference stems from lack of this kind of perspective on communication. We must dig on the frame of reference within which words are used. For instance, the term "nigger," still a racial epithet when used by whites, is actually a term of positive endearment in black raps today. White "overemotionalism" and "excessively" strong feeling become "soul," eagerly embraced and passionately pursued in the world of Black English speakers. "Loud" talk, "too-flashy" dress and behavior become in the black cultural universe the much-valued "stylin and profilin." Of course this is not to say that Black Semantics is grounded in blacks' embracing whatever whites denounce. Although many terms grow out of the conflict and tension of white oppression of black, many aspects of black verbal behavior are Africanized adaptations which can be seen as logical cultural consequences rather than as strictly racially based linguistic terms reflecting black reactions to whiteness. The term "Black Semantics" is broadly conceived to encompass the totality of idioms, terms, and expressions that are commonly used by Black Americans.

There is a popular tendency to think of the Black Semantic contouring of White American English as ethnic slang. Though many terms are "slangish," to dismiss Black Semantics as simply slang talk is a linguistic fallacy. The concept of "slang" does not begin to cover the broad range of semantic referents in the Black English vocabulary. (Anyway, the contemporary world is such that what is slang today can belong to the mainstream tomorrow.) Slang suggests a highly specialized vocabulary used only by a certain group of people; the popular stereotype is that of teenagers, hustlers, hippies, musicians, and various and sundry characters of ill repute. Yet in the black community, the vocabulary of soul crosses generational and class lines and is grounded in black people's common linguistic and cultural history.

There are four traditions that Black Semantics draws from: West African language background; servitude and oppression; music and "cool talk"; the traditional black church.

◆

The Black Semantic language and verbal concepts that come from the West African language background are of three types: words of direct African origin; words that are loan-translations; inflated vocabulary.

With reference to the first type of African linguistic survival, a commonly used example would be the word *yam* (sweet potato) from the Wolof word *nyam,* referring to oversized edible roots found in Africa. Many of these African words were first discovered by black linguist Lorenzo Turner in his fifteen-year study of the coastal region speech of South Carolina and Georgia. Turner found nearly 6,000 words of African origin; although most of these were personal names, many were more general terms.

Some additional examples of common English words that are direct African survivals are: *tote* (to carry); *gorilla; elephant; gumbo; okra; jazz; oasis; sorcery;* the word *juke* in *juke-box; tater; turnip,* the *cola* of *coca-cola; goober* (peanut); *banana; banjo.*

In a recent updating of the African origin of American words,

the (white) British linguist David Dalby added substantially to
Turner's list by citing over eighty words of general American
usage (not personal names) that were borrowings from African
languages. A specialist in African languages, Dalby first publicized his findings in "Americanisms that may once have been
Africanisms," an article that appeared in *The New York Times* in
1969. Immediately, the *Times* was deluged with letters of protest
from American linguists and other just plain Americans. They
were especially angry that Dalby had had the audacity to attribute the good old-fashioned term *okay* to the Dark Continent!
The *Times* allowed Dalby equal time to reply on two or three occasions. The heated and often not-so-polite exchange of letters
and commentaries continued through 1971. The whole business
represents a classic case of racism parading under the guise of
"intellectual truth."

Most of the Americanisms in Dalby's research are word meanings and usage that are derived from the African perspective on
language use; in other words, the speaker does to English what
the West African speaker does to Wolof, Mandingo, Ibo, or
Yoruba — same linguistic process, different language. An
example would be the word *bad* meaning "good" in Black
Semantics. This linguistic reversal process, using negative terms
with positive meanings, is present in a number of African languages — for example, the Mandingo *a ka nyi ko-jugu,* which literally means "it is good badly," that is, "it is very good." This
kind of Black Idiom exemplifies words that are loan-translations
(calques), in which the literal meaning of the African phrase is
retained in Black English, though not always the exact word itself. The calquing process, of course, is not unique to Black English. Many White English words and phrases came into general
Americanese as loan-translations from other Indo-European
languages, particularly Greek, Latin, French, and German. For
example, the expression "your calling" to refer to one's profes-
sion derives from the Latin *vocatio,* a "summoning before a court
of law." The Latin noun *vocatio* itself results from a kind of
internal linguistic calquing, having been derived from the Latin
verb, *vocare,* literally "to call." In this case, English has not only
borrowed the word-for-word translation, but also the specific

term itself, as evidenced by the word *vocation* (your "vocation" is
your "calling").

Some further examples of Black English loan-translations
from African languages are:

> *bad mouth,* to talk about somebody negatively, from Mandingo *da-
> jugu,* literally "bad mouth."
>
> *dig,* to understand or appreciate, from Wolof *dega,* literally "to
> understand."
>
> *hip,* aware, informed, "with it," from Wolof *hepi, hipi,* literally "to
> open one's eyes."
>
> *fat mouth,* to talk too much, especially about somethin you don't
> know nothin bout, from Mandingo *da-ba,* literally "big, fat
> mouth."
>
> *mean,* positive reference to extraordinary person or event; as with
> the Black English use of *bad,* this is derived from the African
> process of using negative terms to denote highly positive qual-
> ities; the positive use of obscenities is another such example.
>
> *skin,* as in *give me some skin,* (also; *give me five* referring to five
> fingers, palm slapping), to reaffirm truth or appropriateness of
> something a person has said, from the West African process of
> using a particular phrase to accompany a handshake, Mandingo
> *i golo don m bolo,* literally "put your skin in my hand."
>
> *bogue,* adjective used in a derogatory sense (as in *He a bogue dude*),
> from Hausa *boko,* literally "deccit" or "fake."
>
> *okay,* both in the sense of "all right," as well as in the sense of "after
> that," connecting sentences in a narrative sequence; from West
> African language form, *kay,* meaning "yes," "of course," "in-
> deed," as in Wolof *waw kay/waw ke,* Mandingo *o-ke;* Fula *'eeyi kay.*
> The meaning "after that" compares with the Mandingo *o-ke-len,*
> literally "that being done."

When blacks use calques like the above, the lingo is negatively
assigned the status of "street" or "hip" talk — in other words,
slang. Yet in the native African languages these are not considered slang expressions. This would suggest that many of the
terms in Black Semantics have been or are improperly labeled
and misperceived by blacks as well as whites not hip to the source
of soul talk.

There is still another level of Black English Semantics which reflects an African language background. Here I refer to the kind of verbal posturing which provides the speaker with inflated word choices for ordinary situations. This use of overelegant vocabulary is prevalent in African discourse and has survived in Black America in the form of exaggerated language or High Talk (also Fine Talk, Fancy Talk). A modern-day African example is provided by the brilliant contemporary African writer, Chinua Achebe, in his second novel, *No Longer at Ease.* The novel's protagonist, Obi Okonkwo, from the Ibo village of Umuofia in Nigeria, is being honored upon his return from England, where the village's Umuofia Progressive Union sent him to "study book." The Union Secretary begins with a welcome, which, Achebe tells us, he "intones from an enormous sheet of paper." The secretary describes Obi as having returned from the "United Kingdom in quest of the Golden Fleece." His welcome continues:

> "The importance of having one of our sons in the vanguard of this march of progress is nothing short of axiomatic . . . [By repaying his debt to the village] our illustrious son and guest of honor . . . [will make it possible that] an endless stream of students will be enabled to drink deep at the Pierian Spring of Knowledge." . . .

Achebe describes the people's overwhelming approval of this Fine Talk:

> Needless to say, this address was repeatedly interrupted by cheers and the clapping of hands. What a sharp young man their secretary was, all said. He deserved to go to England himself. He wrote the kind of English they admired if not understood . . .

By contrast, the returning "hero" is so full of "book" that he has forgotten his village's ancient customs and thus makes several social blunders — the second one of which is his lack of High Talk, his lame verbal response to the Secretary's eloquent plaudits.

> Obi's English, on the other hand, was most unimpressive. He spoke "is" and "was." He told them about the value of education.

"Education for service, not for white collar jobs and comfortable salaries. With our great country on the threshold of independence, we need men who are prepared to serve her well and truly."

When he sat down the audience clapped from politeness. Mistake Number Two.

For examples of Fine Talk in Black America, check out the following from a nineteen-year-old black male: *Naw, it ain true. He being fictitious* (rather than the mundane and limp *He lying*). As another example, Blueboy, the numbers man in *Book of Numbers* by Robert Pharr, shows his appreciation for the surprise treat of corn whiskey that his host sneaks into his hotel room when Blueboy sends for a pitcher of water:

> "Mine dearest host . . . it does this old heart good to meet a boniface who demands good service for his guests. My friend Emily says never to tip your wealthy host so whatever change there is [hands him two dollars] you give it to the sable child of beauty who told you no more dying of thirst."

The condition of servitude and oppression contributed to the necessity for coding or disguising English from the white man. Since slaves were forced to communicate in the white man's tongue, they had to devise ways of runnin it down that would be powerful and meaningful to the black listener, but harmless and meaningless to any whites who might overhear their rap. Thus *Miss Ann* becomes, on a Black Semantic level, a derisive reference to the white woman, and *ofay* (from the Pig Latin for *foe*, the enemy), a derisive term for whites in general. In much the same fashion, slave song lyrics and spirituals had a double-edged meaning. For instance, note the following stanza from an old black folk song:

> You mought be Carroll from Carrollton
> Arrive here night afo' Lawd made creation
> But you can't keep the World from moverin' around
> And not turn her back from the gaining ground.

The phrase "not turn her" in the last line is a concealed reference to preacher-revolutionary Nat Turner. The tradition of slavery and discrimination, then, mark a second source of Black Semantics.

Due to the work of DuBois and others, we now know that the Old Testament–based Negro spirituals wasn't bout no "after here," but "dis heah." The slaves used other-worldly lyrics, yes, but the spirituals had for them this-world meanings. They moaned "steal away to Jesus" to mean stealing away FROM the plantation and TO freedom (that is, "Jesus"). They sang triumphantly "this train is bound for Glory," but the train they were really talking about was the "freedom train" that ran on the Underground Railroad. The symbolic Underground Railroad was actually a revolutionary network of escape routes and schemes devised to assist slaves fleeing to the "glory" of freedom in Canada and the North. "Go down, Moses, and tell Ole Pharaoh to let my people go." Moses — black freedom fighter Harriet Tubman, the "conductor" of the Underground Railroad, who in her lifetime assisted more than 300 slaves to escape. She would "go down" South and by her actions "tell" white slavers ("Ole Pharaoh") to let her people go. The Biblical analogues hit a responsive chord in the black slave community, and the Old Testament, with its themes of oppression, flight, and the tormented wanderings of God's chosen people, became a rich and easily adaptable resource for black songs and sermons of freedom.

Not all spirituals, of course, represented conscious disguises for escaping from slavery. But if the code did not speak to escape as such, the lyrics were nonetheless expressions of feelings about enslavement. Because of fear of the overseer's lash and the possibility of other forms of cruel reprisals, the slave's lament had to be articulated through permissible channels. Religious songs became one such channel, and thus was born the myth of the "happy darkies," idling their time away crooning songs. Nineteenth-century black Abolitionist Frederick Douglass, in his narrative depicting his life as a slave, dispels the notion of the contented singing slave:

> I have often been utterly astonished, since I came to the north, to find persons who could speak of the singing, among slaves, as

evidence of their contentment and happiness. It is impossible to
conceive of a greater mistake. Slaves sing most when they are most
unhappy. The songs of the slave represent the sorrows of his
heart; and he is relieved by them, only as an aching heart is relieved by its tears . . . [The songs] told a tale of woe . . . they were
tones loud, long, and deep; they breathed the prayer and com-
plaint of souls boiling over with the bitterest anguish. Every tone
was a testimony against slavery, and a prayer to God for deliver-
ance from chains . . . To those songs I trace my first glimmering
conception of the dehumanizing character of slavery . . . Those
songs still follow me, to deepen my hatred of slavery, and quicken
my sympathies for my brethren in bonds.

Writing in *Souls of Black Folk* nearly sixty years later, DuBois
referred to the spirituals as the "sorrow songs" and attempted to
locate the situational parallels of their lyrics.

Another [song] whose strains begin this book is "Nobody knows
the trouble I've seen." When, struck with sudden poverty, the
United States refused to fulfill its promises of land to the freed-
men, a brigadier-general went down to the Sea Islands to carry the
news. An old woman on the outskirts of the throng began singing
this song; all the mass joined with her, swaying. And the soldier
wept.

This tradition of a coded dialect of English whose meaning is
veiled from whites persisted even after slavery and can be seen
as the underpinning of urban black "cool" talk, which often
functions as a register of exclusion around whites. The historical
realities of servitude and white oppression explain why this aspect of Black Semantics changes so rapidly, for once a word
gains widespread usage in the White American mainstream, a
new term must be coined; after all, a code is no longer a code if
the enemy is hip to it. Note too that the coding process often operates in the direction of what the African cultural-linguistic
background has provided — for example, the expressions on
page 45. Much of black "cool" talk has been around in the oral
tradition for decades, and thus when we hear what appears
to be a new term, it may simply be a resurfacing of an old
expression.

A word on Pig Latin, which has been in existence in the oral tradition for a very long time. You hear it now usually only among young black children. The linguistic formula for using Pig Latin might be stated as follows: take the first letter of a word, move it to the end, and add *ay*.

$$boy = oybay$$
$$girl = irlgay$$
$$foe = ofay$$

If the word begins with two consonants instead of one, shift both letters.

$$store = orestay$$
$$trip = iptray$$
$$black = ackblay$$

If the word begins with a vowel, don't shift the letter, just add *ay*.

$$evil = evilay$$
$$aunt = auntay$$
$$old = olday$$

If you're dealing with a word of three or more syllables, break the word up into its syllabic parts and deal with two units at a time (three at a time, if one unit is very short).

$$refrigerator = efrigeray, atoray$$
$$elephant = elephay, antay$$
$$understanding = underay, andingstay$$

Seemingly a simple operation when you're only dealing with one word at a time, Pig Latin takes on the complicated sound of a foreign tongue enwhay ouyay areay eakingspay anay olewhay entencesay.

◆

Music and "cool talk" provide a third source of Black Semantics. (I lump music with cool talk because much of the hip or slang aspect of Black Semantics comes from the music world.) By now, it is something of a cliché to speak of the significance of black music in the black experience. Its cultural import and impact on black life are perhaps of such great magnitude because black music is more heavily African than any other single aspect of Black American existence. As Imamu Baraka says in *Blues People:*

> Music, dance, religion, do not have *artifacts* as their end products, so they were saved. These nonmaterial aspects of the African's culture were almost impossible to eradicate. And these are the most apparent legacies of the African past, even to the contemporary Black American . . . blues, jazz and the Negro's adaptation of the Christian religion all rely heavily on African culture . . .

In *Black Talk,* Ben Sidran makes even greater claims for the importance of black music:

> . . . black music is not only conspicious within, but *crucial* to, black culture . . . music is not only a reflection of the values of black culture but, to some extent, the basis upon which it is built . . . the investigation of black music is also the investigation of the black mind, the black social orientation, and primarily, the black culture.

Whether one is willing to make such prodigious claims for music or not, one thing is for sure, as Phyl Garland so aptly and succinctly put it in *The Sound of Soul:*

> The relationship of the black listener to the music that he regards as "his" always has been a very deep and personal one, quite often reflecting a great deal about his subordinate position in the society. In contrast to all the things the black man has not had in this country, he has always had "his" music.

Clarence Major, in the *Dictionary of Afro-American Slang,* minimizes any other influences on Black English vocabulary, and makes black music the paramount source: ". . . more than any other aspect of this experience [the black experience] the language of the black musician has had the greatest total effect on the informal language Americans speak."

Basically, the music world's semantic contribution is of two types: 1) musical expressions from the black folk tradition; 2) terms and expressions coined and used by musicians themselves, either in their lyrics or in their general speech.

The musician will extrapolate figures of speech, idioms and tales from the oral tradition and set them to music, thus exposing black verbal expression to a wider audience. An example is the recording *Stagger Lee* taken from the Toast (black narrative folk poem) about Stack-O-Lee (also Stag-O-Lee) which was popular in the early sixties. Stagger Lee being a fearless, mean dude, it became widely fashionable about this time to refer to oneself as "Stag," as in "I ain got to brag, uhm like Stag." Or, "Don't mess wif me, cause I ain't no fag, uhm Stag." As an extension, "Stag" also became a popular "gangster name" for any cats who exhibited Stag's qualities. (A "gangster name" is an alias by which hustlers are known in the streets, but it also generally refers to a nickname assumed by any blacks wishing to project an image of hipness or toughness.) Another example is the still-popular Black English expression "I cain't kill nothin and won't nothin die," used to refer to the speaker's bad luck. This expression is common in a number of blues songs. Then there are the proverbs which musicians tap for their songs; these resurface for a time and become popular sayings in the black community, such as "Smiling faces sometime tell lies," and "Action speak louder than words."

The black musician, his or her way of life and talk, provide a kind of standard in the Black English–speaking community. (The preacher provides another.) Since the music preserves the Africanness, as well as speaks to the uniqueness of black cultural sensibility, it is only logical for musicians to be elevated to the position of culture heroes. The whole notion of "cool talk" that has come to be associated with the music world suggests a heroic posture of calmness and control, a kind of Hemingwayesque grace under pressure, which was and is vitally necessary for a black man or woman in White America, who's often tested, much arrested, but rarely blessted. Black musicians are cool par excellence as they style and profile to the max. (The Black English word *cool* itself evolved as a loan translation from the Mandingo word for a certain kind of slow-tempoed music: *suma,* literally translated, means "cool.")

Here are some words that musicians have coined and contributed themselves.

> *jazz,* referring to jazz music, but also meaning to speed up, to excite, to act uninhibited, possibly from Mandingo *jasi,* literally, "to act out of the ordinary." Originally, the term was also used to refer to sexual activity; for a poetic example of this use, see Gwendolyn Brooks's poem "We Real Cool," in her *Selected Poems.*
>
> *hot,* referring to fast tempo music, also by extension, to fast movement and action, or excessive energy generated in an activity, as in *The Celtics done got hot now,* meaning *They really playing good basketball;* possibly from the Mandingo *goni,* literally, "fast."
>
> *cool,* referring to slow tempoed music, and by extension, calm, slow, worldly posture; see above.
>
> *cooking,* to play music with intense enthusiasm and fervent excellence, and by extension, to do any activity energetically and with skill. Thus athletes, when really gittin down playing ball, can be said to be *cooking.*
>
> *doin it to death,* seriously playing music, and by extension, seriously performing any activity as if it's a matter of life or death.
>
> *changes,* in jazz music, an interval or departure from the central melodic refrain, during which the musician improvises and innovates; by extension, *going through changes,* or *putting somebody through changes,* refers to problems in one's personal life in which one undergoes sporadic, spontaneous, and unanticipated emotional experiences that seemingly have no connection.
>
> *gig,* reference to jazz musician's job, and by extension, any kind of work; also by musical association, reference to a dance or party.
>
> *funky,* the blue notes or blue mood created in jazz, blues, and soul music generally, down to earth soulfully expressed sounds; by extension, the real nitty-gritty or fundamental essence of life, soul to the max.

Though popular and loved in Black America, the musician has traditionally been an outsider when measured by mainstream White America's standards. Sex, alcohol, drugs . . . They live fast, die young, and have beautiful coffins . . . The musician bees steppin fast, fast, fast, caught up in the cultural whirl of black music as an escape from white oppression. During earlier times when White America refused black musicians both economic and aesthetic "propers" for their art, their music and their lifestyle was an expression of their rejection of White America. Perhaps for this reason, even churchgoers who gave lip-service rejection to the musician's "sinful" ways secretly applauded and supported them, buying their records and attending their shows in clubs and concerts. The musician as rebellious black hero and bad nigger is well expressed by Clay, a bourgeois Negro turned angry black man in Baraka's play, *Dutchman:*

> The belly rub? You wanted to do the belly rub? Shit, you dont even know how .. . . . Belly rub is not Queens. Belly rub is dark places, with big hats and overcoats held up with one arm. Belly rub hates you. Old bald-headed four-eyed ofays popping their fingers . . . and don't know yet what they're doing. They say, "I love Bessie Smith." And don't even understand that Bessie Smith is saying, "Kiss my ass, kiss my black unruly ass." Before love, suffering, desire, anything you can explain, she's saying . . . "Kiss my black ass." And if you don't know that, it's you that's doing the kissing. Charlie Parker? Charlie Parker. All the hip white boys scream for Bird. And Bird saying, "Up your ass, feeble-minded ofay! Up your ass."

Unlike the first half of the twentieth century, when musicians and singers like Bessie Smith and Charlie Parker lived and suffered, in the 1960s there was an explosion of "soul music." White America not only began to dig black music, but white musicians started usurping it on a mass basis. (Witness the Beatles, who to their credit, at least, have acknowledged their musical debt to black musicians.) This mass popularization and commercialization of black folks' music served to put many black singers and musicians on full. Today, black music seems to be shedding its previous aura of sin, dope, rebellion, and the poverty of the chitlin circuit. Groups like the Supremes and the Jackson Five now project a nice, clean, all-American boy or girl image of blacks. The crucial point here is that it was not always so among the older blues and jazz men and women, who suffered far more than most contemporary black music stars will ever know anything about. (The recent film, *Lady Sings the Blues,* depicting the life of the tragic black songstress, Billie Holiday, is a case in point. In this sense, the gutsy, lusty Aretha Franklin, with all her personal suffering and man problems, rather than the nicey, wifey Diana Ross, with her wholesome, overnight-success image, typifies the characteristic black songstress of old. This accounts for the dismay and displeasure voiced by many blacks when it was announced that Motown Movie Productions cast Miss Ross, rather than Lady Soul, for the part of Lady Day.)

Finally, you can readily grasp the pervasiveness of music-derived Black Semantics if you recall that historically music has provided an ever-present and unifying focal point in the total black community. From eight to eighty, black adults, teens, and children have always grooved on the same music and basically done the same dances. From doctor to ditch digger, all classes and manner of black folk done always got down on the same soulful jams and latest steps. Characteristically, every black party always has music and dancing — a social feature that whites just started gittin hip to in the middle 1960s. (Longer ago than I care to remember, a white colleague once pointed out to me that he really dug how there was little awkwardness at black social sets because the music and dancing automatically broke down social barriers and provided a natural and easy way to get acquainted with the opposite sex. This, as he sadly observed, was in direct contrast to white parties where everybody just sat around ill at ease, with drinks in hand, uncomfortably trying to make conversation. Course, all this done changed now since white folks decided to let black folks show 'em where it's at!)

♦

The fourth tradition that helped give birth to Black Semantics is that of the traditional black church. Because of the profound influence of the black religious tradition on black culture, many expressions and semantic concepts in the Black English vocabulary have a religious base (albeit secular users may be completely unaware of the fact). As will be pointed out more extensively in Chapter Four, the traditional black church remains an important source of African cultural survivals and the manifestation of the traditional African world view. Fundamental to this view is the precedence of the spiritual over the material world — the reign of soul over body — but, almost in the same breath, the need for body to connect with soul for true human balance "the way Nature planned it." The popular semantics of "soul" came directly out of the black church. Ironic, though, that some of those who most exuberantly applaud soul would be the first to renounce the little Southern country and urban storefront churches where soul was kept alive during centuries of de-humanization and hopelessness. The belief that the human soul transcends material reality, the firm commitment to the triumph of the human spirit over adversity, the certainty that there's a God on high who may not move the mountain, but will give you strength to climb — such are the fundamental propositions of the traditional African world view transposed to the African-American's Judaeo-Christian context in the New World. It is, after all, only a short distance from "sacred" Clara Ward's "I'm climbin high mountains tryin to git Home" to "secular" Curtis Mayfield's "keep on pushin / cain't stop now / move up a little higher / someway or somehow."

The common "church" and "street" ingredients of soul: long suffering but with a heroic posture of endurance and sheer human will to survive, knowing that "He may not come when you want Him, but He's right on time," and that "If I didn't have bad luck, I wouldn't have no luck at all." Thus preacher and bluesman come to grips with an irrational world where people can be made to suffer just because of the color of their skin. Soul: refusal to wallow in self-pity, secure in the knowledge that a "change is gon come," cause, like, "everybody talkin bout Heaven sho ain goin there"; soul: daring to "show some sign" that "you got good religion" by "gittin the spirit in the dark," as you "reach out and touch" somebody else's "soul," cause that's really what life is all about.

Yeah, all those old darkies shoutin out there in the fields and talkin in tongue — they weren't fooled one bit by the white man's Christianizing efforts to subdue their will to be free. Religion was a way to keep them going with their Africanness intact — they simply found in the white man's religion something close to home.

Here are some of the terms and concepts that came out of the traditional black church:

Sister, Brother, forms of address for black females and males, terms emphasize solidarity and unity. Conceiving of the church as the human family in microcosm, church folk typically address each other in this fashion. Older women are addressed as "Mother," and older men are the church family "Elders." The term *soul-brother* is simply an extension of this concept.

As God is my secret judge, an expression commonly used to reaffirm truth or prove one's validity, as in "As God is my secret judge, man, I din't bust on the Brother."

gittin the spirit, to show deep emotion and express feeling of one's soul by body movements and gestures. The traditional black church retained the African belief in spirit possession.

shout, same as above. Both may be characterized by moans, groans, hollers, whoops, and articulation in a code language known only to God and the saved, that is, talkin in tongue. When this ecstasy is projected into a secular context, as at a soul music concert, it is not unusual for persons to be so overcome with the emotion of the spirit that they momentarily lose consciousness, just like the Brothers and Sisters of the traditional black church.

Lord ham mercy, or *Lord a mercy* (Lord, have mercy), popular idiomatic interjection to indicate surprise or agreement.

Tell the truth!, enthusiastic reaffirming response to the validity of what someone has said or done, popularized by Ray Charles's secular recording by that title. In the traditional black church, the phrase is a typical response heard during a sermon, testifyin, or other such "call."

Well, all right!, same as above. (See Chapter Five for an extended discussion of sacred-secular call-response communication.)

soul clap, clapping hands to music as is done in the church. "Put your hands together" . . . soul music singers thus induce their secular audience to engage in this sacred-based behavior. The genuine *soul clap* is a two-beat rhythmic unit, one clap on the beat, rapidly followed by one off the beat.

soul shake, (also known as the black power handshake) an intricate handshake with a number of variations of the basic four-part structure, which is executed by juxtaposing the right thumbs, first to the right of your partner's thumb; then to the left, next, grasp his or her fingers in your palm, followed by your fingers being grasped in his or her palm. While the term *soul shake* itself is not specifically used in the traditional black church, the concept of an in-group handshake of solidarity identifying oneself as a "club member" was borrowed from the church practice of extending the "right hand of fellowship" to newly-saved members.

testifyin, concept referring to a ritualized form of black communication in which the speaker gives verbal witness to the efficacy, truth, and power of some experience in which all blacks have shared. In the church, testifyin is engaged in on numerous symbolic occasions; newly converted ex-"sinners" testify to the church congregation the experience of being saved, for instance, or on Watch Meeting Night, New Year's Eve, when church folk gather to "watch" the old year go out and the new one come in — they testify to the goodness of the Lord during the past year. A spontaneous expression to the church community, testifyin can be done whenever anybody feels the spirit — it don't have to be no special occasion. Like the Reverend C. L. Franklin, father of Aretha Franklin, might just get up in the pulpit any Sunday morning and testify to the goodness of God. Aretha talks about the greatness of her man and how he makes her feel in her well-known blues recording, *Dr. FEELGOOD,* and that's testifyin too.

Whichever of the four traditions a term in the Black English vocabulary comes from, what is basic here is the fact that Black Semantics represents Black Americans' long-standing historical tendency to appropriate English for themselves and their purposes. Any previously all-white activity or field that blacks enter is colored by a black conceptual approach and terminology, as if to say, this can only be ours if we put our special linguistic imprint upon it. An excellent example of this from a most unlikely field is the use of black lingo in the game of golf. Generally perceived as the "white man's thang," it is not a sport popularly played among the masses of blacks. Yet among those few participating in it, there has developed a special set of black terms, as Edward Boyer's glossary illustrates:

    bunt — a short drive
    ducking the card — scoring below par on a round
    hammer — a golf club
    library game — no talking allowed
    Nellie's belly — playing it as it lies
    pallet — a green

pitch-out — shanking the ball

stick it in the ground — tee up the ball

taking home the iron — winning the trophy

train — several foursomes competing in a daily winner-take-all
  contest

undertaker — a skilled putter who "buries" the ball in the cup

♦

It would be useful now to consider some principles describing the general characteristics of contemporary Black Semantics, that is, certain common properties that can assist the unhip to decode the vocabulary of soul. Here I will try to illustrate what Black Semantics is all about in a descriptive, rather than a historical, sense. Keep in mind, though, that we are still considering both the process and the product of the semantic creation.

When White English words are given a black semantic interpretation, their range of referents increases.

For blacks, English words can have potentially two levels of meanings, one black, one white. Since blacks share in the consensus dialect of the American mainstream, on one level a word's referent is the same for blacks and whites. But since blacks also share a linguistic subculture outside that mainstream, on another level (the Black Semantic level) the same word has multiple meanings and associations. Thus within the black level of meaning there are many sublevels. Take the word *bad*. For blacks and whites, it suggests negativity, unpleasantness, distastefulness. For blacks only, it can also suggest something positive: good, extraordinary, beautiful. *I got a bad cold* means the same thing to blacks and whites, but *He is a bad dude* would suggest to whites the idea of an undesirable character, whereas to blacks it would indicate a highly desirable person. But there are various ways desirability manifests itself: he is highly desirable because . . . the terms should tell us why, clue us in to the quality the dude possesses. To get at these shades of meaning, we must go to the communicative context. Here we can see how one word in the black lexicon can serve many different purposes because Black Semantics is highly context-bound. Thus *That's a bad dress* means in white terms something like a beautiful or pretty dress. Anyone who tells it like it is (such as Angela Davis,

Jesse Jackson, Rap Brown, Malcolm X) is described as *bad,* hence equivalent to *powerful truth-teller.* After watching a Sammy Davis performance, a Brother testified: "Sammy Davis sho did some bad stuff" which translates to *extraordinary* stuff, and *stuff* in turn translates to *performance,* hence, *bad stuff* in this context implies *extraordinary performance.* One dude said to another, noticing how he was dressed: "You sho got on some bad shit," which means he got on good shit, which means he's attractively dressed.

Now this last example represents a. sensitive point in Black Semantics, use of what is considered profanity. I would like to push this point because I think these so-called obscenities are least understood. Even among some persons in the black community the terms are derogatorily dismissed as curse words or as street talk, used only by the low-life — hustlers, pimps, winos on the corner. Yet it is obvious that the four-letter word above does not refer to defecation, nor is it being used to "cuss somebody out," but as a very positive compliment to the person being addressed. The same goes for the black lexicon's most famous word, *motherfucker,* and its euphemistic representations — *M.F., Marilyn Farmer, Mister Franklin, motor scotor, monster, mother.* Yet the word is used in both negative and positive ways, and sometimes as just a filler with no meaning at all. Here are some examples:

> In an urban ghetto, where cars are often valued above people, a Brother described a Cadillac Eldorado as a "bad muthafucka." Here the speaker was obviously expressing approval. Possible translation: "beautiful car."
>
> One middle-class black female commented to another, concerning her man who she'd just discovered was going around with someone else: "That no-good muthafucka." Here the speaker is obviously expressing disapproval. Possible translation: "deceitful man."
>
> One black middle-class male says to another, in a barber shop, "You muthafuckin right I wasn't gon let him do that." Here the speaker is simply emphasizing how correct the listener's assessment is, using the "obscenity" as a grammatical intensifier, modifying "right."

by permission of the artist

> One black student described to another the activities of the night
> before in this way: "We wasn't doin nothin, just messin round
> and shit." Here the "obscenity" is used neutrally, as an expletive
> (filler) to complete the sentence pattern; semantically speaking,
> it is an empty word in this linguistic environment.

The whole-point, of course, is that in none of the first three
does the speaker refer to the act of committing incest with one's
mother, nor does the last example refer to defecation.

Another Black Semantic term that aptly demonstrates the
multiple subjective association process is the oft-used word *nigger*. Whereas to whites it is simply a way of callin a black person
outa they name, to blacks it has at least four different meanings
as well as a different pronunciation: *nigguh*. It may be a term of
personal affection or endearment, as in *He my main nigguh* (*He's
my best friend*), or *You my nigguh if you don't get no bigger, and if you
get bigger, you gon be my bigger nigguh* (*You're my friend/lover no matter what you do*). Sometimes it means culturally black, identifying
with and sharing the values and experiences of black people. At
a black rally, when the Sister shouted out, "*Nigguhs is beautiful,
baby*," she was referring to "shonuff nigguhs," as contrasted to
Negroes, who aspire to white middle-class values. With the recent advent of black consciousness, there is a move on to replace
this use of *nigguh* with *Black* or *Afro-American*. *Nigguh* may also be
a way of expressing disapproval of a person's actions. In this
sense, even white folk, when they are acting inappropriately, are
called *nigguhs*. Finally, the term may simply identify black folks
— period. In this sense, the word has neutral value. "*All the nigguhs in the Motor City got rides*" means simply (and not pejora-
tively) that all persons of African descent that live in the city of
Detroit have automobiles.

Lest we forget, we are talking about terms rooted in the black
cultural experience, the semantics of which depends not only on
the immediate linguistic context but on the sociohistorical context as well. An excellent illustration of this is the word *baby*.
Among whites (and also on one level among blacks) this expression is used by men to refer tenderly, usually romantically, to
women. In the Black Semantic sense, however, it can be used between men. Since black men have historically been emasculated

by White America, black folk place a very high premium on masculinity — I mean to a far greater extent than do whites: like a black cat can get himself offed (killed) by just challenging another cat's manhood — "I'm a man, what you mean, steppin on my toe," and so on like that. What, then, would be the most manly thing a black man could do? Use a term of female address with a male; reverse the whole semantic business as employed by White America and demonstrate that his man thang is so great he "contains multitudes," so much so in fact that he can refer to another dude with a "female" term. In so doing, he is also acknowledging the supermasculinity of the recipient of the term, since in a sense the speaker is saying: you are so much man too that I can say this to you. Claude Brown, in *Manchild in the Promised Land,* aptly explains the semantic import of *baby* in black culture:

> The first time I heard the expression "baby" used by one cat to address another was up at Warwick in 1951 . . . The term had a hip ring to it, a real colored ring . . . I knew right away I had to start using it. It was like saying, "Man, look at me. I've got masculinity to spare." It was saying at the same time to the world, "I'm one of the hippest cats, one of the most uninhibited cats on the scene. I can say 'baby' to another cat, and he can say 'baby' to me, and we can say it with strength in our voices." If you could say it, this meant that you really had to be sure of yourself, sure of your masculinity . . .
>
> The real hip thing about the "baby" term was that it was something that only colored cats could say the way it was supposed to be said. I'd heard gray boys trying it, but they couldn't really do it. Only colored cats could give it the meaning that we all knew it had without ever mentioning it — the meaning of Black masculinity.

Note too that since this is an in-group term, it also connotes togetherness or peoplehood. Thus, by extension, *baby* can be used by a black man to address a strange black woman with no romantic or flirtatious overtones — it's his way of simply acknowledging her place in the black community fold. (By contrast, a white man using *baby* to a strange white woman might get his face slapped.) Remember the late Congressman Adam

Clayton Powell's famous "Keep the faith, baby"? Well, that's what that expression was all about. Just saying "Keep the faith" wouldn't have done it. By adding "baby" Powell was conveying a sense of unity, for he knew black men and women would recognize the term as one of nationalistic endearment. What A. C. Powell's "baby" meant was: "I'm with y'all."

Many Black Semantic terms refer to Afro-American physical characteristics and black-white interactional conflict and are used in this way almost solely by blacks.

While some of the soul terms already mentioned can be and are being used by whites in a somewhat similar fashion, there is another whole category of terminology and concepts that precludes white usage. Such terms are generally limited in meaning to one particular black-based referent. Some have to do with hair, color, skin, and facial features of blacks; others are terms referring to whites.

Kitchen refers to the hair at the nape of the neck, which is inclined to be very kinky. On the whole head of hair, it is therefore the hardest part to keep straightened. In the old days of whiteomania, black women, especially, were extremely self-conscious about their kitchens and would go to great lengths to hide them. Many refused to wear upsweep hairdos because it would expose the kitchen. If you were one of the "lucky" ones who had a straight, silky kitchen, you bragged about it and were often complimented for it. Another part of the hair that was hard to keep straightened was the *edges,* referring to the contour of the hairline that connects with the facial skin.

The word *nappy* refers to extremely kinky hair, once damned but now praised. If your hair was real nappy, it was said to be *bad (meaning "not good")* hair; *good hair,* by contrast, was naturally straight hair akin to that of whites. Naturally everybody who wasn't in the good hair club used some artificial means of achieving that status. For the Sisters, this usually involved the excruciating long process of pulling a heated iron comb (called in black talk a *hot comb,* even when it was cold) through small strands of hair one at a time; this was followed by a curling procedure, again using heated irons for this purpose. Depending on how long and how thick your hair was, the whole job, with washing and drying, could conceivably take up to three hours, and you were lucky if you came through it all with no telltale burns on your face or neck. ("Telltale" since mostly everybody had to get they hair straightened, but pretended it was naturally that way if they could get away with the lie.) When you got your hair done, you tried real hard not to do anything to make you sweat, and you ran like hell when you saw water or rain because that would make you hair *go back* (meaning, to where it came from, its natural state of nappysville). Being obviously unhip to this agonizing possibility, white gym teachers could never understand why black girls made up so many different varieties of excuses to get out of swimming classes. (I remember once in junior high school when a young, inexperienced white teacher got scared to death and rushed one of my classmates to the school nurse because she had been "regular" for a whole month.)

In the twentieth century, a cosmetic genius developed a straightening method using chemicals — this was known as a *permanent*, also *perm*. Because it was, and still is, an expensive process, nothing but the "e-lights" (moneyed, upper-class blacks) had permanents and most working-class women put up with the hot comb method.

A *do*, also called *process*, is a Black Semantic term referring to the black male's artificially straightened hair, once praised but now damned — although the Superfly image, projected by the successful black film of that name, is doing much to bring it back in vogue. Like the Sisters, Brothers used to suffer the torture of trying to achieve whiteness. Because the shortness of their hair prevented use of the hot comb, they used the method of straightening with a basic mixture of lye and hair grease. If the solution was too strong or remained on the hair too long, it could burn out whole patches of hair and penetrate right to the scalp. However, once straight, the Brother's hair could be set in rows of Nat King Cole waves — and faster than you could say Jackie Robinson, he was so outa sight you couldn't hit him in the behind with a red apple! But Brothers, like Sisters, had to avoid water to keep their do's from going back, and they wore a scarf or *stocking cap* (made by simply cutting off the upper half of a

Sister's nylon stocking) to keep the waves in place during sleep. The scarf was called a *do-rag.*

More important than the inconvenience and possibility of damage to the hair, skin, and scalp was the attitude black folks had about their hair back then. From a practical viewpoint, straightening the hair did make it easier to comb because it reduced the snarls and kinkiness to manageable proportions. Especially for those women with very long, thick, kinky hair, it is a monster to comb it in its natural state. I have seen the pain bring tears to the eyes of grown black women, to say nothing of the agony experienced by little black girls who have yet to learn to endure it. But this was not the prime reason for getting your hair straightened, since the hot comb procedure itself was equally, if not more, torturous. No, the plain and simple motivation was a desire to look like Miss Ann, and for the Brothers, like Mr. Charley. The psychic pain caused by black self-hatred was far worse than all the hot combing and lye in the world. In his *Autobiography,* Malcolm X testifies to the psychological degradation of this experience:

> Shorty soon decided that my hair was finally long enough to be conked . . . I . . . went to a grocery store, where I got a can of Red Devil lye, two eggs, and two medium-sized white potatoes. Then at a drugstore near the poolroom, I asked for a large jar of Vaseline, a large bar of soap, a large-toothed comb and a fine-toothed comb, one of those rubber hoses with a metal sprayhead, a rubber apron and a pair of gloves . . . He peeled the potatoes and thin-sliced them into a quart-sized Mason fruit jar, then started stirring them with a wooden spoon as he gradually poured in a little over half the can of lye. "Never use a metal spoon; the lye will turn it black," he told me.
>
> A jelly-like, starchy-looking glop resulted from the lye and potatoes . . . Shorty broke in the two eggs, stirring real fast . . . The congolene turned pale-yellowish. "Feel the jar," Shorty said. I cupped my hand against the outside, and snatched it away. "Damn right, it's hot, that's the lye . . . So you know it's going to burn when I comb it in — it burns *bad.* But the longer you can stand it, the straighter the hair." . . .
>
> The congolene just felt warm when Shorty started combing it in. But then my head caught fire.

I gritted my teeth and tried to pull the sides of the kitchen table together. The comb felt as if it was raking my skin off.

My eyes watered, my nose was running. I couldn't stand it any longer; I bolted to the washbasin. I was cursing Shorty with every name I could think of when he got the spray going and started soap-lathering my head . . .

"The first time's always worst. You get used to it better before long. You took it real good, homeboy. You got a good conk." . . .

My first view in the mirror blotted out the hurting. I'd seen some pretty conks, but when it's the first time, on your *own* head, the transformation, after the lifetime of kinks, is staggering . . . on top of my head was this thick, smooth sheen of shining red hair — real red — as straight as any white man's.

How ridiculous I was! Stupid enough to stand there simply lost in admiration of my hair now looking "white." . . . I vowed that I'd never again be without a conk . . . This was my first really big step toward self-degradation: when I endured all of that pain, literally burning my flesh to have it look like a white man's hair . . . Look around today . . . you'll see the conk worn by many, many so-called "upper class" Negroes, and, as much as I hate to say it about them, on all too many Negro entertainers. One of the reasons that I've especially admired some of them, like Lionel Hampton and Sidney Poitier, among others, is that they have kept their natural hair and fought to the top. I admire any Negro man who has never had himself conked, or who has had the sense to get rid of it — as I finally did.

But before Malcolm's black consciousness makes him get rid of his conk, he experiences one final, ultimate act of self-degradation:

This was the trip to Michigan in the wintertime when I put congolene on my head, then discovered that the bathroom sink's pipes were frozen. To keep the lye from burning up my scalp, I had to stick my head into the stool and flush and flush to rinse out the stuff.

Ashy refers to the whitish coloration of black skin due to exposure to the *Hawk* (cold and wind). Whites get ashy too, but the whiteness shows up more pronouncedly on blacks due to their darker skin pigmentation. Blacks characteristically were (and perhaps are still) ashamed of their ashy skin, and black mothers used to strongly admonish young black children to put hair grease on their faces, arms, and legs so the ashiness wouldn't show up. (Grease, not lotion — ain't enough oil in lotion.)

Saddity is applied to uppity-acting blacks who put on airs; *haincty* to those who are contentious and unpleasant-acting. While *Miss Ann,* also just plain *Ann,* is a derisive reference to the white woman, by extension it is applied to any black woman who puts on airs and tries to act like Miss Ann. The cultural and corresponding semantic corrective to a black Miss Ann is *Big Momma,* referring to the black grandmother, typically a central figure in the black family household who keeps the kids while the parents work. Though white sociology has depicted Big Momma as a big-bosomed emasculating matriarch, she was, in fact, the anchor and core that held the family together through her unselfish sacrifice and warm love that nurtured her grandchildren through the storm and taught them to keep their "eye on the sparrow."

Silks and *pink toes* are positive references to white women, used mostly by black men who, again in the old (?) days, valued the white woman's physical characteristics over those of black women. *Silk* is an obvious allusion to the softness and silkiness of white women's hair, and *pink toes* to the supposed softness and tenderness of their feet, as contrasted to Sapphire's large feet, usually calloused and swollen from standing too long and working too hard in the kitchens and households of pink toes. The term *Sapphire* itself, with its suggestion of black color, refers to the stereotypical evil, complaining, emasculating black woman.

The Man is an ambivalent reference to the white man. While it suggests the fearful notion of "boss" and control in this male-dominated society, black men have always thought they could outsmart and out-man The Man if given only half a chance. The ambivalence lies in the fact that if the white man is The Man, then is the black man unconsciously acknowledging that he is The Boy?

Unlike the more slangy terms easily borrowed by White

America, the foregoing terms are so firmly rooted in the black experiential setting (which includes both servitude and psychological oppression) that they cannot be properly used nor understood outside the black context.

Many Black Semantic concepts enter the American cultural mainstream and serve to enrich the general language of all Americans.

The terms so absorbed are those of direct African origin such as those cited on page 45 and a larger number often (and y'all now know erroneously, right?) labeled "slang," such as *cool, dig, jazz, jive, uptight.* Initially these latter terms moved out of the black community via white musicians and others of the artsy Hip Set (whom Mailer referred to as "white Negroes"). In the late 1950s and early 1960s, this movement out was continued by young whites who participated in the civil rights movement. Today, given the pervasiveness of the mass communications network and the explosion of soul, the process of borrowing general, casual white talk from the black vocabulary is inevitable. An interesting example of such a term is the word *hip* (which was always represented as *hep* in the Archie comic book days of my youth — and interestingly enough, a number of blacks who went to schools with whites were constantly "corrected" for this pronunciation, I among them). In the black community the term has always been rendered as *hip* and used widely in the community, not just among the teeny-bopper set. Well, nowadays, everybody and they momma is talkin bout bein hip and rendering the word with Black America's "mispronunciation." Another example is the word *rap.* All over America, folks is having rap sessions. What you see is not always what you get however, as the translation of the word *rap* demonstrates. In the white mainstream, *rap* is used to mean talk, usually serious, but in its indigenous black meaning, *rap* refers to romantic talk from a black man to a black woman for purposes of winning her emotional and sexual affection. Interestingly enough — but not at all surprisingly, since blacks participate in mainstream white culture — this word has now been recycled in the black community and both the original black meaning and the newer white meaning are now employed.

Black Semantics exists in a dynamic state.

Another property of the black lexicon, especially in relation to more slangy terms, is that it is in a constant state of rapid change. That is, the words given the special Black Semantic slant tend to lose their linguistic currency in the black community if or when they move into the white mainstream. Thus new words must be coined continuously. Since, for example, *hip* was picked up so readily, it was quickly replaced by *together,* which in turn was replaced by *cold* and *mean.* This dynamism is due, in part, to today's rather extreme cultural chauvinism among blacks, which says all whites are lames and if they are using this expression, it's gotten stale and unhip. Or, "Baby, it ain mean enough for me." The other part of the explanation may be due to the historical inimical relations of blacks and whites which dictated the necessity for a black linguistic code. Then, too, the change is more accelerated today than it was in the past, because of the recent cultural closeness between blacks and whites and the rapidity with which terms can be borrowed through mass communications. On a national scale, blacks can easily adapt to these linguistic changes because many of them involve simply semantic substitutions from the black linguistic-cultural universe and are often, in fact, merely the re-emerging of older terms.

Fortunately for the continued healthy survival of Black Semantics, as well as the sustained enrichment of White English, there is a wealth of semantic tradition and rich linguistic resources in black culture that can be drawn upon.

Black Semantics is highly metaphorical and imagistic.

Many Black English vocabulary items manifest a poetically appropriate representation of rather mundane reality. Not only is the black lexicon a tool, its figurative power and rhetorical beauty complement its survival function. Many Black English terms are unusual, innovative ways of articulating rather ordinary events. To *hat up,* for instance, means "to leave," derived from the fact that one usually puts one's hat on when leaving. To *co-sign,* means to verify or affirm what someone has said or done, derived from the frequent necessity — if you're black — of having someone co-sign for you before you can obtain credit. *Lames*

are folks who are out of step and can't keep up. *Players* are
pimps, hustlers, and playboys who are *up on it* and *hip* to *playing
the game* (of life). *Mother's Day* is the day welfare and A.D.C.
mothers (a disproportionate percentage of whom are black) get
their checks.

Black Semantics has fluid social and generational boundaries.
Black vocabulary cuts across generational, sexual, educational,
and occupational lines. Most segments of the black community
use some, if not all, of the terms from the black lexicon, at one
time or another. And certainly most black folk, because they re-
side in the black community, come into contact with Black
Semantics, and if not ready users, can immediately understand
the terms (as opposed to whites, to whom the lingo is "foreign"
unless or until it hits the mainstream). While subsets within the
black community use some terms that represent the special jargon of their group, most of the different semantic concepts simply represent variations on the theme of the fundamental historical and descriptive principles outlined here. For instance,
church folk refer to spirit possession and mystical, religious
ecstasy as *gittin happy*. On Friday, *eagle-flyin* day (pay day), secular
folk look forward to *gittin high*. Musicians and dancers hope to
achieve a spirit-catharsis by *gittin down*. All black groups speak of
gittin ovuh — overcoming strife and pressures of oppression and
thus being in a continuous state of *happiness* and *highness*.

Though Black Semantic terms may vary somewhat from region to region and to some extent within subgroups in the black
community, the Afro-American's intuitive knowledge of Black
Semantics, coupled with his or her participation in the common
black experience, enables that person to interpret or translate
any words, expressions, and idioms not heard before. Thus
blacks from one community have no trouble adjusting to the
black linguistics of another community.*

---

*Consult Appendix C for a glossed summary of selected terms in Black
Semantics.

4

"How I Got Ovuh"

African World View and Afro-American Oral Tradition

My soul look back and wonder
How I got over.

BOTH in the old-time black Gospel song and in black street
vernacular, "gittin ovuh" has to do with surviving. While the religious usage of the phrase speaks to spiritual survival in a sinister world of sin, its secular usage speaks to material survival in a
white world of oppression. Since men and women live neither by
bread nor spirit alone, both vitally necessary acts of gittin ovuh
challenge the human spirit to "keep on pushin" toward "higher
ground." In Black America, the oral tradition has served as a
fundamental vehicle for gittin ovuh. That tradition preserves
the Afro-American heritage and reflects the collective spirit of
the race. Through song, story, folk sayings, and rich verbal
interplay among everyday people, lessons and precepts about
life and survival are handed down from generation to generation. Until contemporary times, Black America relied on word-
of-mouth for its rituals of cultural preservation. (For instance, it
was not until the late nineteenth century that the Negro spirituals were written down, though they date well back to the beginnings of slavery.) But word-of-mouth is more than sufficient because the structural underpinnings of the oral tradition remain
basically intact even as each new generation makes verbal adaptations within the tradition. Indeed the core strength of this tradition lies in its capacity to accommodate new situations and
changing realities. If we are to understand the complexity and
scope of black communication patterns, we must have a clear

understanding of the oral tradition and the world view that un-
dergirds that tradition.

◆

The Black communication system is actualized in different
ways, dependent upon the sociocultural context — for instance,
"street" versus "church" — but the basic underlying structures of
this communication network are essentially similar because they
are grounded in the traditional African world view. In brief, that
view refers to underlying thought patterns, belief sets, values,
ways of looking at the world and the community of men and
women that are shared by all traditional Africans (that is, those
that haven't been westernized).

The mainstream tradition of European scholarship on Africa
has rested on a conceptual framework relative to the so-called
"diversity" of Africa. To be sure, there are differences in the
many tribes, languages, customs, spirits, and deities that exist
throughout the African continent, but these seeming diversities
are merely surface variations on the basic "deep structure"
themes of life acknowledged by traditional Africans. Focusing
on such surface differences as tribal customs or politically defined African boundaries has only served to obscure the existence of the deep structure that is shared by all traditional African people. Robert F. Thompson conducted field studies of
African art in nine different African cultures and was able to
identify common canons of form pervading them all. Similarly,
Daryll Forde's studies of African social values in various tribal
cultures brought him to remark that: "One is impressed, not
only by the great diversity of ritual forms and expressions of beliefs, but also by substantial underlying similarities in religious
outlook and moral injunction." And the West African scholar
Fela Sowande, as well as the East African scholar John S. Mbiti,
present nearly identical descriptions of the African view of the
universe and man's place in the scheme of things. To be sure,
students of African culture have yet to detail *all* of the salient
features that transcend tribal differences and constitute what is
here being called the "traditional African world view." But recent findings and field studies, especially those of African

scholars themselves, point to sufficient patterns of commonality to suggest an interlocking cultural and philosophical network throughout Africa. We can thus assert that similar underlying thought patterns do exist amid the unending diversity of African people, and therefore it is appropriate to speak of traditional African thought as a single entity — albeit with complex and diverse manifestations.

What is the traditional African world view? First, there is a fundamental unity between the spiritual and the material aspects of existence. Though both the material and the spiritual are necessary for existence, the spiritual domain assumes priority.

The universe is hierarchical in nature, with God at the head of the hierarchy, followed by lesser deities, the "living dead" (ancestral spirits), people, animals, and plants. Though the universe is hierarchical, all modes of existence are necessary for the sustenance of its balance and rhythm. Harmony in nature and the universe is provided by the complementary, interdependent, synergic interaction between the spiritual and the material. Thus we have a paradigm for the way in which "opposites" function. That is, "opposites" constitute interdependent, interacting forces which are necessary for producing a given reality.

Similarly, communities of people are modeled after the interdependent rhythms of the universe. Individual participation is necessary for community survival. Balance in the community, as in the universe, consists of maintaining these interdependent relationships.

The universe moves in a rhythmical and cyclical fashion as opposed to linear progression. "Progression," as such, occurs only into the past world of the spirit. Thus the "future" is the past. In the community, then, one's sense of "time" is based on participation in and observation of nature's rhythms and community events. (In the African conception of "time," the key is not to be "on time," but "in time.") And since participatory experiences are key to one's sense of "time," the fundamental pedagogy in the school of life becomes experience, and age serves as a prime basis for hierarchical social arrangements.

Community roles are equally governed by the hierarchical

unity of the spiritual and material aspects of the universe. Since the spiritual realm is the ultimate existence of humankind, those closest to the spiritual realm assume priority in social relationships. Thus, elders are of great importance, and the spiritually developed people serve as rulers and doctors.

Naturally, Black Americans, having had to contend with slavery and Euro-American ways, have not been able to practice or manifest the traditional African world view in its totality. But, as we shall see in closely examining the many facets of the oral tradition, the residue of the African world view persists, and serves to unify such seemingly disparate black groups as preachers and poets, bluesmen and Gospel-ettes, testifiers and toast-tellers, reverends and revolutionaries. Can I get a witness?

Both in slavery times and now, the black community places high value on the spoken word. That community supports a tradition that the anthropologists would call "preliterate." (Although the great Margaret Mead laid the classic bomb on the superiority complex of the Western world when she said that the "influence" of Western culture on non-Western peoples was to make the "preliterate illiterate." In fact, the black oral tradition links Black American culture with that of other oral "preliterate" people — such as Native Americans — for whom the spoken word is supreme.) The persistence of the African-based oral tradition is such that blacks tend to place only limited value on the written word, whereas verbal skills expressed orally rank in high esteem. This is not to say that Black Americans never read anything or that the total black community is functionally illiterate. The influence of White America and the demands of modern, so-called civilized living have been too strong for that. However, it is to say that from a black perspective, written documents are limited in what they can teach about life and survival in the world. Blacks are quick to ridicule "educated fools," people who done gone to school and read all dem books and still don't know nothin! They have "book learning" but no "mother wit," knowledge, but not wisdom. (Naturally, not *all* educated people are considered "educated fools," but if the shoe fits . . .) Furthermore, aside from athletes and entertainers, only those blacks who can perform stunning feats of oral gymnastics become culture heroes and leaders in the community. Such feats are the basic requirement of the trade among preachers, politicians, disc jockeys, hustlers, and lovers. Like the preacher who was exhorting his congregation to take care of themselves and their bodies:

Preacher:	How many of y'all wanna live to a old age?
Congregation:	Hallelujah!
Preacher:	Or is y'all ready to die and go to Heaven?
Congregation:	(uncomfortable; some self-conscious laughter)
	Well, no Lord, not yet, suh!
Preacher:	Y'all wanna stay here awhile?
Congregation:	Praise the Lord!
Preacher:	Well, y'all better quit all this drankin, smokin, and runnin 'round. Cause, see, for me, I got a home in Heaven, but I ain't homesick!

And check out this from a black disc jockey on a "soul" station. He is urging his audience to listen to his station because it's the best, and to call in to win the "top ten" album, therein making the winner eligible for the grand prize: "Super CHB . . . making the music work for you. When one quits, another hits . . . Looking for that seventh caller . . . Caller number seven, call, cop, and qualify."

In any culture, of course, language is a tool for ordering the chaos of human experience. We feel more comfortable when we have names for events and things. To know that "the earth is round and revolves around the sun" might not bring us any closer to solving the riddle of the universe, but at least it helps in imposing an orderly explanation upon a seemingly disorderly world. To use words to give shape and coherence to human existence is a universal human thing — a linguistic fact of life that transcends cultural boundaries. The crucial difference in American culture lies in the contrasting modes in which Black and White Americans have shaped that language — a written mode for whites, having come from a European, print-oriented culture; a spoken mode for blacks, having come from an African, orally-oriented background. As black psychiatrist Frantz Fanon describes it, to "talk like a book" is to "talk like a white man."

The oral tradition, then, is part of the cultural baggage the

African brought to America. The preslavery background was one in which the concept of Nommo, the magic power of the Word, was believed necessary to actualize life and give man mastery over things. "All activities of men, and all the movements in nature, rest on the word, on the productive power of the word, which is water and heat and seed and Nommo, that is, life force itself . . . The force, responsibility, and commitment of the word, and the awareness that the word alone alters the world . . ." In traditional African culture, a newborn child is a mere thing until his father gives and speaks his name. No medicine, potion, or magic of any sort is considered effective without accompanying words. So strong is the African belief in the power and absolute necessity of Nommo that all craftsmanship must be accompanied by speech. And it is not uncommon for a verbal battle to precede or accompany warfare. In the African epic of Sundiata, a renowned king of ancient Mali, the exiled king must wage war to regain his throne, but, as the griot tells us, "those fighting must make a declaration of their grievances to begin with":

"Stop, young man. Henceforth I am the king of Mali. If you want peace, return to where you came from," said Soumaoro.

"I am coming back, Soumaoro, to recapture my kingdom. If you want peace you will make amends to my allies and return to Sosso where you are the king."

"I am king of Mali by force of arms. My rights have been established by conquest."

"Then I will take Mali from you by force of arms and chase you from my kingdom."

"Know, then that I am the wild yam of the rocks; nothing will make me leave Mali."

"Know, also that I have in my camp seven master smiths who will shatter the rocks. Then, yam, I will eat you."

"I am the poisonous mushroom that makes the fearless vomit."

"As for me, I am the ravenous cock, the poison does not matter to me."

"Behave yourself, little boy, or you will burn your foot, for I am the red-hot cinder."

"But me, I am the rain that extinguishes the cinder; I am the boisterous torrent that will carry you off."

"I am the mighty silk-cotton tree that looks from on high on the tops of other trees"

"And I, I am the strangling creeper that climbs to the top of the forest giant."

"Enough of this argument. You shall not have Mali."

"Know that there is not room for two kings on the same skin, Soumaoro; you will let me have your place."

"Very well, since you want war I will wage war against you, but I would have you know that I have killed nine kings whose heads adorn my room. What a pity, indeed, that your head should take its place beside those of your fellow madcaps."

"Prepare yourself, Soumaoro, for it will be long before the calamity that is going to crash down upon you and yours comes to an end."

Thus Sundiata and Soumaoro spoke together. After the war of mouths, swords had to decide the issue.

The above exchange of word-arrows is not unlike that of two bloods squaring off on any street corner or in any cottonfield in the U.S.:

"If you don't quit messin wif me, uhma jump down your throat, tap dance on your liver, and make you wish you never been born."

"Yeah, you and how many armies? Nigger, don't you know uhm so bad I can step on a wad of gum and tell you what flavor it is."

Even though blacks have embraced English as their native tongue, still the African cultural set persists, that is, a predisposition to imbue the English word with the same sense of value and commitment — "propers," as we would say — accorded to Nommo in African culture. Hence Afro-America's emphasis on orality and belief in the power of the rap which has produced a style and idiom totally unlike that of whites, while paradoxically employing White English words. We're talking, then, about a tradition in the black experience in which verbal performance becomes both a way of establishing "yo rep" as well as a teaching and socializing force. This performance is exhibited in the narration of myths, folk stories, and the semiserious tradition of "lying" in general; in black sermons; in the telling of jokes; in proverbs and folk sayings; in street corner, barbershop, beauty shop, and other casual rap scenes; in "signifying," "capping," "testifying," "toasting," and other verbal arts. Through these raps of various kinds, black folk are acculturated — initiated — into the black value system. Not talking about speech for the sake of speech, for black talk is never simple cocktail chit-chat, but a functional dynamic that is simultaneously a mechanism for learning about life and the world and a vehicle for achieving group approval and recognition. Even in what appears to be only casual conversation, whoever speaks is highly conscious of the fact that his personality is on exhibit and his status at stake. Black raps ain bout talkin loud and sayin nothin, for the speaker must be up on the subject of his rap, and his oral contribution must be presented in a dazzling, entertaining manner. Black speakers are flamboyant, flashy, and exaggerative; black raps are stylized, dramatic, and spectacular; speakers and raps become symbols of how to git ovuh.

In his autobiography *Black Boy,* Richard Wright excellently depicts the dynamics of a street corner rap in a Southern town:

"You eat yet?" Uneasily trying to make conversation.

"Yeah, man. I done really fed my face." Casually.

"I had cabbage and potatoes." Confidently.

"I had buttermilk and black-eyed peas." Meekly informational.

"Hell, I ain't gonna stand near you, nigger." Pronouncement.

"How come?" Feigned innocence.

"Cause you gonna smell up this air in a minute!" A shouted accusation.

Laughter runs through the crowd.

"Nigger, your mind's in a ditch." Amusingly moralistic.

"Ditch, nothing! Nigger, you going to break wind any minute now!" Triumphant pronouncement creating suspense.

"Yeah, when them black-eyed peas tell that buttermilk to move over, that buttermilk ain't gonna wanna move and there's gonna be war in your guts and your stomach's gonna swell up and bust!" Climax.

The crowd laughs loud and long.

"Man, them white folks oughta catch you and send you to the zoo and keep you for the next war!" Throwing the subject into a wider field.

"Then when that fighting starts, they oughta feed you on buttermilk and black-eyed peas and let you break wind!" The subject is accepted and extended.

"You'd win the war with a new kind of poison gas!" A shouted climax.

There is high laughter that simmers down slowly.

"Maybe poison gas is something good to have." The subject of white folks is associationally swept into the orbit of talk.

"Man, you reckon these white folks is ever gonna change?" Timid, questioning hope.

"Hell, no! They just born that way." Rejecting hope for fear that it could never come true.

"Shucks, man. I'm going north when I get grown." Rebelling against futile hope and embracing flight.

"A colored man's all right up north." Justifying flight.

"They say a white man hit a colored man up north and that colored man hit that white man, knocked him cold, and nobody did a damn thing!" Urgent wish to believe in flight.

"Man for man up there." Begging to believe in justice.

Silence.

"Listen, you reckon them buildings up north is as tall as they say they is?" Leaping by association to something concrete and trying to make belief real.

"They say they gotta building in New York forty stories high!" A thing too incredible for belief.

"Man, I'd be scareda them buildings!" Ready to abandon the now suppressed idea of flight.

"You know, they say that them buildings sway and rock in the wind." Stating a miracle.

"Naw, nigger!" Utter astonishment and rejection.

"Yeah, they say they do." Insisting upon the miracle.

"You reckon that could be?" Questioning hope.

"Hell, naw! If a building swayed and rocked in the wind, hell, it'd fall! Any fool knows that! Don't let people maka fool outta you, telling you them things." Moving body agitatedly, stomping feet impatiently, and scurrying back to safe reality.

Silence. Somebody would pick up a stone and toss it across a field.

"Man, what makes white folks so mean?" Returning to grapple with the old problem.

"Whenever I see one I spit!" Emotional rejection of whites.

"Man, ain't they ugly?" Increased emotional rejection.

"Man, you ever get right close to a white man, close enough to smell 'im?" Anticipation of statement.

"They say we stink. But my ma says white folks smell like dead folks." Wishing the enemy was dead.

"Niggers smell from sweat. But white folks smell *all* the time."
The enemy is an animal to be killed on sight.

And the talk would weave, roll, surge, spurt, veer, swell, having
no specific aim or direction, touching vast areas of life, expressing
the tentative impulses of childhood. Money, God, race, sex, color,
war, planes, machines, trains, swimming, boxing, anything . . . The
culture of one black household was thus transmitted to another
black household, and folk tradition was handed from group to
group. Our attitudes were made, defined, set, or corrected; our
ideas were discovered, discarded, enlarged, torn apart, and accepted.

While some raps convey social and cultural information,
others are used for conquering foes and women. Through signification, the Dozens*, and boastful talk, a dude can be properly put to rest with words. (Recall the verbal duel in the Sundiata epic.) Hubert "Rap" Brown, the controversial black leader
of the 1960s, describes this cultural phenomenon in his autobiography, *Die Nigger Die!*:

> . . . what you try to do is totally destroy somebody else with words.
> It's that whole competition thing again, fighting each other.
> There'd be sometimes 40 or 50 dudes standing around and the
> winner was determined by the way they responded to what was
> said. If you fell all over each other laughing, then you knew you'd
> scored . . . The real aim of the Dozens was to get a dude so mad
> that he'd cry or get mad enough to fight . . . Signifying is more
> humane. Instead of coming down on somebody's mother, you
> come down on them . . . A session would start maybe by a brother
> saying, "Man, before you mess with me you'd rather run rabbits,
> eat shit and bark at the moon." Then, if he was talking to me, I'd
> tell him:
> Man, you must don't know who I am.
> I'm sweet peeter jeeter the womb beater
> The baby maker the cradle shaker
> The deerslayer the buckbinder the women finder
> Known from the Gold Coast to the rocky shores of Maine
> Rap is my name and love is my game.

Signification refers to the act of talking negatively about somebody through
stunning and clever verbal put downs. In the black vernacular, it is more commonly referred to as *sigging* or *signifyin*. *The Dozens* is a verbal game based on
negative talk about somebody's mother. More on both of these in Chapter Five.

Since it is a socially approved verbal strategy for black rappers to talk about how bad they is, such bragging is taken at face value. While the speakers may or may not act out the implications of their words, the point is that the listeners do not necessarily *expect* any action to follow. As a matter of fact, skillful rappers can often avoid having to prove themselves through deeds if their rap is strong enough. The Black Idiom expression "selling woof [wolf] tickets" (also just plain "woofin") refers to any kind of strong language which is purely idle boasting. However, this bad talk is nearly always taken for the real thing by an outsider from another culture. Such cultural-linguistic misperception can lead to tragic consequences. Witness, for instance, the physical attacks and social repression suffered by black spokesmen of the 1960s, such as the Black Panthers. "Death to the racist exploiters!" "Off the pigs!" "Defend our communities by any means necessary!" — the white folks thought the bloods was not playin and launched an all-out military campaign. These aggressive moves resulted partly from White America's sense of fear that the radical rhetoric (much of which was really defensive, rather than offensive) constituted more than idle threats. The whites were not hip to braggadocio and woof tickets; at any rate, they wasn't buyin none.

While boastful raps are used to devastate enemies, love raps help in gittin ovuh with women. Both, of course, require speakers with intellectual adroitness and a way with words. Since it is believed that the spoken word has power, it is only logical to employ it with what many regard as men's most formidable obstacle — women. Many black rappers specialize in the verbal art of romantic rappin. Like Hubert "Rap" Brown said, love is his game. Examples of such "game," dating from the nineteenth century are provided in the folklore collection of Hampton Institute. Here is one such example which appeared in an 1895 edition of the *Southern Workman,* a journal published by the institute: "My dear kin' miss, has you any objections to me drawing my cher to yer side, and revolvin' de wheel of my conversation around de axle of your understandin'?" A contemporary example is provided in the novel *Snakes* by Al Young, in which Young depicts a heavy love rapper in his main character, Shakes (short for Shakespeare). Exemplifying the rich ability of black speechmakers, Shakes gives propers to another great rapper who taught him that "you can get away with anything if you talk up on it right."

> I just wanna knock out chicks and show these other dudes they aint hittin on doodleysquat when it come to talkin trash. I got it down, jim! You hip to Cyrano de Bergerac? . . . Talk about a joker could talk some trash! Cyrano got everybody told! Didn't nobody be messin with Cyrano, ugly as he was. Some silly stud get to cappin on Cyrano's nose and he dont flinch an inch. He get right up in the stud's face and vaporize him with several choice pronouncements, then he go and waste the cat in a suhword fight. Meantime, there's this little local lame that's tryna make it with Cyrano's cousin Roxanne, so old Cyrano and the lame get back up behind the bushes one night while the chick up there on the balcony. Cyrano whisperin all in the lame's ear what he spose to be sayin, but the lame messin up the lines so bad until Cyrano just sweep him on off to one side and stand up and make the speech his own self. He commence to messin up the broad's mind so bad she ready to out and out say I do. See, she dont know it's her own cousin that's been layin down that incredible rap. And now, to show you what kinda man Cyrano was, after that lady is on the verge of succumbing to the amorous design that his words had traced in the air of that night, so to speak, then he just step off to one side and let her old lame boyfriend move on into the picture and cop, like he the one been doin all that old freakish talk out there under the moonlight.

Contrary to popular stereotype, black men have never really regarded black women as sex objects, pure and simple, for the love rap, based on the African view of the reconciliation of opposites, is a synthesis of emotional and intellectual appeal and has as its ultimate objective the conquest not simply of the woman's body, but her mind as well. As one blood said, "Baby, I don't just want your behind, I want your mind." Romantic raps not only contain sweet and complimentary "nothings" that lovers like to hear, but they must demonstrate the rapper's power and ability at persuasive verbal logic. An excellent example of a unique rap is provided by Woodie King in "The Game," a description of his early life in the streets. In an effort to git ovuh with Edith, a very foxy but "religious broad," Sweet Mac introduces the Bible into the game — surely an unprecedented technique in this tradition:

> . . . for the last couple of weeks I been quoting the Good Book and all that stuff to her; telling her I am now saved myself, you dig . . . I says to her, "Edith, baby, we can't go on like this. I dig you *but* . . . baby I'm one hundred percent man. And baby, from looking at you, you are one hundred percent woman (the broad went for this evaluation) . . . So . . . if that is the case, something or someone is trying to keep us — two pure American religious people of the same order — apart." At this point, I drop a quote or two from the Good Book on her; *"Thou shall not covet thy neighbor's wife;* and baby since you're not anybody's wife, I pleaded, *do unto others as you would have them do unto you . . ."* Next, I whispered to her secretly, doing the ear bit with the tongue, "Baby only something like that no-good Satan would want to stop something as mellow as laying naked in the Foggy Night with MJQ or Ravel on the hi-fi, me there playing with you, only Satan," I says. "He trying to put game on us, momma." The broad is looking dazed like she done seen the handwriting on the wall.

The existence of love rappin in the oral tradition allows a strange black man to approach a strange black woman without fear of strong reprisal. Black women are accustomed to — and many even expect — this kind of verbal aggressiveness from black men. Black culture thus provides a socially approved verbal mechanism with which the man can initiate conversation aimed at deepening the acquaintance. Rappin also accounts for what whites often label as "aggressive," "brash," "presumptive," or "disrespectful" behavior by black men toward black women. "Hey pretty momma, where you goin, wit yo baaaad self? I know you a movie star or somebody important, but could I just have a minute of yo time?" If she's interested, he gets more than a minute, if not, she just smiles and keeps on steppin.

Though this approach was previously reserved for males, with the advent of feminist assertion black women are beginning to develop the art of romantic rappin. However, it is a strictly contemporary, slowly developing trend, and verbal aggressiveness from women is still not approved in any but the most sophisticated social sets.

by Ollie Harrington

"That book ain't gonna teach you no French, Bootsie. You got to live it. Now s'posin' you just had a fine feed at some chick's pad. You bows and says, 'Bon soir mademoisselle, et cetera.' Now that means, 'Good night, Irene. Thanks for the fine scoff. The chitterlings was simply devine and I'll dig you by and by!' "

Black sermons also form an important part of the oral tradition. By now the sermonizing style of traditional black clergy is perhaps rather widely known, especially given the preacher imitations done by popular black comedians Flip Wilson and Richard Pryor. What has not been too well publicized is the devastating raps black preachers run down before and after their sermons. Since the traditional black church service is an emotion-packed blend of sacred and secular concerns, informality is the order of the day. It is not a lax, anything-goes kind of informality, though, for there are traditional rituals to be performed, and codes of proper social conduct must be observed. For instance, if the Spirit moves you, it's acceptable to get up and testify even though that's not on the church program. On the other hand, when the preacher is "taking his text,"* a hushed silence falls over the whole congregation, and it is most out of order to get up, move around in your seat, talk, or do anything until he finishes this brief ritual in the traditional structure of the sermon.

Since the traditional black church is a social as well as a religious unit, the preacher's job as leader of his flock is to make churchgoers feel at home and to deal with the problems and realities confronting his people as they cope with the demands and stresses of daily living. Thus preachers are given wide latitude as to the topics they can discuss and the methods of presentation. Indeed, the congregation virtually demands digressive commentary and episodic rappin as a prelude to the big event. I mean, if you a preacher in a traditional black church you just don't be gittin up and goin right into yo sermon like they does in them other churches. The best preachers use this time wisely, as in the case of the big city "Reb" who was called on the carpet for healing and selling blessings over the radio:

Preacher: I thank God for this radio station.
Congregation: My Lord! Yes, Lord!

*Also referred to as "announcing" his text, this involves a fairly consistent three-part structure: 1) the act of citing the Scriptural reference from which the message of the sermon is to be taken, followed by 2) the reading of the passage, and concluding with 3) a usually cleverly worded statement articulating the "theme" (message) of the sermon.

Preacher:	Y'all know you got some radio directors with two years of edu-ma-cation.
Congregation:	Look out, now! You on the case! Tell it! Tell it! Two years!
Preacher:	And they have decided that they know what you want to hear. Who ever heard of a radio station licensed by the Federal Communications System that's gon tell *you* that you cain't heal?!!
Congregation:	Right on, brother!
Preacher:	Gon tell you that you cain't read a Scripture.
Congregation:	Well, well!
Preacher:	You don't tell them white folks that.
Congregation:	Hallelujah!
Preacher:	So don't tell me that 'cause I don't wonna hear it!
Congregation:	No, Lord!
Preacher:	If Jesus hada healed all the rich folks, he wouldn'ta had no problems!
Congregation:	Amen! Speak on it!

The inclusion of church raps here in practically the same breath as street raps is to demonstrate the sacred-secular continuum in the oral tradition and to dramatize the importance of the black church in the culture and verbal style of black people. Very broadly speaking, and for purposes of illustration only, we can think of black language as having both a sacred and a secular style. The sacred style is rural and Southern. It is grounded in the black church tradition and black religious experience. It is revealed in the spirituals, the Moan, the Chant, the Gospel songs; it is testifyin, talkin in tongue, and bearin witness to the power of God and prayer. It tends to be more emotional and highly charged than the secular style. Though urban and Northern, the secular style also has its roots in the rural South. It is manifested in forms like the Dozens, the Toast, the blues, and folk tales, all of which were transformed to accommodate the urban experience. Within the secular style is the street culture style, the style commonly associated with, but not exclusive to, barbershops, pool halls, and street corners in black communities. More cool, more emotionally restrained than the sacred style, newer and younger in time, the secular style only fully evolved as

by Ollie Harrington

"Smite them down to the third, yea, even unto the fourth generation. Even as King David smote down the mighty Philistines . . . An' watch that left jab!"

a distinct style with the massive wave of black migration to the cities.

Sacred style is an important force in black culture because the traditional black church is the oldest and perhaps still the most powerful and influential black institution. To speak of the "traditional" black church is to speak of the holy-rolling, bench-walking, spirit-getting, tongue-speaking, vision-receiving, intuitive-directing, Amen-saying, sing-song preaching, holy-dancing, and God-sending church. Put another way, this church may be defined as that in which the content and religious substance has been borrowed from Western Judaeo-Christian tradition, but the communication of that content — the process — has remained essentially African. The specific convergence of Judaeo-Christian content and African process is found in Protestant denominations, such as Baptist, Methodist, Holiness, and Sanctified, where the worship patterns are characterized by spontaneous preacher-congregation calls and responses, hollers and shouts, intensely emotional singing, spirit possession, and extemporaneous testimonials to the power of the Holy Spirit.

The traditional black church is peopled by working-class blacks — domestics, factory workers, janitors, unskilled laborers. While today there is an ever-increasing number of high school graduates and college-educated members, most "pillars of the church" have less than a high school education. The preacher of such a church may or may not be university-educated, but he must be able to "talk that talk" (preach in Black English style and lingo). It is within the traditional black church that traditional black folk (blacks who haven't been assimilated into the elusive American mainstream) create much of their reality, which includes the preservation and passing on of Africanized idioms, proverbs, customs, and attitudes. During slavery, the church was the one place Ole Massa allowed the slaves to congregate unsupervised and do pretty nearly as they pleased. Not surprisingly, a number of slave rebellions and revolutionary leaders (such as preacher Nat Turner) were spawned in the church. In addition to serving as a buffer and source of release against white oppression, the traditional black church functions as an important social unit where the rich and needy are helped, community news is exchanged, and black men gain opportunities (as deacons, trustees, officers) to play leadership roles. Speaking to the importance of the church, C. Eric Lincoln, the noted black historian, put it this way:

> The black man's pilgrimage in America was made less onerous because of his religion. His religion was the organizing principle around which his life was structured. His church was his school, his forum, his political arena, his social club, his art gallery, his conservatory of music. It was lyceum and gymnasium as well as sanctum sanctorum. His religion was his fellowship with man, his audience with God. It was the peculiar sustaining force which gave him the strength to endure when endurance gave no promise, and the courage to be creative in the face of his own dehumanization.

Viewing it from this perspective, we can see how the traditional black church became paramount in the history of Black America. But more than that, the embracing of a white God was a natural, cultural response based on the African way of life. Recall that in traditional African society it is believed that there is a unity between the spiritual and material aspects of existence. People are composed of both spiritual and material selves, but the prime force behind the movements of man and the universe is spiritual. This conception of a "spiritual universe" means that man's ultimate destiny is to move on to the "higher ground" of the spiritual world. Concomitant with the African's emphasis on spirituality, "religion" (in the sense in which Westerners use the term) becomes a pervasive dominating force in the society. Throughout Africa, there is no dichotomy between sacred and secular life, and there are no "irreligious people" in traditional African society, for to be "without religion amounts to a self-excommunication from the entire life of society . . . African people do not know how to exist without religion." As "common as daily bread, religion is not a sometime affair. It is a daily, minute involvement of the total person in a community and its concerns. Indeed, the spirit will not come forth with power apart from the community emptying itself (and thus the priest), so that the power can reign without interference . . . The heart of traditional African religions is the emotional experience of being

filled with the power of the spiritual." In the traditional black
church, and in Black American culture generally, this aspect of
the traditional African world view strongly continues in the emphasis on spirituality ("soul") rather than materiality. Black
Americans believe that soul, feeling, emotion, and spirit serve as
guides to understanding life and their fellows. All people are
moved by spirit-forces, and there is no attempt to deny or intel-
lectualize away that fact.

However, while blacks realize that people cannot live by bread
alone, they believe that God helps those who help themselves. As
the church folk say, "don't move the mountain, Lord, just give
me strength to climb." Thus the traditional black church's
other-worldly orientation is balanced by coping strategies for *this*
world. And, like the traditional African God, the Black American God is viewed not only as Someone Who dwells on High but
as One Who also inhabits this mundane earthly world of ours. As
such, He too balances His other-worldly concerns with those of
this world. Black American men and women, like traditional African men and women, are daily "living witnesses" to God's Supreme Power; thus they look up to God while simultaneously
being on regular speaking terms with Him. As comedian
Richard Pryor says, in talking about how a black preacher would
function as an "exorcist": "Now, I knows you's busy, Lord — I
done check yo schedule — but there's a person here who is PO-
sessed."

Given the unity of the spiritual and the material, the sacred
and the profane, in traditional African culture, it is not surprising to find the "circle unbroken" in Black America. None of this
is to say that *all* black people go to and support the church. On
the contrary, the stomp-down shonuff churchgoers are in the
minority in the community. What we are stressing here is the
heavy preservation of Africanisms in the church which have had
an impact on Black American culture at large. For instance,
when a soulful black singer or musician of secular music is really
gittin down, members of the audience unconsciously respond by
"shouting," (also referred to as "gittin happy"), that is, they show
signs of being moved by the musical spirit — hollering, clapping
hands, stomping feet, frenzied dancing, and other kinds of emo-

tional responses. In other words, here is a secular audience gittin the Spirit! That very African tradition — belief in and expression of spirit possession — was retained in the traditional black church. ("If you got religion, show some sign.") Here we are in contemporary times finding this behavior being exhibited by blacks who don't even set foot inside the church door!

Thus, while the secular style might be considered the primary domain of the street, and the sacred that of the church, no sharp dichotomy exists, but a kind of sacred-secular circular continuum. As we have said, the black preacher's rap and traditional black church service tend to be highly informal and both abound in secularisms. For example, it is considered entirely appropriate for a preacher to get up in the pulpit and, say, show off what he's wearing: "Y'all didn notice the new suit I got on today, did y'all? Ain the Lord good to us?" Similarly, there is very often a sacred quality surrounding the verbal rituals of the secular style, with all gathered about the rapper, listening attentively, looking idolizingly and lingering on his or her every word, mystically engrossed in the rap. This is the effect achieved, for instance, by a black-culture poet such as Haki Madhubuti (Don Lee) or Imamu Baraka (LeRoi Jones) verbally performing ("reading") before a black audience. The most striking example of this merging of sacred and secular styles is in the area of black music, where lyrics, musical scores, and singers themselves easily float in and out of both worlds. Black blues and soul artists who came out of the church include the Staple Singers, Sam Cooke, Lou Rawls, Dionne Warwick, Dinah Washington, Nina Simone, Sly Stone — the list goes on and on. One of the deepest of this group is Aretha Franklin, who started singing and playing piano in her father's church at a very young age, went on to make record hits in the secular world, and then "returned" to the church to record the hit album, *Amazing Grace*, with the Reverend James Cleveland. (White America might have just "discovered" Gospel singers and Gospel rock, but they been there all the time in the traditional black church.) Another fantastic move was made by James Brown when he appropriated the preacher's concluding ritual for his secular performances. "Soul Brother Number One" has a classic number that climaxes each performance: he goes off-stage and returns wearing a black cape, reminiscent of the preacher's robe, then he proceeds to do his soulful thing until he gits the Spirit; he keeps on "shoutin" until he has to be pulled away from the mike, fanned, his perspiration toweled down, and his spirit brought back under "normal" control. Can I get a witness?

◆

The language and style that comprise the sacred-secular oral tradition can be characterized in a number of ways. In Chapter Five we shall look at larger, overall patterns — strategies or modes of discourse. Here, we might speak in terms of the rhetorical qualities of smaller, individual units of expression. The qualities are: exaggerated language (unusual words, High Talk); mimicry; proverbial statement and aphoristic phrasing; punning and plays on words; spontaneity and improvisation; image-making and metaphor; braggadocio; indirection (circumlocution, suggestiveness); and tonal semantics. A black rap can have one, all, or any combination of these. Rappers must be skillful in reading the vibrations of their audience and situation, for the precise wording depends on what is said to whom under what conditions. We shall briefly illustrate each.

Exaggerated language. Rappers sprinkle their talk with uncommon words and rarely used expressions. Recall Shakes's lady "succumbing to the amorous design his words had traced in the air of the night." Martin Luther King, Jr., once referred to a matter as being "incandescently clear." A lesser-known preacher said emphatically in his sermon: "When Jesus walked the face of the earth, you know it upset the high ES-U-LAUNCE [echelon]." Sometimes the whole syntax of a sentence may be expressed in an elevated, formal manner, as in this invitation from a working-class black male: "My dear, would you care to dine with me tonight on some delectable red beans and rice?"

Mimicry. A deliberate imitation of the speech and mannerisms of someone else may be used for authenticity, ridicule, or rhetorical effect. For instance, whenever rappers quote somebody, they attempt to quote in the tone of voice, gestures, and particular idiom and language characteristic of that person. A black female complains to a friend about her man, for instance: "Like he come tellin me this old mess bout [speaker shifts to restatin and imitatin] 'Well, baby, if you just give me a chance, Ima have it together pretty soon.' That's his word, you know, always talkin bout having something 'together.' " Occasionally, the mimicking takes the form of a title or line from a song: "Told you she wasn't none of yo friend; [singing] 'smiling faces' . . ."

Proverbial statement. The rapper sprinkles his or her talk with familiar black proverbs and drives home the points with short, succinct statements which have the sound of wisdom and power. While proverbs have been around for ages, we are here referring to the black rapper's tendency to encapsulate and in a sense "freeze" experience through his or her own aphoristic phrasing. "It ain no big thang" originated in this manner; it was followed up by the aphoristic repartee: "But it's growing." Two well-known examples of proverbial-sounding statements often used by churchgoers are: "I been born again" and "My name is written on High."

Many old black proverbs become titles or lines in hit songs — for instance, Aretha Franklin's "Still Water Runs Deep" and Undisputed Truth's "Smiling Faces Sometimes Tell Lies." Many proverbs are quoted by mothers to their children and serve as child-rearing devices to teach rapidly and in no uncertain terms about life and living. "A hard head make a soft behind," "If you make yo bed hard, you gon have to lie in it," and "God don't like ugly" are three such frequently used proverbs. Proverbs and proverbial expressions are significant in the oral tradition because they hark back to an African cultural-linguistic pattern that was retained and adapted to the conditions of the New World. Among the Ibo people of West Africa, according to the African writer Chinua Achebe, "the art of conversation is regarded very highly, and proverbs are the palm-oil with which words are eaten." (Consult Appendix A for a list of well-known proverbs in the oral tradition.)

Punning. While many verbal wits employ this rhetorical strategy, punning in the black heavily depends on the threads of the black experience common to all, and knowledge of black speech. For example, it is commonly believed that black people

are adept with knives and razors as weapons. Thus James
Brown's "I don't know Karate but I know Karazor." Another
such example depends on one's knowledge of how Black English
is pronounced. It goes as follows:

> Knock, knock.
> Who's there?
> Joe.
> Joe who?
> Joe Momma.

This is a good example of playing the Dozens (see pages 130–34)
by punning on the similarity in sound between *yo* (not *your*) and
Joe.

Spontaneity. Though black raps have an overall formulaic
structure, the specifics remain to be filled in. The rapper is free
to improvise by taking advantage of anything that comes into the
situation — the listener's response, the entry of other persons to
the group, spur-of-the-moment ideas that occur to the rapper.
For example, the preacher will say, "Y'all don wont to hear dat,
so I'm gon leave it lone," but if the congregation shouts, "Naw,
tell it, Reb! Tell it!", he will. Rarely does the rapper have a completely finished speech, even in more structured "formal" kinds
of speech-making, such as sermons or political speeches. (Many
a would-be romantic rapper has been known to blow his thang
with a canned rap.) By taking advantage of process, movement,
and creativity of the moment, one's rap seems always fresh and
immediately personalized for any given situation. For instance,
before Malcolm X's prison background became widespread
knowledge, he mentioned to an audience the fact that he had
once been in prison. He read the vibrations of the audience,
sensing their surprise, and quickly reacted. Noting that all black
people in this country were, in a sense, imprisoned, he capped:
"That's what America means: prison."

Image-making. An important criterion of black talk is this use of
images, metaphors, and other kinds of imaginative language
The metaphorical constructs are what give black raps a poetic
quality. Ideas, trivial or small though they may be, must be expressed in creative ways. Preachers especially must be good at

image-making. The Reverend Jesse Jackson refers to the plight of black people as analogous to being on the expressway with all the entrances and exits closed off. Another Baptist preacher compared Christ's work to a "mission: impossible." The figures of speech created in black linguistic imagery tend to be earthy, gutsy, and rooted in plain everyday reality. One blood's distaste for wig-wearing females was expressed as: "They look like nine miles of bad road with a detour at the end."

Braggadocio. The rapper boasts a good deal, as we have seen in earlier examples. The bragging is of various kinds and dimensions. Instead of saying something limp like "If you so bad, gon and start something," one potential fighter boldly rapped: "If you feel froggy, leap!" Of course the badness of heroes must be celebrated, as for instance Stag-O-Lee, who was so bad "flies wouldn't fly around him in the summertime, and even white folks was scared of him." Whether referring to physical badness, fighting ability, lovemanship, coolness (that is, "grace under pressure"), the aim is to convey the image of an omnipotent fearless being, capable of doing the undoable. Consider two contrasting love raps using braggadocio. Smokey Robinson confidently croons:

> I'll take the stars and count them
> and move the mountains
> And if that won't do
> I'll try something new.

But the Temptations, with all their badness, have run into some hard times:

> I can change a river into a burning sand
> I can make a ship sail on dry land
> All these things I'm able to do
> But I can't get next to you.

Indirection. The rapper makes his or her points by the power of suggestion and innuendo. It is left to the listener to decipher and explicate the totality of meaning. Much signifyin works through indirection. For instance, Malcolm X once began a speech in this way: "Mr. Moderator, Brother Lomax, brothers and sisters, friends and enemies: I just can't believe everyone in here is a friend and I don't want to leave anybody out." Not only is Malcolm neatly putting down his enemies in the audience without a direct frontal attack, he is also sending a hidden message (to those hip enough to dig it). Since it is an all-black audience, Malcolm is slyly alluding to the all-too-familiar historical and contemporary pattern of blacks being betrayed by other blacks; traitors in their midst who ran and told the white folks everything they knew. (A number of slave uprisings were foiled because of these "black Judases," and there is a saying that surely dates back to the slave experience: when a blood does something, however small or innocuous, maybe something not even having to do with white folks, he or she will typically say, "Now, run and tell that!")

Indirection gives longer black raps their convoluted style, that is, the rapper will start with a point, then proceed to meander all around it; he may return, circular fashion, to the point, but he typically does not proceed in a straight, linear, point-by-point progression. Unless you are good at circumlocution, it is difficult to win an argument with a rapper skilled in this device. For one thing, such rappers will refuse to confront head-on any contradictory points raised. When dealing with such rappers, it is best to remember that they depend on psychological and experiential logic, rather than some abstract system of logic that maybe exists nowhere but in somebody's head. As an example, Jesse B. Simple is trying to prove he is part Indian, but his friend says he is just plain "colored," and besides, "Jesse is not even an Indian name." Simple counters this with the fact that he had a Hiawatha in his family "but she died," whereupon he is promptly contradicted and threatens to be caught in his lie: "*She*? Hiawatha was no *she*." Not at all undaunted by this correction of facts, Simple reasons that the sex of Hiawatha neither proves nor disproves that he has Indian blood. His experience has taught him that a lot of black people are part Indian. At any rate, he has to win the argument, so he refuses to even deal with the implications of the rebuttal, and in a smooth psych-out move, he promptly proceeds to change the subject: "She was a *she* in our family. And she had long coal-black hair just like a Creole. You know, I started to marry a Creole one time when I was coach-boy on the L & N down to New Orleans. Them Louisiana girls are bee-oou-te-ful! Man, I mean!"

Such indirection and circumlocutory rhetoric are also a part of African discourse strategy, and Afro-Americans have simply transformed this art to accommodate the English language. As an example of this technique in West Africa, Chinua Achebe in his first novel, *Things Fall Apart*, depicts the example of Unoka from the Ibo village of what is now Biafra. Supposedly, Unoka, father of the main character, Okonkwo, is a failure by village social standards; people laugh at him, and they "swore never to lend him any more money because he never paid back." However, "Unoka was such a man that he always succeeded in borrowing more, and piling up his debts." Surely part of his success must be attributable to the fact that Unoka can skillfully employ circumlocutory reasoning in his discourse, as Okoye found out when he came to collect the two hundred cowries that Unoka had been owing him for more than two years.

> As soon as Unoka understood what his friend was driving at, he burst out laughing. He laughed loud and long and his voice rang out clear as the *ogene*, and tears stood in his eyes. His visitor was amazed, and sat speechless. At the end, Unoka was able to give an answer between fresh outbursts of mirth.
>
> "Look at that wall," he said, pointing at the far wall of his hut, which was rubbed with red earth so that it shone. "Look at those lines of chalk"; and Okoye saw groups of short perpendicular lines drawn in chalk. There were five groups, and the smallest group had ten lines. Unoka had a sense of the dramatic and so he allowed a pause, in which he took a pinch of snuff and sneezed noisily, and then he continued: "Each group there represents a debt to someone, and each stroke is one hundred cowries. You see, I owe that man a thousand cowries. But he has not come to wake me up in the morning for it. I shall pay you, but not today. Our elders say that the sun will shine on those who stand before it shines on those who kneel under them. I shall pay my big debts first." And he took another pinch of snuff, as if that was paying the big debts first. Okoye rolled his goatskin and departed.

Tonal semantics. Verbal power can be achieved through the use of words and phrases carefully chosen for sound effects. (Since this can be either a line or a pervasive structure in a total rap, it is briefly mentioned here and will be discussed at length in the next chapter.) In employing tonal semantics, the rapper gets meaning and rhetorical mileage by triggering a familiar sound chord in the listener's ear. The words may or may not make sense; what is crucial is the rapper's ability to make the words *sound* good. They will use rhyme, voice rhythm, repetition of key sounds and letters. Fighter-poet Muhammad Ali was working right in this tradition with his taunting rhymes predicting his opponents' defeats: "They all must fall/in the round I call" and "If he mess wif me, I'll drop him in three." Most Toast-tellers rely on tonal semantics, their verbal ingenuity taxed to the limit in trying to sustain the melodic structure. "I'm Peter Wheatstraw, the Devil's son-in-law," or "I'm sweet peeter jeeter, the womb beater." Obviously, preachers rely on tonal semantics. For example, my father, Reverend Napoleon, once expressed the following theme in a sermon: "I am nobody talking to Somebody Who can help anybody." Other deep-down church folks use tonal semantics too; for instance, they will use the Moan to trigger a responsive chord, establishing a kind of psycho-cognitive reality of one who knows the Lord: "Hmmmmm-mmmmmmmmmmmmm," or "HHHHHHHHHHHHHHHH-mmmmmmmmmm."

5

"The Forms of Things Unknown"

Black Modes of Discourse

With halting progress, Dr. J. Mason Brewer, America's most distinguished Negro folklorist, seemed to move slower than integration as he took the stage.

Some 150 persons stilled in anticipation of old words from the slight man whose appearance was as aged as the stories he tells.

A slight man, Brewer leaned cautiously up toward the microphone.

Suddenly a full, vibrant voice recited a bounding rhyme about the evening's entertainment: "Sit back and relax, dear listeners, and let the joy bells ring in your receptive mind, as I attempt to do my thing."

SHORTLY AFTER Dr. Brewer died on January 24, 1975, a Texas congressman told the foregoing story as part of a commemorative tribute to him before the United States House of Representatives. A black scholar, artist, and collector of Afro-American folklore, J. Mason Brewer devoted his entire life to chronicling and preserving the Black American folk tradition. In the foreword to *American Negro Folklore*, his best-known work, he said:

> The folk literature of the American Negro has a rich inheritance from its African background . . . They brought with them no material possessions to aid in preserving the arts and customs of their homeland. Yet though empty handed perforce, they carried in their minds and hearts a treasure of complex musical forms, dramatic speech, and imaginative stories, which they perpetuated through the vital art of self-expression. Wherever the slaves were

ultimately placed, they established an enclave of African culture
that flourished in spite of environmental disadvantages . . . [The]
regional variations . . . may be regarded as aspects of a historical
whole. The many local patterns of song, story, belief, and speech
all manifest a common cultural background . . . As a result, the
original treasure has diffused and grown, for the enrichment of
themselves and of others.

This grand old dude was a living witness to the black "art of
self-expression." That's why — a septuagenarian, can you dig it?
— he mounted the platform to give what would be one of his last
lectures and ran it down: "Let the joy bells ring . . . as I attempt
to do my thing."

Dr. John Mason Brewer was one of the two men most responsible for recording the Black English folk expression of
African-Americans. The other was Richard Wright, 1908–1960.
While Brewer, the folklore scholar, collected and documented
the "authentic Negro folklore tradition," Wright, the prolific,
self-taught writer and father of all modern Black American literature, used this tradition as literary source material and incorporated it extensively in his novels and short stories.

> These two main streams of Negro expression [are] the Narcissis-
> tic level and the Forms of Things Unknown . . . This division in
> Negro life can be described in psychological as well as in class
> terms. It can be said there were Negroes who naively accepted
> what their lives were, lived more or less unthinkingly in their envi-
> ronment, mean as they found it, and sought escape either in relig-
> ion, migration, alcohol, or in what I've called a sensualization of
> their sufferings in the form of jazz and blues and folk and work
> songs.
> Then there were those who hoped and felt that they would ulti-
> mately be accepted in their native land as free men, and they put
> forth their claims in a language that their nation had given them.
> These latter were more or less always middle class in their ideol-
> ogy. But it was among the migratory Negro workers that one
> found, rejected and ignorant though they were, strangely positive
> manifestations of expression, original contributions in terms of
> form and content . . .
> . . . I feel personally identified with the migrant Negro, his folk

songs, his ditties, his wild tales of bad men; . . . my own life was
forged in the depths in which they live . . . Numerically, this form-
less folk utterance [the Forms of Things Unknown] accounts for
the great majority of the Negro people in the United States . . .

Speaking thus before European audiences in the years 1950–
1955, Richard Wright was attempting to account for the two
broad divisions of Black American experience in these United
States, the one being that experience of the small number of literate, well-educated blacks, the other being the folk-oral tradition of the black masses. The black experience of the former has
typically been expressed in Amercanized English, that of the latter group in Africanized English. We must thus look to the "original contributions" of the folk — their folklore, folk utterances,
songs and tales of folk expression — to complete our definition
and understanding of Black English. Comprising the formulaic
structure of these contributions are verbal strategies, rhetorical
devices, and folk expressive rituals which derive from a mutually
understood notion of modes of discourse, which in turn is part
of the "rich inheritance" of the African background acclaimed
by Brewer. Following Richard Wright, I have chosen to call these
black discourse modes the "Forms of Things Unknown."

We may classify black modes of discourse into the following
broad categories: call-response; signification (of which the Dozens is a strictly secular, "streetified" example); tonal semantics;
narrative sequencing (of which the Toasts is a strictly secular,
"streetified" example). Before we get into the nitty-gritty of
analyzing each of these communicative modalities, two important points must be reaffirmed. First, recall the unity of the sacred and secular in the Black American oral tradition and in the
traditional African world view. Each discourse mode is manifested in Black American culture on a sacred-secular continuum. Second, recall that the traditional African world view
emphasizes the synthesis of dualities to achieve balance and
harmony in the universe and in the community of men and
women. Thus, while the rituals of black discourse have an overall formulaic structure, individuals are challenged to do what
they can within the traditional mold. Centuries-old group norms

are balanced by individualized, improvisational emphases. By
virtue of unique contributions to the group-approved communicative structure, the individual can actualize his or her
sense of self within the confines of the group.

◆

The African-derived communication process of call-response
may be briefly defined as follows: spontaneous verbal and nonverbal interaction between speaker and listener in which all of
the speaker's statements ("calls") are punctuated by expressions
("responses") from the listener. In the traditional black church,
call-response is often referred to as the congregation's way of
"talking back" to the preacher, the most well-known example of
which is "A-men." (However, traditional black church members
also call and respond between themselves as well as the preacher,
and church musicians frequently will get a Thang goin between
themselves and their instruments.) Like most other Africanisms
in Black American life, call-response has been most carefully
preserved in the church. But it is a basic organizing principle of
Black American culture generally, for it enables traditional black
folk to achieve the unified state of balance or harmony which is
fundamental to the traditional African world view. Since that
world view does not dichotomize life into sacred and secular
realms, you can find call-responses both in the church and on
the street. Before we get too far, a few examples to be sure
everybody understand where uhm comin from.

CHURCH

Preacher ("caller"):	My theme for today is Waiting on the Lord.
Congregation ("responders," all speaking simultaneously):	Take yo' time, take yo' time. Fix it up, Reb! Preach it, Reb!
Testifier ("caller," speaking from her seat):	Giving Honor to God, Who is the Head of our lives, to His Son, Jesus, that Man from Galilee, who set *me* free!

Congregation ("responders," again all speaking at the same time):	Go 'head, go 'head, tell about it! Watch youself, now, you fittin to start somethin. Yessuh! Yessuh!

BARBERSHOP

Male "caller": Male "responders" (all talking at the same time):	I done put my money on Clay. *Ali,* nigger. Doan make no difference what you call him, he still the same. Well, the bookies say — Fuck *them,* they white, they don't know they ass from a hole in the ground! He ain finished yet. Frazier doan stan a chance.

BEAUTY SHOP

Female "caller": Female "responders" (all at once):	You know, a whitey ain shit, now this — Who you tellin! Niggers ain shit, either, doan put it all on the white man. Hey, uhm hip to it! Amen, girl, gon, talk bout it!

Now, obviously, some calls and responses are more strictly limited to either church or street; similarly the subject matter of the discourse is different in sacred and secular contexts. But we are here talking about the *process* of communication, not the substance: the communication vehicle or channel is the same, and sometimes the underlying message is also, though the subject matter differs. Below is a summary list of various responses you might hear and observe in black discourse. (Asterisks indicate those which are strictly secular; the others are found in both sacred and secular contexts.)

VERBAL

*Dig it!	Go head!
*No shit!	Look out!
(also bullshit, ain't that	Lord, ha' mercy!
some shit)	Do Jesus!
Amen!	I hear you!
Say so!	Well, Iah be . . .
Tell it!	Mercy!
Speak on it!	*I swear!
Yeah! (also Naw! Aw!)	*Get down man! (baby, girl)
Yessuh!	*Get back!
*Rap on!	Shonuff!
Well, all right!	*Do it, baby! (man, girl)
Un-huh	Teach! Teach! (however,
*Who you humping!	"Preach" is strictly
*Oh, you mean nigger! (said	sacred)
with affinity and ap-	*Hip me!
proval)	*You lyin! (said only
Really!	semiseriously)
You on the case, now!	Tell the truth!

Verbal comments made to people near you, hollering and whooping at the same time the speaker is talking, to affirm approval of what the speaker has said, are not regarded as discourteous behavior.

NONVERBAL

*giving skin	looking from side to side
waving hand in the air	moving around (sometimes in
stomping feet	a dance-like fashion, some-
hitting back of chair (wall,	times when seated, turning
etc.)	to person next to you or in
*black power sign (raised,	back of you)
clenched fist)	nodding head (also shaking
rolling eyes	head)
pursing lips	clapping hands
sucking teeth	jumping up and down (out of
laughing (simply to indicate a	your seat)
strong point has been made,	
not necessarily in response	
to joke or humorous state-	
ment)	

If you observe black speakers interacting, whether in casual conversation or in a "speech-giving" set, you can witness certain specific functions that these various responses serve. We can thus categorize the responses according to the purpose accomplished or the effect achieved:

Co-signing (affirming, agreeing with speaker):
   Amen; Well; Yes; Un-huh; I hear you; Dig that; Praise the Lord
Encouraging (urging speaker to continue in direction he has started):
   Take yo time; Come on up; You on the case; Watch yoself; Speak on it; What?!; Aw, naw! (meaning really Aw, yes!)
Repetition (using same words speaker has said):
   Speaker says: "Some folk ain't got no mother wit." Response is: "No mother wit! That's right, no mother wit!"
Completer (completing speaker's statement, sometimes in response to "request" from speaker, sometimes in spontaneous talking with speaker):
   Speaker says: "And, what did the Lord say about His time, what did He say, church?" Response: "Yassuh, he may not come when you want Him, but He's right on time." Preacher: "And Job said, of my appointed time, uhm gon wait [congregation spontaneously joins in here] till my change shall come."
On T (an extremely powerful co-signing response, acknowledging that something the speaker has just said is dead on time, that is, "psychological" time):
   Shonuff; Yassuh!; Ooooo-weeeee!; Gon wit yo bad self! (Also waving hand in air, giving five; jumping up; hollering; clapping hands.)

Some calls from the speaker might elicit a co-signing response from one person, an encouraging type of response from someone else, a completer response from still another listener. Whatever is being said at a particular moment will affect different listeners in different ways. The dynamics of black communication allow for individual variation within the structure. Thus all responses are "correct"; the only "incorrect" thing you can do is *not respond* at all.

To get a further understanding of call-response in Black English, we should look more closely at the relationship between this communication dynamic and the traditional African world view, as well as its relationship to black music. Now, y'all got to follow me cause it gon git deep right long in here, you dig?

Recall that the traditional African world view conceptualizes a cosmos which is an interacting, interdependent, balanced force field. The community of men and women, the organization of society itself, is thus based on this assumption. Consequently, communication takes on an interactive, interdependent nature. As Oliver Jackson succinctly states it:

> The moral sanctity of . . . life [in African society] derived from the idea that all is spiritual and that the Supreme Power embodies the totality of the cosmos in one spiritual unity . . . the African continuum is essentially harmonious. Men, in building their societies, endeavor to reproduce this 'divine or cosmic harmony.' This is the basis of all ethical and moral behavior in community life. This human microcosm must reaffirm the harmonious modality of the cosmic macrocosm.

Thus, call-response seeks to synthesize speakers and listeners in a unified movement. It permeates Black English communication and reaffirms the "modality of the cosmic macrocosm."

We are talking, then, about an interactive network in which the fundamental requirement is active participation of all individuals. In this kind of communicative system, "there is no sharp line between performers or communications and the audience, for virtually everyone is performing and everyone is listening." The process requires that one must give if one is to receive, and receiving is actively acknowledging another. Robert Farris

Thompson refers to the antiphonal nature of black communication as "perfected social interaction." He elaborates on this concept as follows:

> The arrogant dancer, no matter how gifted or imaginative, may find that he dances to drums and handclaps of decreasing strength and fervor. He may find, and this is damaging to his reputation, that the chorus will crystallize around another person, as in the telling of tales among the Tiv of northern Nigeria. There, we are told by Laura Bohannan, the poor devil who starts a tale without proper preparation or refinement will find the choral answering to his songs becomes progressively weaker until they ultimately reform about a man with stronger themes and better aesthetic organization. He is soon singing to himself. The terror of losing one's grip on the chorus is a real one in some African societies, a poignant dimension of social interaction that for some reason is not mentioned in discourse on singing in African music . . . Thus, call-and-response and solo-and-circle, far from solely constituting matters of structure, are in actuality levels of perfected social interaction.

The power potential and the essence of call-response is such that Thompson conceives of it as the "politics of perfection." This interactive system embodies communality rather than individuality. Emphasis is on group cohesiveness, cooperation, and the collective common good. In the traditional black church, we find that spiritual regeneration depends on the visitation of the Spirit, but the efforts of the total group are needed to bring this about. The preacher say, "Y'all ain wid me today, the church is dead," therein acknowledging that he can't make it by himself. But the fact that communication proceeds by the issuing of calls from *individuals* to the group underscores the importance of *individual* roles. (It should be kept in mind that in a technical sense, a "group" consists of two or more people; thus we are here talking about communication in groups of several people as well as one-on-one conversation.)

Much of what is accomplished by call-response can be witnessed by moving through the hierarchy of the traditional black church. That hierarchy is outlined below:

God (The Father, Spirit, and the Holy Ghost)
Minister, Reverend, Elder (God-sent men)
Mother of the Church
Old folk (Elders)
Deacons (spiritual men who assist the Church Head)
Trustees (lower in hierarchy because of their fiscal concerns)
Saved adults
Adult ushers and nurses
Saved young folk
Unsaved adults and children
Backsliders (former saved people who have resorted to sin)
Sinners

God must send the man who is to lead, and, subsequently, God tells the man what to say and inspires him to say it. From the outset, traditional black church communication takes on a degree of spontaneity since the leader must "wait on the Lord." Simultaneously, it is the beginnings of process, that is, the *call* by God and the man's *response* by taking up the ministry. See, in the traditional black church, you don't go to no school to be no preacher, cause God must "call" you. Once you acknowledge God's call and affirmatively respond (many, to their detriment, have tried to ignore God's call), you must still await God's guidance in the daily conduct of your affairs, as well as in the conduct of the church's affairs. Thus, a traditional black church sermon can't be written and rehearsed in advance; the preacher must await the visitation of the Spirit, and rely on the spontaneous calls-and-responses between himself and God, as well as between himself and his congregation.

The music of black groups (sacred and secular) well exemplifies the call-response tradition. Characteristically, a group is composed of a lead singer ("caller") and his or her background ("responders"). The leader opens the song and sets the initial mood, but the roles may reverse so that the leader responds to the call of the others. The direction and execution of the song depend on the mutual forces of the leader in spiritual combination with his or her background. For instance, note the opening of the well-known Gospel song "How I Got Over":

Leader (call):	How —
Background (response):	How I got over.
Leader (call repeated with emphatic feeling):	I said how —
Background (response building with the lead):	How I got over.
Leader:	My soul —
Background:	My soul look back and wonder —
Leader:	How —
Background:	How I got over.

The next verse usually repeats the words of this opening but with greater feeling and emotional intensity, thereby taking the song to another spiritual level. The total performance of the group is gauged by their skill in manipulating this musical interplay to move their listeners to get the "spirit in the dark."

We find the same musical tradition in the secular world of black singing groups (who became the model for contemporary mainstream white groups). For example, note the opening lines to "Don't You Know I Love You So," a popular song from the early 1950s and the beginnings of black rock 'n roll soul music. The song was recorded by the Clovers, a black group that has perhaps long since been forgotten.

Leader (call):	Oh, don't you know —
Background (response):	I love you, love you so.
Leader (call repeated):	Oh, don't you know —
Background (response):	I love you, love you so.
Background (taking over call):	Oh, don't you know I love you, love you so —
Leader (responding):	And I'll never, never let you go —
Leader and Background together:	Ooo-dee — ooo-duu — do-wah — I love you so.

Not only has the call-response pattern been employed consistently by twentieth century Gospel and rock groups, it has an older history than that, as it is used in the long-metered, hymnal singing style in the traditional black church. This is a style of singing dating way back to slavery times when "church" was anywhere black people were: in the fields, back in the woods, in the "new ground" areas (uncultivated, unplowed land which had to be made ready for seeding). The leader-caller begins by a kind of talk-singing of the opening line for the hymn: "I love the Lord, He heard my cry." The congregation of responders then sing-chant each word, in a long, slow, drawn-out fashion, with the leader joining in with them, becoming part of the group-response. Then the leader calls out the next line: "And pitied every groan." The congregation sing-chants this line, and the song continues in this fashion to the end.

With the lack of cultural distinction between sacred and secular, it is not surprising to find this singing pattern in old plantation work-song styles, as Brewer and other scholars of black folk music have demonstrated. "Many Thousand Go[ne]" is one such example:

Leader: No more peck of corn for me —
Background: No more, no more;
Leader: No more peck of corn for me —
Background: Many t'ousand go[ne]

As another really striking example of song and oral history combined, Brewer recorded the song, "Foller de Drinkin' Gou'd," which is based on the activities of Peg-Leg Joe, a sailor who made trips throughout the South urging slaves to run away. According to Brewer's folk source, Peg-Leg Joe showed the slaves the "mark of his natural left foot and the round hole made by his peg-leg. He would then go ahead of them northward and leave a print made with charcoal and mud of the outline of a human left foot and a round spot in place of the right foot . . . Drinking gou'd is the Great Dipper." The structure of this song shows another aspect of the call-response pattern, where an entire verse is sung by the leader, then the background joins in with the leader to sing the chorus. Here is an excerpt:

Leader: When de sun come back,
                  When de firs' quail call,
                  Den de time is come —
                  Foller de drinkin' gou'd.

Background: Foller de drinkin' gou'd,
Foller de drinkin' gou'd;
For de ol' man say,
"Foller de drinkin' gou'd."

Call-response is present not only in the singing style of black music, but also in the music itself. With a contemporary group such as War, one hears the call and response of the various instruments in a fashion reminiscent of the African drums. Listening to Stevie Wonder, one hears a "one-man band." He plays a multiplicity of instruments, calling and responding to himself, the instruments, and the listener. He may begin with a plaintive wail on the piano and respond with his harmonica, building until he achieves a plateau of exaltation, that is, balance and harmony. The concept is described in the lyrics of "The Birth of the Blues" — "breeze in the trees, a blue note from a whipper-will, put through a horn 'till it was born into a new note." Various elements are thus combined one by one — call and response — to create harmony and balance.

To shed even further light on call-response, we can observe how the baaadest black writers use this folk material. As mentioned earlier, Richard Wright employed black folk expression extensively. In the following example of a funeral sermon from his novel *The Long Dream,* note how Wright has captured the congregation's various insistent and emotional responses which the preacher needs to concretely drive home the abstract notion of death.

"Tell it! Tell it!"
"Look down on us, Lawd!"
"Mercy, mercy, have mercy, Jesus!"
"Who dares," the reverend asked in a wild cry, "say 'No!' when that old Angel of Death calls? You can be in your grocery store ringing up a hundred-dollar sale on the cash register and Death'll call and you'll have to drop the sale and go! You can be a-riding around in your Buick and Death'll call and you have to go! You about to git out of your bed to go to your job and old Death'll call and you'll have to go! Mebbe you building a house and done called in the mason and the carpenter and then old Death calls and you have to go! Cause Death's asking you to come into your *last* home! Mebbe you planning on gittin married and your wonderful bride's

a-waiting at the altar and you on your way and old Death calls: 'Young man, I got another bride for you! Your *last* bride!' "

"Lawd, it's true!"

"Gawd's Master!"

"Be with us, Lawd!"

The Reverend demanded: ". . . Who understands the Divine Plan of Justice? On the Fourth of July, Gawd reared back and said: 'Death, come here!'

"Wonderful Jesus!"

    'Death, go down to that place called *America!*'

"Lissen to the Lawd!"

    'Death find that state they call Mississippi!'

"Gawd's a-talking!"

    'Death, go to a town called *Clintonville!*'

"Lawd, Lawd, Lawd!"

    'Death, I want you to tell Tyree Tucker that I want to see 'im!'

"Have mercy, Jesus!"

A black woman gave a prolonged scream and began leaping about; ushers rushed to her and led her bounding body out of the church.

    'Death, tell Tyree that I don't care *what* he's doing, he's *got* to come home!'

In an actual church service, when this process gets more and more involved, spiritual forces take over. Shouting breaks out all over the church. Older saved people and children with "special gifts" start speaking in tongue. The preacher moves on up to his climax, and the congregation suddenly breaks out in song. Now Reverend can't quit. The Spirit won't let him stop. He runs down out of the pulpit. Nurses are fanning those shouters who have passed out. The musicians and the choir begin to take over as the Spirit has driven the physical bodies to exhaustion. "My, my, my!" . . . "My, my, my!" . . . "Yes! yes!" . . . "Oo-koo-Koomaba-sigh!" . . . "Ak-baba-hunda!" . . . Thus, community is achieved. God has moved from the minister through the elders and the total congregation, and with the involvement of the saved, the "doors of the church are opened" to the unsaved.

For a secular literary example, we turn to another mean black writer, Ralph Ellison, author of *The Invisible Man.* In "Mister Toussan," Ellison uses call-response between two small black dudes to tell the story of the Haitian general, Toussaint L'Ouverture, who in.1791 led the only successful slave revolt in history. Buster starts out narrating the story. Riley punctuates and reinforces each line of the story (Buster's "call") with varied "A-men" type responses, occasionally, as he probably does in church, repeating the exact words of the "call," other times issuing forth with exclamatory "Jesus"es and "Yeah"s, and sometimes even adding the completer to Buster's "call" statements.

"Riley, you know all them African guys ain't really that lazy," he said.

"I know they ain't," said Riley, "I just tole you so!"

"Yeah, but my teacher tole me, too. She tole us 'bout one of them African guys named Toussan what she said whipped Napoleon!"

Riley stopped scratching in the earth and looked up, his eyes rolling in disgust:

"Now how come you have to start lying?"

"Thass what she said."

"Boy, you oughta quit telling them things."

"I hope God may kill me."

"She said he was a *African*?"

"Cross my heart, man . . ."

"Really?"

"Really, man. She said he come from a place named Hayti."

Riley looked hard at Buster and seeing the seriousness of the face felt the excitement of a story rise up within him.

"Buster, I'll bet a fat man you lyin'. What'd that teacher say?"

"Really, man, she said that Toussan and his men got up on one of them African mountains and shot down them peckerwood soldiers fass as they'd try to come up. . . ."

"Why good-God-a-mighty!" yelled Riley.

"Oh boy, they shot 'em down!" chanted Buster.

"Tell me about it, man!"

"And they throwed 'em off the mountain. . . ."

" . . . Goool-leee! . . . "

" . . . And Toussan drove 'em cross the sand. . . ."

" . . . Yeah! And what was they wearing, Buster? . . . "

"Man, they had on red uniforms and blue hats all trimmed with gold, and they had some swords all shining what they called sweet blades of Damascus. . . ."

"Sweet blades of Damascus! . . . "

" . . . They really had 'em," chanted Buster.

"And what kinda guns?"

"Big, black cannon!"

"And where did ole what-you-call-'im run them guys? . . . "

"His name was Toussan."

"Toussan! Just like Tarzan. . . . "

"Not *Taar*-zan, dummy, *Toou*-zan!"

"Toussan! And where'd ole Toussan run 'em?"

"Down to the water, man. . . . "

" . . . To the river water. . . . "

" . . . Where some great big ole boats was waiting for 'em. . . . "

" . . . Go on, Buster!"

"An' Toussan shot into them boats. . . . "

" . . . He shot into em. . . . "

" . . . Shot into them boats. . . . "

"Jesus!! . . . "

"With his great big cannons. . . . "

" . . . Yeah! . . . "

" . . . Made a-brass. . . . "

" . . . Brass. . . . "

" . . . An' his big black cannon balls started killin' them pecker-woods. . . . "

" . . . Lawd, Lawd. . . . "

" . . . Boy, till them peckerwoods hollowed *Please, Please Mister Toussan we'll be good!*"

"An' what'd Toussan tell em, Buster?"

"Boy, he said in his big deep voice, *I oughta drown all a-you bastards.*"

"An' what'd the peckerwoods say?"

"They said, Please, Please, *Please, Mister Toussan.* . . . "

" . . . We'll be good," broke in Riley.

"Thass right, man," said Buster excitedly. He clapped his hands and kicked his heels against the earth, his black face glowing in a burst of rhythmic joy.

"Boy!"

"And what'd ole Toussan say then?"

"He said in his big deep voice: *You all peckerwoods better be good, 'cause this is sweet Papa Toussan talking and my nigguhs is crazy 'bout white meat!*"

"Ho, ho, ho!" Riley bent double with laughter. The rhythm still throbbed within him and he wanted the story to go on and on . . .

At this point, Riley has become uncontrollably ecstatic about the story and superconfident that he knows how to "put the right stuff" to story-telling. So they switch roles, Riley becoming the "caller," Buster the "responder," and thus the moving rhythm of this story within a story is sustained to its climax.

Riley stood, his legs spread wide, and stuck his thumbs in the top of his trousers, swaggering sinisterly.

"Come on, watch me do it now, Buster. Now I bet ole Toussan looked down at them white folks standing just about like this and said in a soft easy voice: 'Ain't I done begged you white folks to quit messin' with me?' . . . "

"Thass right, quit messing with 'im," chanted Buster.

"But naw, you'all all had to come on anyway. . . . "

" . . . Jus' 'cause they was black. . . . "

"Thass right," said Riley. "Then ole Toussan felt so damn bad and mad the tears come a-trickling down. . . . "

" . . . He was really mad."

"And then, man, he said in his big bass voice: 'Goddamn you white folks, how come you-all cain't let us colored alone?' "

" . . . An' An he was crying. . . . "

" . . . An' Toussan tole them peckerwoods: 'I been beggin' you-all to quit bothering us.' . . . "

" . . . Beggin' on his bended knees! . . . "

"Then, man, Toussan got real mad and snatched off his hat and started stompin' up and down on it and the tears was tricklin' down and he said: 'You-all come tellin' me about Napoleon.' . . . "

"They was tryin' to scare him, man. . . . "

"Said: 'I don't give a damn about Napoleon.' . . . "

" . . .Wasn't studyin' bout him. . . . "

" . . . Toussan said: 'Napoleon ain't nothing but a man!' Then Toussan pulled back his shining sword like this, and twirled it at the peckerwoods' throats so hard it z-z-z-zinged in the air!"

"Now keep on, finish it, man," said Buster. "What'd Toussan do then?"

"Then you know what he did, he said: 'I oughta beat the hell outa you peckerwoods!' "

"Thass right, and he did it too," said Buster. He jumped to his feet and fenced violently with five desperate imaginary soldiers, running each through with his imaginary sword. Buster watched him from the porch, grinning.

"Toussan musta scared them white folks almost to death!"

"Yeah, thass 'bout the way it was," said Buster. The rhythm was dying now and he sat back upon the porch, breathing tiredly.

Calling-responding; stating and counterstating; acting and reacting; testing your performance as you go — it is such a natural, habitual dynamic in black communication that blacks do it quite unconsciously when rapping with other blacks. But call-response can be disconcerting to both parties in black-white communication, presenting a real case of cross-cultural communication interference. When the black person is speaking, the white person, because call-response is not in his or her cultural heritage, does not obviously engage in the response process, remaining relatively passive, perhaps voicing an occasional subdued "Mmmmmhhhm." Judging from the white individual's seeming lack of involvement, the black communicator gets the feeling that the white isn't listening, and thus may repeatedly punctuate the "call" with questions, such as "Are you listening to me?", "Did you hear me?" In an extended conversation, such questions become annoying to the white, and he or she may exclaim, "Yes, I'm listening, of course, I'm listening, I'm standing right here!" Then when the white communicator takes over the "call," the black person, as is customary, begins to get all into it, responding with verbal expressions, like "Dig, it!", "Tell it," "I hear you," "Go head, run it down," and moving and dancing around when he hears something that he thinks is really dynamite. Judging from all this apparent "interference," the white person gets the feeling that the black person isn't listening, because he "keeps interrupting and turning his back on me." (There is also the possibility that the black person will not be his or her natural self and respond at all; hence also preventing maximum communication.)

◆

Signification, our second mode of discourse, refers to the verbal art of insult in which a speaker humorously puts down, talks about, needles — that is, signifies on — the listener. Sometimes signifyin (also siggin) is done to make a point, sometimes it's just for fun. This type of folk expression in the oral tradition has the status of a customary ritual that's accepted at face value. That is to say, nobody who's signified on is supposed to take it to heart. It is a culturally approved method of talking about somebody — usually through verbal indirection. Since the signifier employs humor, it makes the put-down easier to swallow and gives the recipient a socially acceptable way out. That is, if they can't come back with no bad signification of they own, they can just laugh along with the group.

For example, the following dialogue took place in a group of six black adolescents:

Sherry:	I sho am hongy. Dog!
Reginald:	That's all you think bout, eating all the time.
John (Sherry's brother):	Man, that's why she so big.
Sherry:	Aw, y'all shut up!
John:	Come on, Sherry, we got to go. We'll catch you later, man.
Reginald (to John):	Goodnight Sleep tight Don't let Sherry Eat you up tonight.

(Everybody laughs — including Sherry — and gives skin.)

In ending his little ditty the way he does, Reginald has cleverly substituted signification for the original lines of this folk rhyme, which goes: "Goodnight / Sleep tight / Don't let the bed bugs bite." Though not addressing Sherry directly, Reginald is obviously still on her case about her enormous appetite which, he suggests, is so huge that even her brother may be in danger! His farewell to Sherry and John, playful, exaggerated, and quick-witted, is approved by all as good signifyin. Thus excellence and skill in this verbal art helps build yo rep and standing among yo peers.

Some Black Semantic terms that are somewhat synonymous with signification are: dropping lugs; joanin; capping; sounding. All are characterized by exploitation of the unexpected and quick verbal surprises. The difference is that signification tends to be more subtle and circumlocutory than the other verbal activities. For example, one traditional black church preacher hurled the following linguistic social corrective at his congregation: "Seen some mens out drankin and gamblin last night — I know I ain gon get no A-men!" He didn't get too much response; it was a *lug,* pure and simple. By contrast "Reben Nap" did it this way: "Y'all know, the Lord sees and watches everythang we do; whether we be in the church or out. And I just wanta let y'all know one thang: Everybody talkin bout Heaven ain goin there!" This effective siggin got both laughter and applause.

Another unique characteristic of signification is that it can be both light and heavy. Sounding, capping, joaning, and lugging are generally lightweight, that is, for verbal posturing. Signifying, on the other hand, can also be heavy, that is, a way of teaching or driving home a cognitive message but — and this is important — without preaching or lecturing. An example of lightweight siggin or cappin is provided in the playful name-calling rituals, such as: "You so ugly look like you been hit by a ugly stick," and "Yo natural look like this broad on the wall" (pointing to a picture of Medusa). Here are some examples of heavy siggin:

> Stokely Carmichael, addressing a white audience at the University of California-Berkeley, 1966:
>> "It's a privilege and an honor to be in the white intellectual ghetto of the West."
>
> Malcolm X on Martin Luther King, Jr.'s nonviolent revolution (referring to the common practice of singing "We Shall Overcome" at Civil Rights protests of the sixties):
>> "In a revolution, you swinging, not singing."
>
> Reverend Jesse Jackson, merging sacred and secular siggin in a Breadbasket Saturday morning sermon:
>> "Pimp, punk, prostitute, preacher, Ph.D. — all the P's — you still in slavery!"
>
> A black middle-class wife to her husband who had just arrived home several hours later than usual:
>> "You sho got home early today for a change."

The point of the above examples, like all effective heavy signification, is to put somebody in check, that is, make them think about and, one hopes, correct their behavior. Note, too, that heavy signification, though it may include elements of sarcasm, is not as venomous or personally debilitating as sarcasm.

As can be seen from the examples given, signification has the following characteristics: indirection, circumlocution; meta-phorical-imagistic (but images rooted in the everyday, real world); humorous, ironic; rhythmic fluency and sound; teachy but not preachy; directed at person or persons usually present in the situational context (siggers do not talk behind yo back); punning, play on words; introduction of the semantically or logically unexpected.

Signifyin can be a witty one-liner, a series of loosely related statements, or a cohesive discourse on one point. It can exhibit all or a combination of characteristics just cited. As an example of a one-line verbal quip, two middle-class black males, Bob and Art, had been heatedly debating child-rearing techniques when Art suddenly had to go to the bathroom. While he was *supposedly* out of the room, Bob used the opportunity to observe how "sick" Art was. Art evidently overheard it and the conversation resumed as follows:

Art: Nigguh, I heard that! Yo momma is sick.
Bob: Hey man, I thought you said you was goin to the bathroom.
Art: Yeah, but like, the bathroom ain outdoors.
Bob: Well, but, like, what you came back with was outdoors, so you know.

The siggin of Bob's last line shows humor, punning, and is directed at the person present.

These next two passages come from the card-playing scene in Richard Wright's novel *Lawd Today*. The first one illustrates signifyin in a series of statements:

"You's one down, *re*doubled!" boomed Slim, marking down the score.
"Easy's taking candy from a baby!" laughed Al.
"Smoother'n velvet!" laughed Slim rearing back in his seat and blowing smoke to the ceiling.
"Like rolling off a log!" sang Al, shuffling the cards.
"Like sliding down a greasy pole!"

"Like snapping your fingers!"
"Like spitting!"
"Like falling in love with a high yellow!"

In siggin on the losers, Al and Slim's verbal repartee shows metaphor (beating Jake and Bob is like "taking candy from a baby,"); humor; rhythmic fluency (all the "like" statements have the same structure with "ing" and three in a row start with "s"); it is directed at persons present (that is, their opponents); it plays on the logically unexpected (surely Jake and Bob didn't expect their losing to elicit all that!).

The following is a one-liner that reflects humor, plays on the semantically and logically unexpected, and is directed at the person present.

"Let's go," said Slim.
"One Notrump," said Al.
"I ain't got a Gawddamn thing," whined Jake, squirming in his chair.
"Don't confess to me!" said Slim haughtily. "I ain't no priest!"

The next set of examples illustrate extended uses of signification as an overall discourse strategy with a single focal point.

The first passage, which contains all eight features of signifyin, comes from Coffin Ed and Grave Digger, two hilarious black Harlem detectives created by black novelist Chester Himes. (This fantastic pair was re-created in living color in the 1970 film *Cottom Comes to Harlem*.) Grave Digger and Coffin Ed appear as main characters in several of Himes's novels. In *Hot Day, Hot Night*, their white superior has assigned them the task of discovering who started a riot in Harlem. Their answer is baaaaad signifyin all the way:

"I take it you've discovered who started the riot," Anderson said.
"We knew who he was all along," Grave Digger said.
"It's just nothing we can do to him," Coffin Ed echoed.
"Why not, for God's sake?"
"He's dead," Coffin Ed said.
"Who?"

"Lincoln," Grave Digger said.

"He hadn't ought to have freed us if he didn't want to make provisions to feed us," Coffin Ed said. "Anyone could have told him that."

At this point, Anderson tries to put forth a feeble counterstatement, but he is no match for this baaaad rappin pair. They continue to sig and circumlocute all the way, and Anderson never does get a direct answer to his query about the riot.

"All right, all right, lots of us have wondered what he might have thought of the consequences," Anderson admitted. "But it's too late to charge him now."

"Couldn't have convicted him anyway," Grave Digger said.

"All he'd have to do would be to plead good intentions," Coffin Ed elaborated. "Never was a white man convicted as long as he plead good intentions."

"All right, all right, who's the culprit this night, here, in Harlem? Who's inciting these people to this senseless anarchy?"

"Skin," Grave Digger said.

Coffin Ed and Grave Digger show skillful use of indirection to convey their message that rioting is caused by historical conditions of enslavement and white oppression ("Lincoln" and liberal white "intentions" which haven't really done anything to solve the problem on a mass basis. The "liberal" North pulled out of the South in 1877 and left newly freed black slaves to fend for themselves. When blacks left the South in massive numbers after each of the World Wars, they looked to their "liberal friends" in the North but found even greater discrimination and racial oppression "up South.") The method of circumlocution is used to teach Anderson but not in a sermonizing way. The siggin is directed at Anderson as a representative white liberal type in the Lincoln tradition, and thus it's being run on him to his face, not behind his back. The two detectives are obviously introducing the unexpected, both in a logical and semantic sense. (Lincoln should have kept us enslaved if he wasn't going to make any provisions for us other than the many Harlems of the United States; thus an eating slave is better than a starving free man.

Further, Anderson has asked a perfectly normal whodunit investigatory type question and instead gets a surprise sociological explanation.) There is rhythmic fluency in the use of "freed us/ feed us." The extended metaphor of a mock trial is used to indict Lincoln and White America generally, as if to say they should be on trial and not the rioters. (Note courtroom terms like "charge him," "plead," "convicted.") Further, there is the metaphorical allusion to the old saying, "the road to Hell is paved with good intentions." Finally, Grave Digger and Coffin Ed use metaphor, irony, and play on words with their final *circumlocutory* response that "skin" is responsible for the "senseless anarchy." By "skin" they are suggesting color, oppression, Lincoln, white liberal attitudes — in short, giving the same answer they have been giving all along, in a different way and in one word. Like I said, they's baad!

The second example of extended signification, again displaying the characteristics of deep signifyin, comes from the church. The preacher begins with the usual episodic prelude. Here he uses it as an opportunity to advertise a blessing he has available and to put down other folk in the sacred and secular worlds who *say* they can help you but really can't. (The person or persons being alluded to may not be present in the church at the time, but since this particular church service is being broadcast over radio, the individuals are still technically in the situational context.)

Preacher:	I say this thang I got, this thang, yeah this thang, it ain like what the other folks telling you bout.
Congregation:	Yeah! Yeah!
	Tell about it!
	Say so! You on the case!
Preacher:	This thang will make a way outa no way, and, lissen to me church, you ain got to go no long way to git it, not *my* thang.
Congregation:	Yessuh!
	I hear you!
Preacher:	You ain got to catch no bus, you ain got to fly no airplane, go no long ways, just come on over here and git this thang and help yoself.

Congregation:	Say the word!
	Talk about it!
Preacher:	You see, like I was sayin, talk is cheap, plenty
	peoples go round sayin what they gon do for you
	and they ain got nothin theyself.
Congregation:	Look out, now!
	Well, come on out with it!
	Un-huh, un-huh!
Preacher:	I say, what I look like askin you to pray for me
	and you ain got a pot nor a window!
Congregation:	Watch yoself, doc!
	You gon tell it in a minute!
	Go head, go head!
Preacher:	Y'all know what uhm talkin bout, that's a word my
	grandmomma use to say. Come on over here to
	14873 Puritan and git my thang!

Here, the preacher-signifier is using indirection to teach his message, which, stated more bluntly, is something like this: Don't let folks try to sell you on what they can do to help you if they are not in good financial and material conditions themselves. After all, God help those who help themselves, and action speak louder than words. As mentioned, the preacher is not talking behind anybody's back since he's making public statements over a mass communications channel. The people being sigged on are a variety of con types found in black communities. They include: preacher-charlatans selling blessings in the form of candles or incense, which supposedly will better one's condition; numbers men whose implicit sales pitch is that if you play the numbers, you can hit and get rich quick; hoo-doo workers (those supposedly skilled in the art of voodoo); dope men trying to solicit additional pushers; pimps recruiting women to work for them. All such types either implicitly or explicitly use a rap that tries to convince the individual that they can help him or her git ovuh cause they got the "answer." (Course, skeptics can't help but wonder what is so different and powerful about this preacher's "thang"!) There is humor, irony, and metaphor in the preacher's allusion to an old secularly worded black proverb ("You ain got a pot to piss in or a window to throw it out of").

This is also unexpected since the church audience had not anticipated the introduction of such a real-world vernacular image — but for this reason, it is highly effective, as if the Reb is saying, "Look, uhm hip to what's happenin out there." Further imagery is provided in the use of buses and airplanes to suggest that if something is good and somebody really wants you to have it, then you should not have to go through a lot of changes to get it. Rhythmic fluency and sound is provided by use of the preacher's ritualized cadenced tone and breathy pausing after each structural phrase. This obviously cannot be conveyed on paper, but the preacher, in effect, "preached" this signification, with vocal flourishes, much as he later preached the sermon for the day.

The last example of extended signifyin demonstrates all characteristics except the teaching aspect. It's the end of the card-playing session between Wright's characters, Jake, Bob, Al and Slim.

"So you got a new shirt, hunh, Al?" asked Jake quietly, tentatively, sucking his teeth and throwing his leg over the arm of the chair.

Al modestly stroked the collar of his shirt with his fingers.

"Yeah, I picked it up yesterday."

"Where you steal if from?"

"Steal it? Nigger, you can't steal shirts like this!"

"You didn't buy it!"

"How come I didn't? Ain't I got money?" said Al. He was sitting upright, his round black face flushed with mock indignation.

"What did you ever buy?" asked Jake.

Al rose, rammed his hands deep into his pockets, and stood in front of Jake.

"You go into Marshall Field's and steal a shirt! It takes kale to wear clothes like this!"

"Marshall Field's?"

"Yeah. Marshall Field's!"

"The closest you ever got Marshall Field's was the showwindow," said Jake.

"That's a Gawddamn lie!" said Al.

Slim and Bob listened silently, hoping for a bout of the dozens between the two.

"Whoever heard of a nigger going into Marshall Field's and buying a green shirt?" asked Jake, as though to himself.

"Aw, nigger, quit signifying! Go buy *you* a shirt!"

"I don't need no shirts. I got aplenty!"

"This nigger setting here wearing his purple rag around his throat talking about he's got aplenty shirts. Somebody wake 'im up!"

Slim and Bob laughed.

"I can change *five* shirts to your *one*," boasted Jake.

"The onliest way you can do that is to pull off the one you has on now and put it on five times," said Al.

Slim and Bob laughed again.

"Listen, nigger," said Jake. "I was wearing shirts when you was going around naked in Miss'sippi!"

Slim and Bob opened their mouths wide and slumped deep into their seats.

"Hunh, hunh," said Al. "That was the time when you was wearing your hair wrapped with white strings, wasn't it?"

"White strings? Aw, Jake. . . . Hehehe!" Bob could not finish, the idea tickled him so.

"Yeah," said Jake. "When I was wearing them white strings on my hair old Colonel James was sucking at your ma's tits, wasn't he?"

"Jeesus," moaned Slim, pressing his handkerchief hard against his mouth to keep from coughing. "I told a piece of iron that once and it turned *redhot*. Now, what would a poor *meat* man do?"

Al glowered and fingered his cigarette nervously.

"Nigger," Al said slowly, so that the full force of his words would not be missed, "when old Colonel James was sucking at my ma's tits I saw your little baby brother across the street watching with slobber in his mouth. . . ."

Slim and Bob rolled on the sofa and held their stomachs. Jake stiffened, crossed his legs, and gazed out of the window.

"Yeah," he said slowly, "I remembers when my little baby brother was watching with slobber in his mouth, your old grandma was out in the privy crying 'cause she couldn't find a corncob. . . ."

Slim and Bob groaned and stomped their feet.

"Yeah," said Al, retaliating with narrowed eyes. "When my old grandma was crying for that corncob, your old aunt Lucy was round back of the barn with old Colonel James' old man, and she was saying something like this: 'Yyyou kknow . . . Mmmister Cccolonel . . . I jjjust ddon't like to ssssell . . . my ssstuff. . . . I jjjust lloves to gggive . . . iit away. . . .'"

Slim and Bob embraced each other and howled.

"Yeah," said Jake. "I remembers when old aunt Lucy got through she looked around and saw your old aunt Mary there watching with her finger stuck in her puss. And old aunt Lucy said, 'Mary, go home and wash your bloomers!'"

Slim and Bob beat the floor with their fists.

Al curled his lips and shot back:

"Hunh, hunh, yeah! And when my old aunt Mary was washing out her bloomers the hot smell of them soapsuds rose up and went out over the lonesome graveyard and your old greatgreatgreat grandma turned over in her grave and said: 'Lawd, I sure thank Thee for the smell of them pork chops You's cooking up in Heaven. . . .'"

Slim grabbed Bob and they screamed.

"Yeah," drawled Jake, determined not to be outdone, "when my old greatgreat*great* grandma was smelling them pork chops, your poor old greatgreatgreatgreat grandma was a Zulu queen in Africa. She was setting at the table and she said to the waiter: 'Say waiter, be sure and fetch me some of them missionary chitterlings. . . .'".

"Mmmm . . . miss . . . missionary chitterlings?" asked Slim, stretching flat on the floor and panting as one about to die.

"Yeah," said Al. "When my greatgreatgreatgreat grandma who was a Zulu queen got through eating them missionary chitterlings, she wanted to build a sewerditch to take away her crap, so she went out and saw your poor old greatgreatgreatgreat*great* grandma sleeping under a coconut tree with her old mouth wide open. She didn't need to build no sewerditch. . . ."

"Jeesus!" yelled Slim, closing his eyes and holding his stomach. "I'm dying!"

Jake screwed up his eyes, bit his lips, and tried hard to think of a return. But, for the life of him, he could not. Al's last image was too much; it left him blank. Then they all laughed so that they felt weak in the joints of their bones.

◆

The passage began with some light, for-fun siggin and slid down into a heavy exchange of verbal Dozens — and I mean the Dirty Dozens. The Dozens is a form of signification, but as a discourse mode it has some rules and rituals of its own, thus it constitutes a kind of subcategory within the signification mode. A crucial difference, though, is that the Dozens is found only in

"A is for 'Amen' . . . B is for 'Black and Beautiful' . . .
C is for the 'Changes' . . . er . . . D is for the 'Dozens' . . ."

by permission of the artist

"NOW DON'T YOU GO MAKING DECISIONS ON YOUR OWN!"

by permission of the artist

secular contexts (not that church folk don't play them, they just don't play them in the church). What you do in playing the Dozens is sig on a person's kinfolk — usually the mother, the closest kin — instead of siggin on the person. The player can extend the put-down, by analogy, to include other immediate relatives, and even ancestral kinfolk — like Al does in the sounding session from *Lawd Today,* where he reaches all the way back to drop a lug on Jake's "greatgreatgreatgreat*great* grandma sleeping under a coconut tree" somewhere in Africa. However, like Hughes's Jesse B. Simple, most black folk "don't play the Dozens that far back." The objective of the Dozens is to better your opponent with more caustic, humorous "insults." Played for fun or viciousnesss — and it can be either — the Dozens is a competitive oral test of linguistic ingenuity and verbal fluency. The winner, determined by the audience's responses, becomes a culture hero.

The most common specific verbalism of the Dozens is the simple retort: *Yo momma* (also *Ask yo momma*). When someone says something you dislike, the rejoinder can be in this simple form. A literary use of the Dozens is provided by Langston Hughes in the title of his longest poetic work: *Ask Your Mama.* The work contains pointed and often bitter references to racial oppression. In playing the Dozens in the title, Hughes is slyly alluding to America's unacknowledged racially mixed genealogies. (With rampant miscegenation in this country, who is to say who is really black or white? Ask yo momma!)

Another literary example of the Dozens is provided by Ralph Ellison in *The Invisible Man.* Ellison's nameless black hero is confronted by Brother Jack, his so-called "liberal" but really white racist Communist colleague. Brother Jack is criticizing the hero for having taken some action on his own initiative. The following dialogue ensues:

> "His personal responsibility," Brother Jack said.
> "Did you hear that, Brother? Did I hear him correctly?
> "Where did you get it, Brother," he said. "This is astounding, where did you get it?"
> "From your Ma —" I started and caught myself in time.

In its indigenous folk style, the Dozens consists of set responses in versified form, usually rhymed couplets. Some refer to various sexual acts committed with "yo momma" — the mother of whoever is being addressed. The term "Dozens" probably comes from the fact that the original verses involved twelve sex acts, each stated in such a way as to rhyme with the numbers 1 to 12. Other folk verses refer to aspects of "yo momma's" sexuality rather than to direct sexual activities. As an example, Richard Wright's short story "Big Boy Leaves Home" opens with a group of young black Southern cats playing the Dozens on their way to the swimming hole.

> *Yo mama don wear no drawers . . .*

Clearly, the voice rose out of the woods, and died away. Like an echo another voice caught it up:

> *Ah seena when she pulled em off . . .*

Another, shrill, cracking, adolescent:

> *N she washed 'em in alcohol . . .*

Then a quartet of voices blending in harmony, floated high above the tree tops:

> *N she hung 'em out in the hall . . .*

Laughing easily, four black boys came out of the woods into cleared pasture. They walked lollingly in bare feet, beating tangled vines and bushes with long sticks.

"Ah wished Ah knew some mo lines t tha song."

"Yeah, when yuh gits t where she hangs em out in the hall yuh has t stop."

"Shucks, whut goes wid *hall*?"

"*Call*."

"*Fall*."

"*Wall*."

"*Quall*."

They threw themselves on the grass, laughing.

"Big Boy?"

"Huh?"

"Yuh know one thing?"

"Whut?"

"Yuh sho is crazy!"

"Crazy?"

"Yeah, yuh crazys a bed-bug!"

"Crazy bout whut?"

"Man, whoever hearda *quall*?"

"Yuh said yuh wanted somthing to go wid *hall*, didn't yuh?"

"Yuh, but whuts a *quall*?"

"Nigger, a *qualls* a *quall*."

They laughed easily, catching and pulling long green blades of grass with their toes.

"Waal, ef a *qualls* a *quall*, whut IS a *quall*?"

"Oh, Ah know."

"What?"

"Tha ol song goes something like this:

> *Yo mama don wear no drawers,*
> *Ah seena when she pulled em off,*
> *N she washed em in alcohol,*
> *N she hung em out in the hall,*
> *N then she put em back on her QUALL!"*

As blacks have become more urbane, the Dozens have become more sophisticated and today the game is played with fewer of its original programmatic responses. The player who reaches into his or her linguistic bag and comes up with something fresh and original is given heavy audience approval. The most recent popular addition to the game, though now somewhat dated, was: "I fucked yo momma for a solid hour / Baby came out hollin 'Black Power.' "

In the original basic form, the Dozens is a game played usually by black males. Females will use the phrase "yo momma" or "ask yo momma," but they rarely get off into an extended scene like the Brothers do. The following dialogue between two adult black middle-class females shows an example of the limited use of the Dozens practiced by women. The two, both social workers, have just arrived at their office:

Shirley (obviously expressing disapproval): Girl, what's the matter with you today? You look a mess!

Martha (in no mood to be criticized today, not even by a friend and co-worker): Aw, yo momma. [Your mother is the one who looks a mess]

Since the Dozens can be a potentially explosive game, it would be well to pay attention to its fundamental rule: the "insult" hurled must not represent an accurate statement of reality, or a battle — a shonuff one — will ensue. (Since the speakers are "playing" the Dozens, even in the original sexually "insulting" versions, nobody has actually had intercourse with anybody else's mother.) For example, I once overheard my son Tony and his partners get into the Dozens.

> Ralph (to Duane about Duane's unmarried mother): Least my momma don't take no birth control pills.
> Duane (getting mad and hurt since this was a true statement): Okay, now, muthafu —
> Tony (to Ralph, who's from a very poor family of ten children): Well, yo momma need to take some.
> Ralph (to Tony): Least my momma don't buy her furniture from the Good Will.
> (Tony was really hurt, since I had indeed bought his T.V. table from the Good Will, which he never forgave me for. Now the whole thing was about to blow up, with everybody squaring off and cursing, and me thinking I would have to intervene, but Robert, level-headed and older, ended it.)
> Robert: Hey, y'all cool it 'foe we get into some trouble. And anyway, ain non of y'all got no business dishing it out since can't nobody take it.

◆

Tonal semantics, the third category of discourse, refers to the use of voice rhythm and vocal inflection to convey meaning in black communication. In using the semantics of tone, the voice is employed like a musical instrument with improvisations, riffs, and all kinds of playing between the notes. This rhythmic pattern becomes a kind of acoustical phonetic alphabet and gives black speech its songified or musical quality. Black rappers use word sound to tap their listeners' souls and inner beings in the same way that the musician uses the symbolic language of music to strike inward responsive chords in his listeners' hearts. The speech rhythms and tonal inflections of Black English are, of course, impossible to capture in print. But you have heard these rhythms in the speech-music of James Brown and Aretha Franklin, in the preaching-lecturing of Martin Luther King, Jr., and Jesse Jackson, in the political raps of Stokely Carmichael and Malcolm X, in the comedy routines of Flip Wilson and Richard Pryor. The key to understanding black tonal semantics is to recognize that the sound of what is being said is just as important as "sense." Both sound and sense are used to deliver the Word. Reverend McKenzie of Memphis intoned: "I say Lo-rd, Lo-rd, Lo-rd, do you hear me, do you hear — ear-ear-ear — me-mee-mee." And Martin Luther King, Jr., once said, "Lord, we ain what we ought to be, and we ain what we want to be, we ain what we gon be, but thank God, we ain what we was." In tonal semantics then, strictly semantic meaning is combined and synthesized with lyrical balance, cadence, and melodious voice rhythm. The effect achieved is the conveyance of a psycho-cognitive message. These songified patterns of speech reach down to the "deep structure" of life, that common level of shared human experience which words alone cannot convey.

To both understand and "feel" tonal semantics requires the listener to be of a cultural tradition that finds value and meaning in word sound. In Black America, that tradition, like other aspects of Black English style, is located in the African background. From a strictly linguistic viewpoint, we may note that West African languages are *tone languages*. That is, speakers of these languages rely on the tone with which they pronounce syllables, sounds, and words to convey their meaning. The closest example of tone used to distinguish meaning in English is the difference in word pairs like: permit/permit (pronounced one way, you have the verb, pronounced another way, it's a noun); suspect/suspect (again, difference in pronunciation signals whether the verb or noun form is being used). Whereas English is quite limited in its use of the features of tone to signal meaning, African languages have a very complex, highly sophisticated system of tone. Caught between a tone language (i.e., their native African tongue) and a "toneless" language (i.e., the English they were forced to adopt), Africanized English speakers seem to have mediated this linguistic dilemma by retaining in their cultural consciousness the abstract African concept of tone while applying it to English in obviously different ways. The anthropologist Melville Herskovits, in *The Myth of the Negro Past*, commented on the survival of tone in Black speech:

Such matters as the fate in the New World of the tonal elements in West African speech, where, as has been indicated, tone has semantic as well as phonemic significance, remain to be studied. It is a most difficult problem requiring a long-term and highly technical analysis of Negro speech in various parts of the New World. That the peculiarly "musical" quality of Negro-English as spoken in the United States and the same trait found in the speech of white Southerners represent a nonfunctioning survival of this characteristic of African languages is entirely possible, especially since this same "musical" quality is prominent in Negro-English and Negro-French everywhere. One Negro who was faced with the practical task of distinguishing the registers in the tonal system of a West African language has stated that he was greatly aided in this task by reference to the cadences of Negro speech he knew from Harlem. When he was confronted with the need of mastering the especially difficult combinations of tones in Ifek, the registers of such a phrase as "Yeah, boss," (⏋—) greatly simplified his task. That such an experience may offer a methodological hint for future research on the survival of tone in the speech of New World Negroes, and especially those of the United States, is not out of the range of possibility.

By applying a contemporary sociolinguistic perspective to the use of tone in Black English, we can see that it is highly functional. That is, since there is an interaction between what is said, how it is said, who says it, to whom it is said, and the sociocultural context in which it is said, listeners are affected by *all* this information — not just the "pure" words — in interpreting a speaker's utterance. In looking at just one of these components — how it is said — we can see that though Black English speakers are not directly applying the African linguistic rules for tone, what they are doing amounts to a variation on the same theme. Not only are Black English speakers and listeners affected by linguistic meaning and linguistic sound, but there is an expectation that Black speech utterances will depend on and employ tonal contouring. In fact, given that (to paraphrase Baraka) word sound and word use trip a familiar social chord, it is nearly impossible to filter out the strictly linguistic-cognitive abstract meaning from the sociocultural psycho-emotive meaning. This is all the more applicable to the communication system of a people with a cultural base in which the two realities are considered to be one. Thus in the socio-cultural context (where *all* languages are used, interpreted, and tested anyway), what Herskovits calls this "musical quality" — tonal semantics — is meaningful and hence functional.

As stated, the retention of tone as a register of meaning in Black English was buttressed by two cultural forces. First, the emphasis on balance and the synthesis of opposites in the traditional African world view, hence emotion and intellect, word *sound* and word *meaning,* are combined in Afro-American communication dynamics. The second cultural force relates to the use of the drum in African culture. Not only does the drum function to convey cognitive messages, it has a sociopsychological purpose as well. In *Indaba My Children,* African scholar Credo Mutwa put it this way:

> The drumbeat can summon tears from the springs of our eyes and drive our souls deep into the caverns of sorrow, or it can raise us to the very peak of elation . . . Drums can be sounded in such a way that they have a soothing effect, and create a restful feeling. The beat of the drums can cure what no medicines can cure! It can heal the ills of the mind — it can heal the very soul. Where Americans and Europeans have their evil drugs and the couches of their psychiatrists, the Africans still have their drums.

Although Afro-Americans no longer have their drums, they have retained this African cultural concept in the use of word-sound combinations to achieve spiritual equilibrium and psychological balance.

Tonal semantics has many varied representatations in black speech. These may be grouped according to the following types: talk-singing, repetition and alliterative word play, intonational contouring, rhyme. Given the limitations of print, it will be difficult to illustrate these properly. But we gon do our best!

◆

Talk-singing in tonal semantics achieves its meaning from the listener's association of the tone with the feeling of being "happy" and gittin the Spirit. (That feeling, as we've noted, is

behaviorally expressed in the black cultural ritual of "shouting.")
By extension, then, talk-singing is associated with any state of
feeling good (whether you "shout" or not). The black preacher's
vocalization is the most widely known example of talk-singing.
He combines straightforward talk with the cadence and rhythm
of traditional black preaching style. This style is characterized by
elongated articulation of single words, by heavy breathing, by
lengthy pauses between words and phrases, and by constant in-
terjections of the standard key expressions "ha," "aha," and
"un-huh." Characteristically, the style signals the dramatic high
point of the sermon, the preacher shifting into this level and
style of communication to excite his congregation and move
them with the power of the Word (as he too is being moved). An
example is provided by this excerpt from the sermon "The Mid-
night Prayer Meeting."

> . . . So there was Paul and Silas, had been thrown into jail for
> preaching and converting the peoples unto the Word of the Lord.
> And it was gittin on into the midnight hour, they went to singin,
> prayin, and callin on God. Church, I wonder what did they say
> when they cried out unto the Lord. Some folk say they said: I-I-I-
> I-I-I love the-uh-uh ha-the Lord, the Lord, He heard, he hear ——
> — d my-y-y-y-y cry. But, naw, I don't think that was it. Somebody
> else said they said: AAAAA-maz-Amazing Grace, un-huh, uh, ha,
> how sweet, how sweet, yassuh, the sound. But naw, I don't think
> that was it, either.
>
> [By now, the preacher's congregation is ecstatically tense, poised
> on edge, nearing their emotional plateau, and waiting to see what
> kind of "on time" call the preacher is going to issue forth in
> expounding what *he* thinks Paul and Silas must have said. The
> preacher continues and shifts to talk-singing right in the middle
> of his sentence]:
>
> I believe, church, I believe, yassuh, help me Lord, I believe, un-
> huh, I believe that ol Paul and Silas, looked up toward Heaven,
> and said, ha, sa —— id, Father, Faaaa — ther, I-I-I-I-I stretch
> my hand, aha, to to —— to — toooooooo — to Thee, cause, Lo —
> —— rd, no other, no other, help I-I-I-I-I kn —— ow.

Popular treatment of the traditional black preacher creates
the impression that talk-singing is limited to the ritualistic struc-

ture of the sermon. However, this synthesis of talking and singing is more pervasive and widespread than that. In the church,
a deacon, tesitifer, or any old body who just feels like it, may get
a rhythm going throughout the church: "I-I-I-I-I, Oh, yeah,
I-I-I-I-I heard the voice of Jesus saying . . . " Or the caller of
tonal semantics can just get on one word and render it with as
many different rhythmic riffs and musical sounds as possible:
"Jeeeeeeeesus, oh, yeah, Lord Jessssssssssssssus, Je-Je-Je-Je-Je-
Jeeeeeesus . . . " Often the Moan and Chant are used in this
manner: "Hmmmmmmmmmmmmmmm, or HHHHHHHHH-
HHHmmmmmmmmmmmmm." With each "note," the speaker
builds the congregation to an emotional fervent climax . All such
vocal channels send the logical-emotional message of one who
knows the Lord.

The preacher himself uses talk-singing at times other than
when he is giving his sermon. He may sprinkle his off-the-cuff
general remarks with it (as the signification example over on
page 125 shows). He may be discussing church business or finance
and shift into talk-singing. He may also use it in exhorting the
members to pay attention to upcoming church events. The point
is that talk-singing is not restricted to Sunday morning sermons,
nor is it limited to the preacher. From a practical viewpoint,
perhaps it is widely used because it is an excellent attention-
getting device. The listener recognizes the shift from straight
talk to talk-singing and becomes extra alert and attentive to the
speaker, since the tone derives meaning from its use as a signal
that the ritual of intense emotion and spirit possession is about to
come down. Whether it comes down or not, the fact is that the
listener is moved to sit up and take notice.

Today, talk-singing is not as prevalent in secular settings. The
most frequent contemporary uses are found in musical and poetic performances. Black soul singers and groups incorporate
raps along with musical melody and singing, sometimes
throughout a song, sometimes at the peak of the song. Among
the well-known musical artists who employ this technique are
Isaac Hayes (especially on his *Hot Buttered Soul* album), Barry
White, Smokey Robinson, B. B. King, James Brown, and Aretha
Franklin. Like the preacher, the black singer may combine sing-

ing and talking at the high point of his or her rendition of a musical piece. Having built up to an emotional climax, the singer
attempts to sustain the mood by riffing and improvising with
verbal sing-type statements about the theme or message of the
music; statements repeating the lyrics of the song; statements
about how he or she feels at the moment or about how the audience feels. For example, the lead singer of the Spinners uses this
form of tonal semantics to reiterate the theme of the group's
well-known song, "Mighty Love." Essentially the message has to
do with the necessity for and power of eternally strong and profound love between men and women. Although there is no neat
mathematical formula or how-to directions for finding this vital
ingredient of life, the Brothers believe that with soul you can
create the male-female bond of "mighty love." Calling and responding among themselves, the background pushes the lead
singer to his musical max; the result: a concluding "sermon" on
love:

> [background, repeating throughout this brief "sermon"]: Mighty
> love, doo-doo-doo-oooo-ooo-ooo / Mighty love, doo-doo-doo-
> oooo-ooo-ooo [lead, singing]: Mighty love Jones comin down on
> me baby, see baby, with a mighty love you can sometimes turn the
> world around, with a mighty love you can turn the world around
> sometimes, yes you can, it makes music have a [talk-singing] haa-
> aaaaaaaaapy sound . . . I-I-I-I-I gon, gon, gon, gon git yo lovin . . .
> hey baby, hey, hey, got to love ya . . . I-I-I-I-gooooooooot to love ya
> [singing] I knew when I first met you that you had a mighty love,
> baby [talk-singing] uhm gon wait on ya, gon wait on ya [higher]
> gon wait on ya . . . Just giiiiiiiiiiiive me yo loooooooooove . . . [ca-
> denced "preaching"] miiiiiiiiighty, miiiiiiiiighty, miiiiiighty, miiiiii-
> ighty, miiiiiiiiighty, miiiiiiighty, miiiiiighty, miiiighty, hear what I
> say, saaaaaaaay, now, now, now, now, baby [subtle shift into
> Moan-Hum] ooooo-ummmmmm-ooooo-hhhhhhhhmmmmmmmm
> . . . comeonononononononononon on now . . .

Another example is provided by Aretha Franklin and Ray
Charles in their *Live at Fillmore West* album. Aretha has just completed a soulful rendition of "Dr. FEELGOOD," her earthly man
who cures all her "pains and ills." Then she shifts ever so subtly

and gently into talk-singing about the Heavenly Dr. FEELGOOD, who moves her and Ray Charles right on into their soulful duet "Spirit in the Dark":

> Oh, good God Amighty, that man sho makes me feel real good . . . yeah, yeah, yeah [picking up] Yeah! Yeah! Ohhhhhhhh yeah! [into the Moan and Chant] Hmmmmmmmmmm . . . Hmmmmmm . . . [higher] HHHHHHHHHHHHHHHHHHmmmmmmmmmmm . . . it's gon beeeeee all right . . . I just wanna say yeah! Ohhhhhh yeah! [soft Moan] Hmmmmmmmmm . . . I get a little fearful about thangs that I don't understand sometime . . . sometime it's good, oh, hear me now, it's good, to sit back, cross yo arms, cross yo legs, look out up to Heaven and say yeah! oh, yeah! yeeeeeeee eah! . . . Can I hear you say yeah, if you understand soul, why can't I hear you say yeah! [this is purely rhetorical since audience has been yeahing, whooping, and shouting all the time] . . . say it one mo time . . . it feels all right, feels mighty, mighty nice to me right now, yes, it does . . . come onnnnnnn Lord, and watch over meeeeeee, yeah . . . [subtly into straight singing] are you gittin the Spirit in the dark . . .

Talk-singing is also found in contemporary black poetry, in the incorporation of musical lyrics and lines to be sung within the structure of a poem. For example, Imamu Baraka draws upon James Brown's first hit recording, "Please, Please, Please," in the poem "The Nation Is Like Ourselves." He pleads for the return of middle-class blacks to the community fold. He employs the entreaty "please" at the beginning of each plea, and when read, he sings it in James Brown fashion ("please mister liberated nigger," "please mr. ethnic meditations professor," "doctor nigger, please"). Then he concludes the poem with:

> yes the sweet lost nigger
> you are our nation sick ass assimilado
> [sings] please come back
> like james brown say
> [talk-sings] please please please.

Another example comes from Haki Madhubuti. His title poem "Don't Cry, Scream" is a tribute to John Coltrane, in which

Haki simulates a John Coltrane solo with poetic words. The marginalia of the poem contains instructions for how the poem is to be read-sung, such as "sing loud & high with feeling" and "sing loud & high with feeling letting yr / voice break." Occasionally, interspersed throughout the poem itself are words and phrases to be sung. For instance, at the end of the stanza quoted below, you are supposed to sing the Ray Charles–Temptations version of "Yesterday" for full effect:

> swung on a faggot who politely
> scratched his ass in my presence.
> he smiled broken teeth stained from
> his over-used tongue, fisted-face.
> teeth dropped in tune with ray
> charles singing 'yesterday.'

An even more striking example is provided by Haki's "Poem to Complement Other Poems, in which the poet exhorts black folk to enter into a new state of consciousness by changing their reality and perceptions. The poet details the types of changes required and the necessity for change, beginning or ending each statement with the word *change*. Then in the last stanza, the poet whups it on us with a climax resembling Aretha Franklin singing her song about the "chains of love." Here he repeats the word *change* twenty-three times in near succession, playing off on the similarity in sound between *change* and *chain*. It's obvious what kind of "chains" the poet is singing about as he hits us hard with the concluding musically poetic lines:

> change change change your enemy
> change change
> change change your change change change
> your mind nigger.

◆

Another feature of tonal semantics is repetition and alliterative word-play. Key words and sounds are repeated in succession, both for emphasis and effect. Believing that meaningful sounds can move people, the black speaker capitalizes on effective uses of repetition: the disc jockey's "call, cop, and qualify"; Jesse Jackson's "pimp, punk, prostitute, preacher, Ph.D."; the preacher's "I am nobody talking to Somebody Who can help anybody"; the preacher's repetition of words and sounds of emotion, especially in the shift to talk-singing; the phrasal structured repetition of King's "we ain what we ought to be, and we ain what we want to be, we ain what we gon be, but thank God, we ain what we was."

There are three additional examples of tonal semantic repetition that should be cited here. In the early sixties, when blacks were pushing hard in the South for the right to vote, Malcolm X cautioned America that it would be either voting or violence. He expressed it in the simple alliterative dichotomy: "the ballot or the bullet." An extended example is provided by his "Message to the Grass Roots" speech. In the first passage quoted he drives home his point by repeating the structural unity "you don't catch hell because . . ." finally concluding with an explanation of why you do catch hell.

> What you and I need to do is learn to forget our differences. When we come together, we don't come together as Baptists or Methodists. You don't catch hell because you're a Baptist, and you don't catch hell because you're a Methodist. You don't catch hell because you're a Methodist or Baptist, you don't catch hell because you're a Democrat or a Republican, you don't catch hell because you're a Mason or an Elk, and you sure don't catch hell because you're an American; because if you were an American, you wouldn't catch hell. You catch hell because you're a black man. You catch hell, all of us catch hell, for the same reason.

In the following excerpt, instead of repeating a whole phrasal unit, Malcolm uses the technique of repeating the key words "bloodshed" and "land."

> Look at the American Revolution in 1776. That revolution was for what? For land. Why did they want land? Independence. How was it carried out? Bloodshed. Number one, it was based on land, the basis of independence. And the only way they could get it was bloodshed. The French Revolution — what was it based on? The

"NOW THERE WAS A GREAT AMERICAN-MARTIN LUTHER KING."

landless against the landlord. What was it for? Land. How did they get it? Bloodshed. Was no love lost, was no compromise, was no negotiation. I'm telling you — you don't know what a revolution is. Because when you find out what it is, you'll get back in the alley, you'll get out of the way.

The Russian Revolution — what was it based on? Land; the landless against the landlord. How did they bring it about? Bloodshed. You haven't got a revolution that doesn't involve bloodshed.

◆

Intonational contouring is the specific use of stress and pitch in pronouncing words in the black style. For example, *yeah* and *un-huh,* when pronounced in a certain way characteristic of black speakers, take on special meaning. Namely, that of registering a notion of sarcastic disbelief or contradiction about what somebody has just said. Hence, depending on context, the speaker can mean the exact opposite of "yeah" and "un-huh." This use of voice inflection does not always operate on a strictly semantic level, but can be used to trip a familiar socio cultural type of semantic lever. That is, the special black pronunciation may not register a different meaning, but it locates the speaker dead into the Black Thang, thus giving greater psychological weight to his words. As one brother said, "it ain the police — it's the PO-lice." (Whereupon another brother turned around and gave the word a truly semantically distinct pronunciation, contending: "Naw, it's the po-lice" [poor lice].)

Preachers employ intonational contouring in their deliberately halting, slow, exaggerated pronunciation of important words. Rather than saying simply "God," they will say "Godt." Or, "There is a PURson here who is PO-sessed."

◆

Modern free verse notwithstanding, rhyme remains a basic ingredient of poetry. Its widespread cultural use and approval in nonpoetic contexts is unique to Black English speakers. While both sacred and secular speech employ rhyme, it is more frequently used in secular discourse. When it is used in sacred contexts, it is usually found in the incorporation of Gospel and old standby hymn lyrics into a sermon, testifying, church speech, or welcome on a church program. A newly "saved" member joining the church said: "I thank God for being here today. And I want y'all to know today that it's a sweet sound cause I once was lost but now uhm found." (The reference is to the church song "Amazing Grace": "Amazing Grace / how sweet the sound / I once was lost / but now am found.")

Occasionally, in the church context, speakers will compose their own rhymes. For instance, a visiting minister who was invited to say a few closing remarks began this way: "Giving Honor to God, Christ Jesus, pulpit associates, members, and friends. I'm glad to be here today, just to say: that God is the way. When we leave here and hit the sky, going to that great Bye and Bye, I want to be among that number."

Turning to the use of rhyme in secular style, where it is most prevalent, we should note that some of the rhyming sounds form semantically meaningful words, others constitute so-called nonsense rhymes. Yet all make sense on one level of meaning or another when located in the cultural tradition that applauds good rappin rhymers. (Thus Wright's Big Boy gets heavy approval for his rhyming ability when he comes up with the word "quall."). William Wells Brown's nineteenth-century novel *Clotel* gives us an early example of rhyme which can still be heard today among older blacks:

> Ought's a ought
> figure a figure
> All for the white man,
> none for the nigger.

Modern-day examples of the black rapper's overwhelming preference for rhymes include the following: "See you later, alligator . . . After while, crocodile . . . Split the scene, jelly bean." And: "You dead, skillet head . . . You ain nowhere, square." Or: "I would if I could, but I ain't cause I cain't."

The most effective signifyin and cappin have rhyme as a prime ingredient. For instance, Malcolm X's heavy sig on the non-violent revolution: "In a revolution, you swinging, not singing." (Referring to the common practice of singing "We Shall

Overcome" in Civil Rights marches and protests of the sixties). And Muhammad Ali's cap on Sonny Liston: "Yes, the crowd did not dream when they laid down their money / that they would see a total eclipse of the Sonny."

An extended example of rhyme as a total discourse mode is provided by the introduction to the record album *The Best of Frankie Crocker: The 8th Wonder of the World.*

> "Say, baby, this is an album that's bound to put more dips in your hips; more cut in your strut; more glide in your stride. If you don't dig it you know you got a hole in your soul; don't eat chicken on Sunday. Punch, girl! Other cats be laughin an jokin; Frankie Crocker's steady takin care a business, cookin' an' smokin'. For there is no other like this soul brother — tall, tan, young, and fly; unnhh' oww! Anytime you want me, baby, I'm your guy. Unhhh! Oww! Young an' single an' I love to mingle — can I mingle with you, baby? Unhh! Ohh! Closer than white's on rice; closer than cold's on ice; closer than the collar's on a dog; closer than a ham is on a country hog. Woooo! Gonna get next to you, mamma! Say, Scooter, thank you very much for buying our first oldies album. Frankie loves you for it. Each and every groove will make you move 'cause you know what I say, baby: you get so much with the Frankie Crocker touch. After all — how can you lose with the stuff I use? Truly the Eighth Wonder of the World; before me there was none; after me there shall be no more. Aren't you glad you live in the town — you can hear the Frankie Crocker sound when the sun goes down. Lemme rap to you, momma: if I'm all you got, I'm all you need. Enjoy the album. I hope it brings many pleasure listening hours. Frankie loves you."

◆

Narrative sequencing is the final mode of discourse to be considered. The story-telling tradition is strong in Black American culture and is most often associated with Toasts and other kinds of folklore, as well as the plantation tales of old. But alongside these more ritualized kinds of story-telling is narrative speech as a characteristic register of black communication generally. Black English speakers will render their general, abstract observations about life, love, people in the form of a concrete narrative — as the saying goes, "a nigguh always got a story." The relating of events (real or hypothetical) becomes a black rhetorical strategy to explain a point, to persuade holders of opposing views to one's own point of view, and in general to "win friends and influence people." This meandering away from the "point" takes the listener on episodic journeys and over tributary rhetorical routes, but like the flow of nature's rivers and streams, it all eventually leads back to the source. Though highly applauded by blacks, this narrative linguistic style is exasperating to whites who wish you'd be direct and hurry up and get to the point.

That the story-telling tradition harks back to an African past is fairly well-established by now. In Chapter Four we spoke of the role of the griot in African tribal culture. This revered person, always an elder, was responsible for maintaining tribal history. Comprising this history was not merely the chronicles of who did what when, but composite word-pictures of the culture, belief, ethics, and values of the tribe. As part of their training for this sacred position, the story-tellers took oaths never to alter the history, customs, and truths of their people. Village story-tellers are like walking museums. The "old ones" tell their stories to "boys and girls seated with open mouths around the spark-wreathed fire in the center of the villages in the dark forests and on the aloe-scented plains of Africa." Thus, as the Akan saying goes, "the words of one's elders are greater than an amulet," for African elders constitute the "repository of communal wisdom." (In Black American culture, this reverence for elders can be witnessed in the rearing of children, who are told that they "bet not be sassin dem ol folks — don't somethin bad happen to you." However, in the chaos and contemporary disintegration of black urban life, one does not hear this expression nor witness this practice as often.)

Every black neighborhood in every city in the United States comes equipped with its own story-tellers. Some can be found on street corners with fifths of whiskey in their hands. Bars, churches, hospitals, unemployment lines, welfare lines — all are possible places where one might find story-tellers. The ghetto porch is home base for some of these "walking historians." In speaking of this tradition and the "front porch" as the stage upon which it was maintained in the South, Frenchy Hodges, a Georgia poet, wrote in her collection *Piece De Way Home:*

Front porches
Were
    "Did-I-ever-tell-yall-
    How-I-met-yo'-mama"?
Or
    "I-put-the-igg-on-yo'-Daddy-
    One-Sunday-in-de-church."
Front porches
Were . . .
If-you-do-this-that'll-happen-stories,
The-dead-who-visit-the-living-stories,
Daddy-you-made-it-and-wrong-stories,
Tell-that-one-again-stories,
That-don't-make-no-sense-stories.

In Black America, modern-day yarn spinners, like their ancient African counterparts, become the words they convey. That is, they are not content just to sit back and rattle off the words to a story; rather, they use voice, body, and movement as tools to bring the tale to life. If the story is about animals (like "Brer Rabbit," or "The Signifying Monkey"), the story-teller becomes the animal and takes on all of that animal's characteristics in the narration of events. If the story is about God and Biblical persons, or about historical heroes like "Mister Toussan," the story-teller mimics the voice, gestures, and posture of each person in the text. (See the conversation between Buster and Riley on pages 115–18). If the "story" is in response to an actual comment or question in a real-life situation, the "story-teller" comes on with a dramatic narration, rather than a succinct, tight response. ("What happened to you last night?" "Oh, well, dig, like I was on my way over here, and so, like this ride came out of this side street, and like it was my main man, and I said, what's happenin? And then we got to rappin . . . ")

Examples of narrative sequencing, as a mode of discourse in black communication, may be found in the following forms: preaching and testifying; folk stories, "tall" tales, and Toasts; narrative rendering of abstractions and responses to events in the real world. Each of these types is a complete "story" in itself; here we can but briefly expound and illustrate them.

◆

To testify is to tell the truth through "story." In the sacred context, the subject of testifying includes such matters as visions, prophetic experiences, the experience of being saved, and testimony to the power and goodness of God. In the secular context, the subject matter includes such matters as blues changes caused by yo man or yo woman, and conversely, the Dr. FEEL-GOOD power of yo man or yo woman; experiences attesting to the racist power of the white oppressor; testimonials to the power of a gifted musician or singer. The retelling of these occurrences in lifelike fashion recreates the spiritual reality for others who at that moment vicariously experience what the testifier has gone through. The content of testifying, then, is not plain and simple commentary but a dramatic narration and a communal reenactment of one's feelings and experiences. Thus one's humanity is reaffirmed by the group and his or her sense of isolation diminished.

The rendering of sermons in the traditional black church nearly always involves extended narration as a device to convey the theme. Rarely will black preachers expound their message in the linear fashion of a lecture. Rather, the thematic motif is dramatized with gestures, movement, plot, real-life characterization, and circumlocutory rhetorical flourishes. The preacher thus becomes an actor and story-teller in the best sense of the word. When he makes reference to Peter "building the church on solid rock," rather than "on shifting sand," the preacher will lift his foot in the air and put it back down firmly to symbolize Peter placing the church on solid ground. When the preacher alludes to the crucifixion, he will throw his handkerchief over his shoulder, to symbolize the cross, and then walk up and down the aisle or across the floor in a stooped position to re-create for his congregation the image of Jesus climbing Mount Calvary. If he refers to the experience of being saved, he may say that "God put running in my feet" and do a kind of slow run across the floor.

The preacher knows that his congregation needs guidance in the conduct of daily affairs, as well as spiritual inspiration to keep on pushin. But the interactive communication process puts on him constraints and demands that he must fulfill. The orchestration of the sermon requires that Biblical persona be brought to life and the events recast into present-day context. Yet, no matter how contemporary the theme, the congregation expects the message of the sermon to be grounded in Biblical textual reference. At the same time, despite the narration of events far removed from their present world and experience, they expect the preacher to make them feel the Spirit. (You ain done no preachin if don't nobody shout!) Since the preacher is the one who must bring it all together — the story, the message, Scriptural clarity, and the Spirit — his imagination and communicative ability is taxed to the max. But most come through. In fact, some sermon-stories are so vividly and dynamically narrated that they become popular and widely known throughout the church community in a given city or town. An example is the sermon "The Eagle Stirreth Her Nest," created by the Reverend C. L. Franklin of Detroit. Immensely popular several years ago, "The Eagle Stirreth Her Nest" was such a frequently requested sermon that Reverend Franklin recorded it for distribution. (He has also recorded several other sermons but this was by far the most popular.) The Scriptural reference for the sermon is the Book of Deuteronomy, Chapter 32 (especially verses 11ff.), in which Moses, in the last days of his life, is instructing the children of Israel to keep God's commandments and admonishing them because of their tendencies to forget God in times of good fortune. Alluding to the story of Jacob, the Scripture reads as follows: "As an eagle stirreth up her nest, fluttereth over her young, spreadeth abroad her wings, taketh them, beareth them on her wings: so the Lord alone did lead him [Jacob], and there was no strange god with him." Having established this background for his congregation, the renowned Reverend Franklin begins to put the story, message, and Spirit all together for his flock. First, he notes that many aspects of the natural world have been used as metaphors for God, and the eagle is simply one such metaphor:

> Many things have been used as symbolic expressions to give us a picture of God or some characteristic of one of his attributes. The ocean with her turbulent majesty — the mountain — the lion —

many things have been employed as pictures of either God's
strength or God's power or God's law or God's mercy! . . . . So the
eagle is used here as a symbol of God.

Next, he establishes an analogy between the eagle stirring her
nest and the history of human development. (The "uh"s,
"yeah"s, and other exclamations in the following excerpts are attempts to capture the deliberate vocalized pauses and soulful
expressions of Spirit that characterize black preaching style.)

Now, uh, in picturing God as an eagle stirring her nest, I believe
history has been one big nest that God has been eternally stirring
to make man better, and to help us achieve world brotherhood . . .
Now, the Civil War, for example, and, uh, the struggle in connection with it was merely the promptings of Providence, uh, to lash
man to a point of being brotherly to all men. In fact, all of the wars
that we have gone through, we've come out with new outlooks and
new views and better people. So that throughout history, God has
been stirring the various nests of circumstances surrounding us so
that he could discipline us, help us to know ourselves and help us
to love one another, and to help us hasten on the realization of the
kingdom of God.

Now he proceeds to return to his first point, having to do with
images and symbols for God, and elaborates further on that
motif, by noting that although many metaphors have been used
for God, the eagle is an especially appropriate image for the
Master.

The eagle symbolizes God because there is something about an
eagle that, uh, is a fit symbol of things about God. In the first place,
the eagle is the king of fowl. It is a regal, a kingly bird. In that
majesty, he represents the kingship of God or symbolize the kingship of God. Uh, listen, if you please. For God is not merely a king
— he is THEE King. Somebody has said that He is the King of
Kings. For, you see, these little kings that we know, they got to have
a king over them . . . God is THEE king, and if the eagle is a kingly
bird, in that way he symbolizes the regalness and kingliness of our
God.
   In the second place, the eagle is strong! Somebody has said that,
uh, as the eagle go weaving his way through the air, he can look
down on a young lamb, grazing by a mountainside, and can fly

down and just with the strength of his claw, pick up this young lamb and fly away to yonder's cliff and devour him, because he is strong. If the eagle is strong, then, in that, he is a symbol of God, for our God is strong. Our God is strong! Somebody has called Him a fortress so that when the enemy is pursuing me, I can run behind Him; somebody has called Him a citadel of protection and redemption; somebody else has said that He's so strong until they call Him a leaning post, that thousands can lean on Him, and He'll never give away. I don't believe you praying with me. People have been leaning on Him eve'y since time immemorial! Abraham leaned on Him, Isaac and Jacob leaned on Him, Moses and the Prophets leaned on Him, all the Christians leaned on Him, people are leaning on Him all over the world today, and He's never given away! He's strong — that strong — isn't it so?

Other attributes of this kingly bird, such as swiftness and extraordinary sight, are explicated, with analogous application to the world of man and God. The nest-building practice of the eagle and its relationship with the "eagleletts" is of special significance:

It is said that, uh, an eagle builds a nest unusual. It is said that, uh, the eagle select rough material basically for the construction of its nest an' then as the nest graduate toward a close or a finish, the material become finer and softer like down at the end. And then, uh, he go about to, uh, set up residence in that nest and when the little eagleletts are born, she go out and bring in food to feed them, but when they get to the point where they old enough to be out on they own, why, uh, the eagle will begin to pull out some of that down and let some of those thorns come through so that the nest won't be, you know, so comfortable so when they get to loungin' round and, uh, rollin' round, the thorns prick 'em here and there. Pray with me if you please. I believe that God has to do that to us sometime, things are going so well and we're so satisfied that we just lounge around and forget to pray — you walk around all day and enjoy God's life, God's health, and God's strength and go climb in the bed without sayin' "Thank you Lord for another day's journey!" We'll do that. God has to pull out a little of the plush around us, a little of the comfort around us, and let a few thorns of trial and tribulation stick through the nest to make us pray sometime! Isn't it so?

Knowing that he has now got his congregation on fire, Franklin moves to his climax with a story about an eagle growing up among chickens on a poultry farm. Here he makes his final symbolic assertion that not only is the eagle representative of God, it also symbolizes the soul of man, the implication being that they are one and the same, that is, God is in man and man is born of God — in fact, that is what differentiates the human "animal" from other earthly animals.

It is said that, uh, there was a man who had a poultry farm and that he raised chickens for the market, and, uh, one day in one of his broods, he discovered a strange looking bird that was very much unlike the other chickens on the yard. And, uh, the man didn't pay too much attention, but he noticed as time went on, that, uh, this strange looking bird was unusual. He outgrew the other little chickens, his habits was stranger and different, Oh, Loooord, but he let it grow on, let it mingle with the other chickens. Oh, Lord! And then one day, a man who knew eagles when he saw 'em, came along and saw that little eagle walking in the yard, and, uh, he said to his friend, "Do you know that you have an eagle here?" AAAA-mmmmmmm, the man said, "Well, I didn't really know it," AAAA-mmmmmmm, "but I knew he was different from the other chickens," and, uh, "I knew that it way were different," and, uh, "I knew that his habits were different," and, uh, "he didn't act like the other chickens," AAAA-mmmmmmm, "but I didn't know that he was eagle." AAAA-mmmmmmm, but the man said, "yeeeeah! you have an eagle here on yo' yard." AAAA-mmmmmmm, "and after while, when he's a little older, he gonna get tired of the ground, yes he will, he's gonna rise up on the pin of his wings." Yeeeeah! AAAA-mmmmmmm, and, uh, "as he grow, why, uh, you can change the cage, and, uh, make it a little larger as he grow older and grow larger." AAAA-mmmmmmm, the man went out and built a cage and, uh, every day he go in and feed the eagle, AAAA-mmmmmmm, but, uh, he grew a little older, AAAA-mmmmmmm, and a little older, yes, he did, his wing begin to scrape on the side of the cage, and, uh, he had to build another cage and open the door of the old cage and let him into a larger cage, yes he did, Oh, Looooord! . . . So one day when the eagle had gotten grown, Lord God, and his wings begin to get restless in the cage, yes, he did, he begin to walk around and be uneasy, AAAA-mmmmmmm, while he heard noises in the air, AAAA-mmmmmmm, a flock of eagles flew over and he heard their voice, and, uh, though he never been around eagles there was something bout that voice that he heard, AAAA-mmmmmmm, that moved down in him, AAAA-mmmmmmm, and made him dissatisfied, Oh, Lord! And the man watched him, he walk around uneasy, AAAA-mmmmmmm, Oh, Loooooord, he said, "Lord, my heart goes out to him, I believe I'll go and open the door," AAAA-mmmmmmm, "and set the eagle free," AAAA-mmmmmmm . . . the eagle . . . flew in yonder's tree, yeeeeeeah! and then he went on up a little higher, the king of the mountain, yeah, yeah, OOOOOOOOOh, one of these days, one of these days, my soul is an eagle in the cage that the Lord hath made for me. My soul, my soul, my soul is caged in this old body, children, and one of these days, the man who made the cage will open the door and let my soul go free . . . OOOOOOOOOOh, yeeeeeeeah, did you hear me church, I'll fly away and be at rest. Loooooord, yeeeeeeah, Lorrrrrd . . . one of these ol' days, one of these ol' days, the soul will take wings, yeeeeah, Loooooooord, one of these ol' days.

In the oral tradition, there are a number of different narrative forms that tell a kind of folk story revelatory of the culture and experiences of Black America. Some of these are ghost stories (such as "Uncle Henry and the Dog Ghost"); some are general human interest stories (such as "The Palacious Rancher and the Preacher"); some are stories explaining the origin of events and men (such as "Why the Negro is Black"). One well-known narrative form is the folk tale about underdog animals who outsmart their larger-sized enemies. An example of this type is the "Brer Rabbit" cycle of stories in which the rabbit always outfoxes the fox. Some black folklorists attribute an African origin to the Brer Rabbit tales. To be sure, many people question the authenticity of these stories made popular by the Southern white writer, Joel Chandler Harris, who distorts the context of the stories in a number of ways — for instance, by adding a black Uncle Remus figure as a "playmate" for the young whites. But Harris, in fact, did not invent these stories. All his life he had heard them from black people who had adapted their African folk tale to American slave conditions. Thus the cunning and deceit of the rabbit personifies the slave outwitting his more powerful master.

Another type of folk tale in this category is the trickster tale, with a black male, usually known as "Buck" or "John," as central figure. A well-known cycle of stories of this type are the "High John de Conquer" stories. Masters of duplicity and guile, capable of working hoo-doo, witchcraft, and conjuration, these characters do it to death to the white man. Using this kind of material as literary source, nineteenth-century black writer Charles Waddell Chesnutt developed his brilliant short story "The Goophered Grapevine." In the story, Uncle Julius, a "venerable-looking colored man," vainly tries to dissuade a white Northerner from buying the vineyard that has been Uncle Julius's hustle all these years. Julius's "story" deals with the way the vineyard has been "goophered — cunju'd, bewitch."

Another type of narrative folklore based on the values and techniques used by the trickster is the less formalized but no less significant tradition of lying. Meant to be taken semiseriously, the lie is a contrived story about some unusual event or outstanding feat that usually has an element of truth in it — somewhere. (Recall that Riley accuses Buster of working out of this tradition when he begins to narrate the story of Toussaint L' Ouverture.) Contemporary examples are found in the "game" used by hustlers, con men, and rappers in general, who will invent intricate and complex narratives designed to get what they want or to provide "rational" excuses for their behavior. "Shucking and jiving" is a variation on this theme.

All of these folk narrative forms have as their overriding theme the coping ability, strength, endurance, trickeration capacity, and power of black people. An excellent example is provided by Mrs. Josie Jordan, born a slave in Tennessee, who was seventy-five years old at the time she related the following story which her mother had told to her:

> . . . I remember Mammy told me about one master who almost starved his slaves. Mighty stingy, I reckon he was.
>
> Some of them slaves was so poorly thin they ribs would kinda rustle against each other like corn stalks a-drying in the hot winds. But they gets even one hog-killing time, and it was funny, too, Mammy said.
>
> They was seven hogs, fat and ready for fall hog-killing time. Just the day before Old Master told off they was to be killed, something

happened to all them porkers. One of the field boys found them and come a-telling the master: "The hogs is all died, now they won't be any meats for the winter."

When the master gets to where at the hogs is laying, they's a lot of Negroes standing round looking sorrow-eyed at the wasted meat. The master asks: "What's the illness with 'em?"

"Malitis," they tells him, and they acts like they don't want to touch the hogs. Master says to dress them anyway for they ain't no more meat on the place.

He says to keep all the meat for the slave families, but that's because he's afraid to eat it hisself account of the hogs got malitis.

"Don't you all know what is malitis?" Mammy would ask the children when she was telling of the seven fat hogs and seventy lean slaves. And she would laugh, remembering how they fooled Old Master so's to get all them good meats.

"One of the strongest Negroes got up early in the morning," Mammy would explain, "long 'fore the rising horn called the slaves from their cabins. He skitted to the hog pen with a heavy mallet in his hand. When he tapped Mister Hog 'tween the eyes with that mallet, 'malitis' set in mighty quick, but it was a uncommon 'disease, even with hungry Negroes around all the time."

The narratives mentioned thus far are told in prose, conversational style. The Toast is a variation on the trickster, bad nigguh theme done in poetic form. While the High John and Brer Rabbit stories are rural and older in time, the Toast is a modern urban continuance of this tradition. In contrast to the lack of profanities and sexual allusions in the older folk stories, Toasts are replete with funk in practically every rhymed couplet. While the older stories reveal black power in subtle forms (such as blacks deceiving white folks), the Toasts let it all hang out. The hero is fearless, defiant, openly rebellious, and full of braggadocio about his masculinity, sexuality, fighting ability, and general badness. Narrated in first person, this epic folk style is a tribute — that is, a "toast" — to this superbad, omnipotent black hustler, pimp, player, killer who is mean to the max:

> I'm m - e - a - n . . .
> . . . mean/mean/mean . . .
> I been walking the streets
> trying to find

> Miss hard time,
> But all I seen
> Was the dust off her feet
> As she was running from me.

Toasts are usually kept alive in black culture by males, although some females, having heard Toasts from their male friends or relatives, will recite them occasionally (such as the present writer, who learned them from her male cousins, much to the dismay of her Baptist preacher father!). You used to hear Toasts quite regularly in the pool halls, barbershops, and on the street corners in the community; nowadays they are mostly heard among black prisoners who sit around for hours passing the time away reciting various Toasts learned in their adolescence. Some of the most famous Toasts are: "The Pimp and Bulldaggers' Ball"; "Frankie and Albert" (which was rendered in popular song under the title "Frankie and Johnnie"); "The Signifying Monkey"; "Stag-O-Lee" (which was brought out in song and became a best-selling black recording several years ago); "Shine and the Sinking of the Titanic" (supposedly based on the Titanic's refusal to give passage to black prizefighter Jack Johnson; in a kind of poetic justice, the only survivor was the legendary Shine, stoker on the Titanic); "Dolemite" (recently popularized in the recording by comedian Rudy Ray Moore). Something of the rhythmic flavor of this narrative form can be gleaned from some of the less funky lines of the Toasts.

> The Twelfth of May was a hell of a day
> The news went around all the towns
> That the great Titanic had gone down.
>   — "Shine and the Sinking of the Titanic"
>
> Down in the jungle where the coconut grows
> Lived a signifying monkey
> Who was a bad-ass hole
>   — "The Signifying Monkey"
>
> At the age of one, he was drinking whiskey and gin,
> At the age of two, he was eating the bottles it came in.
>   — "Dolemite"

In recent years, folklorists and linguists have popularized the
Toasts, much to the chagrin of some blacks who disdain this display of our "bad side." Yet viewed from another perspective,
Toasts represent a form of black verbal art requiring memory
and linguistic fluency from the narrators. Akin to grand epics in
the Graeco-Roman style, the movement of the Toast is episodic,
lengthy, and detailed. While exactness of wording is not demanded, creative use of language is. The Toast-teller must be
adept at linguistic improvisation in order to capture the
rhythmic structure and narrative sense of each line in his or her
own words. Since the overall narrative structure is loose and
episodic, there is both room and necessity for individual rhetorical embellishments and fresh imaginative imagery. Moreover,
critics of this narrative form forget that the material is simply an
extension of black folk narrative in the oral tradition. Thus
contemporary black writers in the black consciousness movement
have used this material since it reflects much of the fundamental
essence of Afro-American values (such as belief in black male
superiority over white males, stress on black verbal ability, coolness, and grace under pressure). Employing this material as an
artistic framework for the conveyance of black ideology, contemporary writers capture the spirit, intent, and poetic power of the
Toasts without "problem" words. As an example, Nikki Giovanni,
in her "Ego Tripping" gives us an innovative and powerful poetic
Toast to the archetypal black person, source of the creative
principle:

> I was born in the congo
> I walked to the fertile crescent and built
>   the sphinx
> I designed a pyramid so tough that a star
>   that only glows every one hundred years falls
>   into the center giving divine perfect light
> I am bad
> . . . . . .
> I sowed diamonds in my back yard
> My bowels deliver uranium
>   the filings from my fingernails are
>   semi-precious jewels

On a trip north
I caught a cold and blew
My nose giving oil to the arab world
I am so hip even my errors are correct
I sailed west to reach east and had to round off
          the earth as I went
The hair from my head thinned and gold was laid
          across three continents

I am so perfect so divine so ethereal so surreal
I cannot be comprehended
          except by my permission

I mean . . . I . . . can fly
          like a bird in the sky . . .

As another example, black prose stylist Julius Lester has recast the Stag-O-Lee Toast into prose form, with updated hip Black Semantic terms, and no sexual references. Lester's version, which appears in his *Black Folk Tales*, is a brilliant accomplishment, well exemplifying the Toast tradition. According to Lester,

Stagolee was, undoubtedly and without question, the baddest nigger that ever lived. Stagolee was so bad that the flies wouldn't even fly around his head in the summertime, and snow wouldn't fall on his house in the winter. He was bad, jim.

In keeping with the legend, Lester portrays Stagolee as a dude so bad that even white folks feared him and only God was able to kill him. Even then it took "3,412 angels working 14 days, 11 hours, and 32 minutes to carry the giant death thunderbolt to the Lord." When Stagolee dies, he decides that Heaven isn't for him since it's too quiet and there are only a few colored folks there — the "nice, respectable," types, the others having been sent to Hell because they were too emotional and bluesy sounding in St. Peter's church service. He tells St. Peter, "Hey, man. You messed up . . . This ain't Heaven. This is Hell," and takes off straight for Hell where

the barbecue [was] cooking . . . the jukeboxes playing . . . and . . . a big BLACK POWER sign [was] on the gate. [Stag] rung on the bell, and the dude who come to answer it recognized him immediately, "Hey, everybody! Stagolee's here!" . . .

"Hey, baby!"

"What's going down!"

"What took you so long to get here?"

Stagolee walked in, and the brothers and sisters had put down wall-to-wall carpeting, indirect lighting, and, best of all, they'd installed air conditioning. [Stag said] "Yeah. Y'all got it together. Got it uptight! . . . Any white folks down here?"

"Just the hip ones, and ain't too many of them. But they all right. They know where it's at."

Stag challenges the Devil to a duel, but the Devil hasn't "learned how to deal with niggers yet" and refuses the challenge. So Stag commences to rule Hell all by himself.

◆

The story element is so strong in black communicative dynamics that it pervades general everyday conversation. An ordinary inquiry is likely to elicit an extended narrative response where the abstract point or general message will be couched in concrete story form. The reporting of events is never simply objectively reported, but dramatically acted out and narrated. The Black English speaker thus simultaneously conveys the facts and his or her personal sociopsychological perspective on the facts.

Now naturally, when you tellin a story, you include details, characterization, plot, and related digressions. Unaware of the black cultural matrix in which narrative sequencing is grounded, whites, as mentioned earlier, often become genuinely irritated at what they regard as "belabored verbosity" and narration in an "inappropriate" context — thus we have yet another case of cross-cultural communication interference. A fascinating look at this type of interference comes from the courtrooms in which young black males are tried for criminal offenses. In many urban areas, the overload of trial cases is overwhelming, and the judges anxiously try to move the cases as quickly and judiciously as possible. Naturally they don't reckon on the narrative style of the young bloods before them.

A twenty-year-old black male, charged as an accessory to

armed robbery, appears before a white judge at the pretrial hearing. His court-appointed attorney had already entered a plea of guilty for him, and, as is customary in trial proceedings, the judge had a copy of the defendant's statement before him. From all indications, it's an open-and-shut case, and the judge need do nothing more than go through the legal motions, ordering the defendant to be bound over for trial. Yet, in the interests of humanitarian fairness, or perhaps due to judicial conscience, the judge makes the cultural "mistake" of soliciting information from the defendant himself. He inquires whether the defendant wishes to add anything in his behalf. The blood begins:

> Well, sir, like the lawyer said, I guess uhm guilty since I *was* there when everythang went down. But see, Your Honor, what happen was that Keif and Mac — Keif, he bout, I say bout this high, with a big natural and Mac, he drive a Deuce, but his car wasn't working. So I went to the job — they work at, Dodge Main and see, I work there too, but I work the midnight shift. So I went to pick 'em up — oh, yeah, Mac, he real tall with a fly [superfly hair do]. And so I pick 'em up from work and Keif, he say he wahn't feelin good so he want to go straight on home. Then Mac ask Keif what he mean, he wahn't feelin good, he look okay to him. And so Keif was the one had the gun, but I didn't know what was goin down, or what they had been rap — discussin — before I got there.
>
> Judge: You say this Keifer had a gun?
> Defendant: Yes, sir.
> Judge: Well, why didn't you leave then?
> Defendant: Well, see, like, I didn't know that, cause Keif — he had on his maxie leather, and the gun was inside. And so Mac, he had a knife, I think, I mean, I found out later, that's what the police said. So Mac said he was gon stop at the credit union and get his check. And I said, what check? And Keif start lookin funny, and I figure he was really sick like he said, and —
> Judge (interrupting, again, with a tone of surprise in his voice): Just a minute, who did you say had the gun — Keifer? Who is he? His name doesn't appear on the record here.
> Defendant: Yes, it was Keif, Your Honor.
> Judge: Keif, or Keifer?
> Defendant: Keif, sir, K-E-I-T-H.
> Judge (with an I-give-up-attitude): Oh . . .

At this point, thoroughly exasperated, and perhaps realizing that this "story" is going to go on and on to its detailed max, the judge asks the attorney and defendant to approach the bench, after which he orders the defendant bound over for trial and goes on to the next case, which is . . . yeah, you guessed it . . . another young black male on a similar charge.

With more patience, time, and black cultural awareness than the white judge, a small group of black men listen intently as one of their partners narrates a scene from the Harlem riot in Ellison's *The Invisible Man.* During the height of the rebellion, the fierce black nationalist leader Ras (race), clad in the dress of an "Abyssinian chieftain . . . fur cap upon his head, his arm bearing a shield, a cape made of the skin of some wild animal around his shoulders," rides a "great black horse" through the Harlem streets like a general leading his troops in battle. Here's the way the "story" is told:

> "This is some night . . . Ain't this some night?"
> "It's 'bout like the rest."
> "Why you say that?"
> "Cause it's fulla fucking and fighting and drinking and lying — gimme that bottle."
> "Yeah, but tonight I seen some things I never seen before."
> "You think you seen something? Hell, you ought to been over on Lenox about two hours ago. You know that stud Ras the Destroyer? Well, man, he was spitting blood."
> "That crazy guy."
> "Hell, yes, man, he had him a big black hoss and a fur cap and some kind of old lion skin or something over his shoulders and he was raising hell. Goddam if he wasn't a sight, riding up and down on this old hoss, you know, one of the kind that pulls vegetable wagons, and he got him a cowboy saddle and some big spurs."
> "Aw naw, man!"
> "Hell, yes! Riding up and down the block yelling. 'Destroy 'em! Drive 'em out! Burn 'em out! I, Ras, commands you! You get that, man' he said, 'I, Ras, commands you to destroy them to the last piece of rotten fish!' And 'bout that time some joker with a big ole Georgia voice sticks his head out the window and yells, 'Ride 'em, cowboy. Give 'em hell and bananas.' And man, that crazy sonofabitch up there on that hoss looking like death eating a sandwich, he reaches down and comes up with a forty-five and

starts blazing up at that window — And man, talk about cutting
out! In a second wasn't nobody left but ole Ras up there on that
hoss with that lion skin stretched straight out behind him. Crazy,
man, everybody else trying to git some loot and him and his boys
out for blood!" . . .

"I was over there," another voice said. "You see him when the
mounted police got after his ass?"

"Hell, naw . . . Here, take a li'l taste."

"Well that's when you shoulda seen him. When he seen them
cops riding up he reached back of his saddle and come up with
some kind of shield."

"A shield?"

"Hell, yes! One with a spike in the middle of it. And that ain't all;
when he sees the cops he calls to one of his goddam henchmens to
hand him up a spear, and a little short guy ran out into the street
and gave him one. You know, one of the kind you see them African guys carrying in the moving pictures . . ."

"Where the hell was you, man?"

"Me? I'm over on the side where some stud done broke in a store
and is selling cold beer out the window — done gone into business,
man . . . I was drinking me some Budweiser and digging the doings
— when here comes the cops up the street, riding like cowboys,
man; and when ole Ras-the-what's-his-name sees 'em he lets out a
roar like a lion and rears way back and starts shooting spurs into
that hoss's ass fast as nickels falling in the subway at going-home
time — and gaawd dam! that's when you ought to seen him! Say,
gimme a taste there, fella.

"Thanks. Here he comes bookety-bookety with that spear stuck
out in front of him and that shield on his arm, charging, man. And
he's yelling something in African or West Indian or something and
he's got his head down low like he knew about that shit too, man;
riding like Earle Sande in the fifth at Jamaica. That ole black hoss
let out a whinny and got his head down — I don't know where he
got that sonofabitch — but, gentlemens, I swear! When he felt that
steel in his high behind he came on like Man o' War going to get his
ashes hauled! Before the cops knew what hit 'em Ras is right in
the middle of 'em and one cop grabbed for that spear, and ole Ras
swung 'round and bust him across the head and the cop goes down
and his hoss rears up, and ole Ras rears his and tries to spear him
another cop, and the other hosses is plunging around and ole Ras
tries to spear him still another cop, only he's too close and the hoss

is pooting and snorting and pissing and shitting, and they swings around and the cop is swinging his pistol and every time he swings ole Ras throws up his shield with one arm and chops at him with the spear with the other, and man, you could hear that gun striking that ole shield like somebody dropping tire irons out a twelve-story window. And you know what, when ole Ras saw he was too close to spear him a cop he wheeled that hoss around and rode off a bit and did him a quick round-about face and charged 'em again — out for blood, man! Only this time the cops got tired of that bullshit and one of 'em started shooting. And that was the lick! Ole Ras didn't have time to git his gun so he let fly with that spear and you could hear him grunt and say something 'bout that cop's kinfolks and then him and that hoss shot up the street leaping like Heigho, the goddam Silver!"

"Man, where'd you come from?"

"It's the truth, man, here's my right hand."

Finally, let's listen to a black rapper using narrative sequencing to demonstrate a general principle about human behavior. The focus of the debate has been on ways to solve the problems of the black poor. One blood has proposed a solution based on the redistribution of economic goods, whereupon his sincerity is challenged: "Say, man, you mean, just give up my shit and share with everybody who ain got nothin? And turn around and we all be poor? Y'all go for that?"

The proponent of the idea reaffirms his belief in this solution. But the blood who posed the challenge is not convinced and goes on to show that when you propose a solution to a problem, you should be wary of just saying something or fronting, because things can boomerang on you.

Well, man, I tell you, nigguhs gon git enough of proposin this and that and not bein able to go through with it. Just like I tell you, back when I's hustlin, I had this thang set up to play head-up with Mose, big-time bookie and number man — he dead now. So anyway, we's gon play five hundred dollar table stake, me and him. Now Mose wahn't hip to me, and he dug my glasses and say, "Naw, man, you cain't play me wid dem glasses on." I say, "Nigguh, what's the matter wit you? These is *glasses*. I cain't see without 'em on." So Mose, he took 'em and look at 'em, but still he say "No bet, baby."

Now, dig this, now, Mose, he wearin glasses too, great big ol suckers, just like mine, and he dam near jes bout blin, without his glasses, jes like me. So then I gits this idea, I say, "Okay, if I cain't play wit my glasses on, then you cain't play wit yours." Now, I call myself runnin that through jes as a tester, knowin the nigguh ain gon agree to that, cause he know he cain't see *shit* without his glasses, and so I figure that cool him out and we can gon and git the game on — see, I know I can beat the nigguh, just on the square, on the strength of the hand, cause in dem days, I was known as the baddest young muthafucka on the West Coast when it come to cards. But do you know what that sucker did? This old, blin, decrepit-ass muthafucka *agreed* to that shit. He say, "Okay, that's a deal, you take off yo glasses, and uhma take off mine." So there we sat, bofe of us, blin as a bat, playin head-up, five hundred dollars a wop!

6

Where It's At

Black–White Language Attitudes

Simple: What're you doing with all those timetables and travel
           books, baby?

Joyce: Just in case we ever should get married, maybe I'm pick-
           ing out a place to spend our honeymoon — Niagara
           Falls, the Grand Canyon, Plymouth Rock . . .

Simple: I don't want to spend no honeymoon on no rock. These
           books is pretty, but, baby, we ain't ready to travel yet.

Joyce: We can dream, can't we?

Simple: Niagara Falls makes a mighty lot of noise falling down. I
           likes to sleep on holidays.

Joyce: Oh, Jess! Then how about the far West? Were you ever
           at the Grand Canyon?

Simple: I were. Fact is, I was also at Niagara Falls, after I were at
           Grand Canyon.

Joyce: I do not wish to criticize your grammar, Mr. Simple, but
           as long as you have been around New York, I wonder
           why you continue to say, I were, and at other times, I
           was?

Simple: Because sometimes I were, and sometimes I was, baby. I
           was at Niagara Falls and I were at the Grand Canyon —
           since that were in the far distant past when I were a
           coachboy on the Santa Fe. I was more recently at Niag-
           ara Falls.

Joyce: I see. But you never were "I were"! There is no "were."
           In the past tense, there is only "I was." The verb *to be* is
           declined, "I am, I was, I have been."

Simple: Joyce, baby, don't be so touchous about it. Do you want
           me to talk like Edward R. Murrow?

Joyce: No! But when we go to formals I hate to hear you say-
           ing, for example, "I taken" instead of "I took." Why do
           colored people say, "I taken," so much?

Simple: Because we are taken — taken until we are undertaken, and, Joyce, baby, funerals is high!

Joyce: Funerals *are* high.

Simple: Joyce, what difference do it make?

Joyce: Jess! What difference *does* it make? Does is correct English.

Simple: And do ain't?

Joyce: Isn't — not ain't.

Simple: Woman, don't tell me ain't ain't in the dictionary.

Joyce: But it ain't — I mean — it isn't correct.

Simple: Joyce, I gives less than a small damn! What if it aren't?

Joyce: You say what if things aren't. You give less than a damn. Well, I'm tired of a man who gives less than a damn about "What if things aren't." I'm tired! Tired! You hear me? Tired! I have never known any one man so long without having some kind of action out of him. You have not even formally proposed to me; let alone writing my father for my hand.

Simple: I did not know I had to write your old man for your hand.

Joyce: My father, Jess, not my old man. And don't let it be too long. After all, I might meet some other man.

Simple: You better not meet no other man. You better not! Do and I will marry you right now this June in spite of my first wife, bigamy, your old man — I mean your father. Joyce, don't you know I am not to be trifled with? I'm Jesse B. Semple.

Joyce: I know who you are. Now, just sit down and let's spend a nice Sunday evening conversing, heh? . . . Oh, Sweety! Let me make you a nice cool drink. Lemonade?

Simple: Yes, Joyce, lemonade. Lemonade! Baby, you ain't mad with me, is you? (JOYCE *smiles and shakes her head, no*) Because I know you know what I mean when I say, "I is" — or "I are" or "was" or whatever it be. Listen, Joyce, honey please. (*He sings.*)

> When I say "I were" believe me.
> When I say "I was" believe me, too —
> Because I were, and was, and I *am*
> Deep in love with you.
>
> If I say "You took" or "taken,"

Just believe I have been taken, too,
Because I were, and am, and I *is*
Taken by you.

If it *is* or it *ain't* well stated,
And it *ain't* or it *aren't* said right,
My love still must be rated
A love that don't fade over night.

When I say "I am" believe me.
When I say "I is" believe me, too —
Because I were, and was, and I *is*
Deep in love with you.

Damn if I ain't!

Joyce: A small damn?

ONCE AGAIN, Langston Hughes's folk hero, Jesse B. Simple, uses his rappin ability and verbal quickness to win an argument (and his woman as well). But life, unlike literature, rarely provides us with such happy endings. The conflict between the two characteristic language attitudes Simple and Joyce represent continues unresolved in Black American life.

On the one hand, you have those blacks who feel that black speech is just as functional as white speech in communicating meanings. "Ain't" or "isn't" — as Simple says, "what difference do it make?" Within this group you have many blacks who argue that our Africanized English should be retained because it's part of the black cultural heritage. Besides, Black English expressions are often superior to those of Americanized English because black talk captures certain subleties and expressive nuances more effectively. This is the point Simple attempts to make by distinguishing the pastness of "were" from that of "was." While his particular example should not be taken seriously, there is, of course, a kernel of truth in what Simple is saying. That is, some Africanized English verb patterns do convey nuances and subtle meanings that Americanized English verbs do not — the difference in meaning between *be* and *non-be,* for instance.

The other characteristic language attitude you find in the

black community is represented by Simple's girlfriend Joyce. This is the notion that "colored people" should use "correct English," meaning, of course, "correct" by White English standards. Furthermore, so holders of this view argue, black speech is associated with being "country," down-Southish. This is the underlying point Joyce is hitting on when she wonders why, as long as Simple has been around New York, he continues to use bad grammar. ("You can take the nigguh out of the country, but you cain't take the country out of the nigguh," as the black saying goes.) Note too that Joyce not only objects to Simple's Black English syntax, but his vocabulary as well. For instance, she checks him for referring to her father as her "old man." Thus Joyce reflects the typical black attitude that rejects the totality of black speech, whether linguistic or stylistic. (There is a message in the fact that many whites reading the Joyce-Simple dialogue assume that Joyce is white.)

Joyce and Simple's two distinctly different language attitudes reflect continuance of the "push-pull" dynamic in Black American history. The ambivalence they symbolize not only exists in the black group at large, it can be found in any *one* black individual. As DuBois said in *Souls of Black Folk:*

> After the Egyptian and Indian, the Greek and Roman, the Teuton and Mongolian, the Negro is a sort of seventh son, born with a veil, and gifted with second-sight in this American world — a world which yields him no true self-consciousness, but only lets him see himself through the revelation of the other world. It is a peculiar sensation, this double-consciousness, this sense of always looking at one's self through the eyes of others, of measuring one's soul by the tape of a world that looks on in amused contempt and pity. One ever feels his two-ness — an American, a Negro; two souls, two thoughts, two unreconciled strivings; two warring ideals in one dark body, whose dogged strength alone keeps it from being torn asunder.

Earlier, we briefly examined language conditions in the slave community as a way of understanding this "double-consciousness" in black language attitudes. Further insight can be provided by locating these ambivalent linguistic attitudes in the psychology of the colonized personality.

An individual's language is intricately bound up with his or her sense of identity and group consciousness. In the history of man's inhumanity to man, it is clearly understandable why the conqueror forces his victim to learn his language, for as black psychiatrist Frantz Fanon said, "every dialect is a way of thinking." Certainly this principle has been operative in the history of colonized people, where the colonizer's language and culture occupy a position superior to that of the colonized, even among the oppressed persons themselves. (The fact that America was once a colony of England goes a long way toward explaining why British English still commands such great prestige in this country — despite the real communication barrier it poses for most Americans. Fanon would label this the "colonized mentality" of White America.)

In analyzing the colonized African mind, Fanon points to the denigration of the African's native language (and subsequent creole versions) as a basic manifestation of the cultural rejection of Africa by both Europeans and Africans. Speaking of the "Negro and language" in the French West Indies, Fanon characterized the situation thus:

> To speak means . . . to assume a culture . . . The Negro of the Antilles will be proportionately whiter . . . in direct ratio to his mastery of the French language . . . Every colonized people — in other words, every people in whose soul an inferiority complex has been created by the death and burial of its local cultural originality — finds itself face to face with the language of the civilizing nation . . . The middle class in the Antilles never speak Creole except to their servants. In school the children . . . are taught to scorn the dialect . . . Some families completely forbid the use of Creole . . . The educated Negro adopts such a position with respect to European languages . . . because he wants to emphasize the rupture that has now occurred. He is incarnating a new type of man that he imposes on his associates and his family.

In the American context, the negative attitude toward black speech is but a variation on this same theme. Historically, Black English has been the usage pattern associated with plantation figures like Uncle Remus and Uncle Tom. Contemporaneously, it is the dialect associated with black urban "ghetto" types. Consistently, it has been labeled "poor English." While blacks have demonstrated ambivalence about it, whites have characteristically rejected it out of hand. In a 1973 article on the subject, a white professor denounced Black English as the "shuffling speech of slavery." In earlier times, whites believed that Black English was the result of lazy lips and tongues, or at best the result of a kind of baby talk. For instance, toward the end of the nineteenth century, writer Ambrose Gonzales collected black stories from the Georgia-Carolina area and later published them in *Black Border*. In the preface to that work he stated:

> The [Gullah] words are, of course, not African, for the African brought over or retained only a few words of his jungle-tongue, and even these few are by no means authenticated as part of the original scant baggage of the negro slaves . . . Slovenly and careless of speech, these Gullahs seized upon the peasant English used by some of the early settlers and by the white servants of the wealthier Colonists, wrapped their clumsy tongues about it as well as they could, and, enriched with certain expressive African words, it issued through their flat noses and thick lips as so workable a form of speech that it was gradually adopted by the other slaves and became in time the accepted Negro speech of the lower districts of South Carolina and Georgia. With characteristic laziness, these Gullah Negroes took short cuts to the ears of their auditors, using as few words as possible, sometimes making one gender serve for three, one tense for several, and totally disregarding singular and plural numbers.

In a 1924 article, "The English of the Negro," and later in his 1925 *English Language in America*, linguist George Philip Krapp attributed the origin of Black English to "archaic" Old English forms and to "baby-talk" between master and slave.

> . . . from the very beginning the white overlords addressed themselves in English to their black vassals. It is not difficult to imagine the kind of English this would be. It would be a very much simplified English — the kind of English some people employ when they talk to babies. It would probably have no tenses of the verb, no distinctions of case in nouns or pronouns, no marks of singular or plural. Difficult sounds would be eliminated, as they

are in baby-talk. Its vocabulary would be reduced to the lowest possible elements . . . As the Negroes imported into America came from many unrelated tribes, speaking languages so different that one tribe could not understand the language of another, they themselves were driven to the use of this infantile English in speaking to one another . . . it is reasonably safe to say that not a single detail of Negro pronunciation or Negro syntax can be proved to have any other than an English origin.

Since the Civil War, and in the twentieth century especially, upward mobility for Black Americans has come to mean the eradication of black language (and black culture) and the adoption of the linguistic norms of the white middle class. (In point of fact, other minority groups and lower-class whites as well have had to assimilate the language patterns of the dominant white middle class — more on this later in the chapter.) As one black writer put it in 1963, "Negro dialect" was the "last barrier to integration." Even the young are not exempt from these negative attitudes toward black speech. A 1968 study of the speech of inner-city black junior high students asked the students what they thought about their language. Most felt that the way they spoke was "wrong," and that black people "broke verbs," and "didn't talk right." (Yet when asked if they would change their patterns of speech, all said, in effect, "ain no way.")

The recent push for bi-dialectalism (fluency in both Black and White English) aims at being a mitigating force against the rejection of black language. This view would have blacks using Black English with black people and White English with whites. Yet that does not really solve the linguistic dilemma. In fact, bi-dialectalism has been termed the "linguistics of white supremacy" (by a white linguist, no less) who argues that whites don't have to learn to talk like blacks to gain upward mobility in America. Moreover, some blacks contend that being bi-dialectal not only causes a schism in the black personality, but it is also like saying black talk is "good enough" for blacks but not for whites. A striking example is provided by black writer Claude Brown. He comments positively about the "language of soul" both in his autobiography *Manchild in the Promised Land* and in an article on the subject:

The language of soul — or, as it might also be called, "Spoken Soul" or "Colored English" — is simply an honest vocal portrayal of Black America . . . "Spoken Soul" is more a sound than a language. It generally possesses a pronounced lyrical quality which is frequently incompatible to any music other than that ceaseless and relentlessly driving rhythm that flows from poignantly spent lives. Spoken soul has a way of coming out metered without the intention of the speaker to invoke it. There are specific phonetic traits. To the soulless ear the vast majority of these sounds are dismissed as incorrect usage of the English language and, not infrequently, as speech impediments. To those so blessed as to have had bestowed upon them at birth the lifetime gift of soul, these are the most communicative and meaningful sounds ever to fall upon human ears: the familiar "mah" instead of "my," "gonna" for "going to," "yo" for "your." "Ain't" is pronounced "ain"; "bread" and "bed," "bray-ud" and "bay-ud"; "baby" is never "bay-bee" but "bay-buh"; Sammy Davis, Jr., is not "Sammee" but a kind of "Sammeh"; the same goes for "Eddeh" Jefferson. No matter how many "man's" you put into your talk, it isn't soulful unless the word has the proper plaintive, nasal "maee-yun."

Yet in virtually the same breath, Brown tells us how he was ashamed of his parents when they went to juvenile court, before a white judge, using the pronunciation and other dialect features of Black English.

Some blacks try to solve the linguistic ambivalence dilemma by accepting certain features or types of black speech and rejecting others. This amounts to the exclusion of those black subgroups using the nonacceptable features of Africanized English. You know, a lil bit of blackness is cool, but not too much. Obviously, this does not solve the problem, for it leads to even greater disunity in what the Reverend Jesse Jackson has called the "great divide" in the community — middle class blacks, for example, accepting the black semantics of musicians and hipsters but rejecting the black syntax of working class blacks — despite the fact that all are, as the Reb would say, "still in slavery."

It continues to be the painful and trying task of the black consciousness movement to destroy the ambivalence about black language and culture and replace the old pejorative associations with new positive ones. Throughout the 1960s and on into the seventies, the clarion call of black politicians, artists, leaders, and intellectuals has been ethnic, their style revolutionary, their language black. Undoubtedly this has been in recognition of the fact that language is interwoven with culture and psychic being. Thus to deny the legitimacy of Africanized English is to deny the legitimacy of black culture and the black experience. The father of the black arts literary movement and leader-spokesman for the National Black Political Assembly, Imamu Baraka, speaks to the unity of black language with black identity:

> I heard an old Negro street singer last week, Reverend Pearly Brown, singing, "God don't never change!" This is a precise thing he is singing. He does not mean "God does not ever change!" He means "God don't never change!" The difference is in the final human reference . . . the form of passage through the world. A man who is rich and famous who sings, "God don't never change," is confirming his hegemony and good fortune . . . or merely calling the bank. A blind hopeless black American is saying something very different. Being told to "speak proper," meaning that you become fluent with the jargon of power, is also a part of not "speaking proper." That is, the culture which desperately understands that it does not "speak proper," or is not fluent with the terms of social strength, also understands somewhere that its desire to gain such fluency is done at a terrifying risk. The bourgeois Negro accepts such risk as profit. But does *close-ter* (in the context of "jes a close-ter, walk wi-thee") mean the same thing as *closer*? *Close-ter*, in the term of its user is, believe me, exact. It means a quality of existence, of actual physical disposition perhaps . . . in its manifestation as a *tone* and *rhythm* by which people live, most often in response to common modes of thought best enforced by some factor of environmental emotion that is exact and specific. Even the picture it summons is different, and certainly the 'Thee' that is used to connect the implied 'Me' with, is different. The God of the damned cannot know the God of the damner, that is, cannot know he is God. As no Blues person can really believe emotionally in Pascal's God, or Wittgenstein's question, "Can the concept of God exist in a perfectly logical language?" Answer: "God don't never change."

Fanon spoke in a similar vein in describing the situation of the Creole-speaking Antilles Negro educated in France:

In every country of the world there are climbers, "the ones who forget who they are," and, in contrast to them, "the ones who remember where they came from." The Antilles Negro who goes home from France expresses himself in the dialect if he wants to make it plain that nothing has changed.

In coming home to the community that gave them birth and nourished them till they got ovuh, E. Franklin Frazier's "black bourgeoisie" and W. E. B. DuBois's "talented tenth" bees makin it plain that nothin done change by using a mode of speech that reflects not only those who have not yet got ovuh but themselves as well. Some examples have been noted earlier in discussing the Black English speaking style of spokesmen like Rap Brown, Malcolm X, Martin Luther King, Jr., and Jesse Jackson. Some blacks have gone even further to incorporate the style and flavor of black speech into their writings (as much as this bees possible at least!). For instance, in a piece of literary criticism by Carolyn Rodgers, one finds the following:

> . . . all black poems ain't the same kind . . . certain poets hip you to something, pull the covers off of something or run it down to you, or ask you to just dig it — your coat is being pulled . . . every poet has written a bein poem. In fact, most poets start off writing them. Just writing about the way they be, they friends be, they lovers be, the world be . . . We do not want subhumans defining what we be doing . . . black poetry is becoming what it has always been but has not quite beed.

And in a sociological essay on the need for an "ideology of black social science," Gerald McWorter, holder of a doctorate from the University of Chicago, says:

> Robert Park was just another cat walkin' and workin' . . . now this was a white dude trying to trick us into diggin' what some slave owners developed about us (remember that they counted us as three-fifths of a man) . . . Park was the man most responsible in the social sciences for developing a liberal white game to run on Black people . . . in other words, we need to get this shit on, and for that we need a revolutionary script for the terrible black drama of cosmic forces that we're about to rain down on these pitiful ofays.

◆

It is perhaps the new black poets who have not only made most extensive use of Black English in written form, but have also had the greatest impact on black readers. To give them they propers in this respect, we should say a word about their contributions to the eradication of negative black attitudes toward Black English.

◆

The Black Arts Movement emerged during the past decade as the appropriate artistic counterpart to the politics of black power. The black arts writer redefined the role of the artist and presented a new perspective on what constitutes art. The creator of black arts literature envisions himself or herself as a necromancer, a skillful manipulator of the art of shonuff black magic whose job it is to "heal" black folks through the evocative power of art, and transform their suffering into constructive political action. According to black fiction writer Ishmael Reed, in his introduction to *19 Necromancers from Now,*

> the condition of the Afro-American writer in this country is so strange that one has to go to the supernatural for an analogy. Manipulation of the word has always been related in the mind to manipulation of nature. One utters a few words and stones roll aside, the dead are raised and the river beds emptied of their content . . . The Afro-American artist is similar to the Necromancer . . . He is a conjuror who works JuJu upon his oppressors; a witch doctor who frees his fellow victims from the psychic attack launched by demons of the outer and inner worlds.

There is a striking difference between this contemporary black arts revival and an earlier literary trend, the Harlem Renaissance movement of the 1920s. This movement brought to the fore what Alain Locke termed a "new Negro," and established Harlem as a literary mecca for such black writers as Countee Cullen, Claude McKay, and Langston Hughes. The Harlem Renaissance was a period when, according to Locke, the "Negro was in vogue." It was a time when whites flocked to Harlem clubs and cabarets to soak up the sensual energy and live-for-today vitality of black life, and to hear the creative expressions of the new black artists — artists who, having thrown off the shackles of

black self-rejection, were loudly proclaiming their African ances-
try and heaping curses and threats of vengeance upon whites.
"If we must die, let it not be like hogs / Hunted and penned in an
inglorious spot / While round us bark the mad and hungry dogs /
Making their mock at our accursed lot." And so on, like that, said
Claude McKay, in his famous "If We Must Die" poem of 1919, a
sort of landmark protest poem, undoubtedly motivated by all
the black blood that flowed in the race riots of what W. E. B.
DuBois termed the "Red Summer" of 1919. (Ironically, the late
Sir Winston Churchill used this poem in his public appeals for
Allied support during World War II, and further, a white
American soldier, who had died on the Russian front, purport-
edly had this poem among his possessions.)

Both the Harlem Renaissance and the Black Arts Movement
are similar in that each involved a rediscovery and legitimizing
of the black cultural heritage and a more vigorous political protest stance on the part of black writers. However, the movements
differ in two major respects.

First, the Harlem writers conceived of themselves as writers
first, last, and only. They were a rather cliquish group, sharing
their works mainly with other black writers and their white pa-
trons. They made no attempts to align themselves with the black
community and would never have thought of taking their works
there. Today's black artists, by contrast, are not content to be
simply writers, sounding their protests only through their art.
They see themselves as black first, and thus as active participants
in the struggle for black liberation (which explains why an artist
like Baraka became involved in local and national black politics).

In the second place, the Renaissance artists, for all they bad-
mouthin of America and white folks, apparently "loved this cul-
tured hell that tested [they] youth," for the literature they
created is very much in the Euro-American tradition. During a
period when the Lost Generation crowd of the White American
literati-intelligentsia was experimenting with new verse forms,
Claude McKay, for instance, consistently cast his protest in the
conventional sonnet form. And so it was with most of his black
contemporaries: their versification styles were very Western, and
in their art they quite consciously neglected the rich reservoir of
Afro-American folk forms and the black cultural tradition. (Of

all the Renaissance "niggerati," Langston Hughes and poet-teacher Sterling Brown stand out as important exceptions who opted for poems about common black folk expressed in the "forms of things unknown.")

Today's black writers are making Herculean efforts to create a literature that will reach and reflect common black folks. They are going into the community — on the street, in the churches, in the recreation centers, and wherever black folk be. The art they are taking with them, they have decided, must be functional and relevant to the lives and daily struggles of black people. This art, which is to be born out of the agony and sweat of the black spirit, must manifest a cultural reality that is uniquely Afro-American. The objective is to prevent today's black consciousness movement from becoming like that of the Harlem Renaissance, which, according to Langston Hughes, ordinary Harlemites had not even heard of, and if they had, "it hadn't raised their wages any."

The new black poetry is the dominant creative expression of this present-day literary renaissance. While the black theater movement, with Ed Bullins at its head, and excellent works of fiction by Ishmael Reed and John Oliver Killens are clearly in the mainstream of the Black Arts Movement, it is the poetic genre which has seen the most prolific outpouring of the new art. To examine why this is so, recall the highly oral nature of black culture. To get the written word to the black nonreading, still essentially preliterate community, the new black writer must, as Haki Madhubuti says,

> move into the small volume direction . . . small black works that can be put into back pockets and purses, volumes that can be conveniently read during the 15 minute coffee break or during the lunch hour . . . we as black poets and writers are aware of the fact that the masses (and I do not use the word lightly for I am part of the masses) of black people *do not read books.*

Then there is the importance of music as a cultural dynamic in Black America. Black writer-critic Larry Neal put it this way:

> . . . the key to where the black people have to go is in the music. Our music has always been the most dominant manifestation of

what we are and feel, literature was just an afterthought, the step
taken by the Negro bourgeoisie who desired acceptance on the
white man's terms. And that is preciseiy why the literature has
failed. It was the case of one elite addressing another elite.

But our music is something else. The best of it has always oper-
ated at the core of our lives, forcing itself upon us as in a ritual. It
has always, somehow, represented the collective psyche. Black Literature must attempt to achieve that same sense of the collective
ritual . . .

As a literary genre, poetry, both traditionally and now, is written
to be recited, even in a sense "sung," in such a way that its creator
becomes a kind of performing bard before the group. Thus
poetry is the form that can most effectively go where black
people are at, for it combines orality, music, verbal performance,
and brevity — and when performed before a black audience it
evokes the "collective ritual."

In taking their poetry to the people, the new black poets recognize that the grass roots, since they lack the black bourgeoisie's
white middle-class aspirations, have been the bearers and sus-
tainers of black culture through the centuries. In representing
the masses, this new art is expressive of the uniqueness of
Afro-American culture. It has a style rooted in the artistic trap-
pings of the Afro-American cultural sensibility — a style that has
emerged as an identifiable black aesthetic. On no level is this
aesthetic more strikingly revealed than in the *language* of the
new black poetry: the poets bees not only tappin the reservoir of
the black cultural universe but doing so in the Black Idiom.
Within the limitations of written form, today's poets are attempting to capture the flavor of Black American speech — its
rhythms and sounds, its dialect and style. They use Black English not only to project the voice of a black character in a poem,
but even when they are speaking in their own poetic voices in a
given poem. Through their artistic efforts, the poets seem to be
saying: if the message is new, the medium must be new also. As
Haki put it, "blackpoets [will] deal in . . . black language or
Afro-American language in contrast to standard english . . . will
talk of kingdoms of Africa, will speak in Zulu and Swahili, will
talk in muthafuckas and 'can you dig it.' "

In previous chapters, I cited some poetry written in the black, and poetry performances utilizing the dynamics of black communication (such as call-response). Here we might note additional examples. In her collection *We A BaddDDD People,* Sonia Sanchez uses Black English language features extensively in her "chant for young brothas & sistuhs" in which she warns them of the destructiveness of dope in the black community:

```
yall
          out there.          looooken so cooool
in yo / highs.
               yeah yall
                         rat there
          listen to me
screeaamen this song.
                              did u know i've
seen yo / high
               on every blk / st in
wite / amurica . . .
          listen to this drummen.
this sad / chant.
                    listen to the tears
flowen down my blk / face
                              listen to a
death/song being sung on thick/lips
by a blk/woman . . .
yall
          out there          looooken so cooool
in yo / highs.
               yeah.                    yall
                         rat there
c'mon down from yo / wite / highs
               and live.
```

In a poetic tribute to Malcolm X, Haki Madhubuti uses Black Semantics throughout, but especially when he describes Malcolm as being "from a long line of super-cools, doo-rag lovers and revolutionary pimps." Super-cools and pimps, living outside the bounds of the white man's laws and customs, are often viewed as culture heroes, and in the old pre-naturals days they

were distinguished by their meticulously coiffured "do's." What
Haki is alluding to, of course, is Malcolm X's early life as a criminal, dope pusher, and pimp. However, the fact that Haki calls
him a "revolutionary" pimp suggests that the leadership and
black political consciousness Malcolm later exhibited lay within
him all the time. By extension, the poet is also implying that the
same revolutionary potential lies in other black pimps.

In her collection *Just Give Me a Cool Drink of Water 'fore I
Diiie,* Maya Angelou plays not the Dozens, but the Thirteens,
with separate but stylistically parallel versions denouncing the
untogetha actions of both blacks and whites.

THE THIRTEENS (BLACK)

Your Momma took to shouting
Your Poppa's gone to war,
Your sister's in the streets
Your brother's in the bar,
The thirteens. Right On.

Your cousin's taking smack
Your Uncle's in the joint,
Your buddy's in the gutter
Shooting for his point
The thirteens. Right On.

And you, you make me sorry
You out here by yourself,
I'd call you something dirty,
But there just ain't nothing left,
cept
The thirteens. Right On.

THE THIRTEENS (WHITE)

Your Momma kissed the chauffeur,
Your Poppa balled the cook,
Your sister did the dirty,
in the middle of the book,
The thirteens. Right On.

Your daughter wears a jock strap,
Your son he wears a bra

Your brother jonesed your cousin
in the back seat of the car.
The thirteens. Right On.

Your money thinks you're something
But if I'd learned to curse,
I'd tell you what your name is
But there just ain't nothing worse
than
The thirteens. Right On.

In *Poems From Prison,* poet Etheridge Knight has two outstanding Toast poems, one of which, mentioned earlier, is a poetic
version of "Shine and the Sinking of the Titanic." The other is a
Toast to black prisoner Hard Rock, who was "known not to take
no shit / From nobody . . . and he had the scars to prove it." I
mean Hard Rock was so bad that "he had once bit / A screw on
the thumb and poisoned him with syphilitic spit." But bad as this
black hero had done been, the "WORD was that Hard Rock
wasn't a mean nigger / Anymore, that the doctors had bored a
hole in his head / Cut out part of his brain, and shot electricity /
Through the rest." With a sensitive stroke of poetic understate-
ment, Knight portrays the effect of the dethroning of this new-
style black hero, the black prisoner:

The testing came to see if Hard Rock was really tame.
A hillbilly called him a black son of a bitch
And didn't lose his teeth, a screw who knew Hard Rock
From before shook him down and barked in his face.
And Hard Rock did nothing. Just grinned and looked silly,
His eyes empty like knot holes in a fence.

And even after we discovered that it took Hard Rock
Exactly 3 minutes to tell you his first name,
We told ourselves that he had just wised up,
Was being cool; but we could not fool ourselves for long,
And we turned away, our eyes on the ground. Crushed.
He had been our Destroyer, the doer of things
We dreamed of doing but could not bring ourselves to do.
The fears of years, like a biting whip,
Had cut grooves too deeply across our backs.

As a final, really outstanding poetic example, I cite Haki's "But he was cool: or he even stopped for green lights," a signifyin poem, showing all the features of heavy signification and rich in Black Semantics, sound, and syntax.

super-cool
ultrablack
a tan/purple
had a beautiful shade.

he had a double-natural
that wd put the sisters to shame.
his dashikis were tailor made
& his beads were imported sea shells
    (from some blk/country i never heard of)
he was triple-hip

his tikis were hand carved
out of ivory
& came express from the motherland.
he would greet u in swahili
& say good-by in yoruba.
woooooooooooooo-jim he bes so cool & ill tel li gent
        cool-cool is so cool he was un-cooled by other
           niggers' cool
        cool-cool ultracool was bop-cool/ice box cool so
           cool cold cool
        his wine didn't have to be cooled, him was air
           conditioned cool
        cool-cool/real cool made me cool — now ain't that
           cool
        cool-cool so cool him nick-named refrigerator.

cool-cool so cool
he didn't know,
after detroit, newark, chicago &c.,
we had to hip
        cool-cool/ super-cool/ real cool
   that
to be black
is
to be
very-hot.

What the new black poets have done, then, is to take for their conceptual and expressive tools a language firmly rooted in the black experience. Such terms and expressions enable the poets to use cultural images and messages familiar to their black audiences, and with great strokes of brevity, Black English lines and phrases reveal a complete story. (Such, of course, is the way any good poet operates; what is unique here is the effective execution of the operation in a black way.)

◆

I alluded earlier to the linguistic assimilation forced upon other "outsiders" in American life. While much of the contemporary sound and fury on "nonstandard" speech focuses on the linguistic behavior of the largest minority group (blacks), traditionally there has always been a significant social dimension undergirding the racial component which throws the whole question of standard-nonstandard English into a wider realm ultimately affecting whites as well. Although our focus here has been on racial and oppressive attitudes toward *black* language behavior, language has been a tool of oppression wielded against other social and ethnic groups. Anyone familiar with Mark Twain's masterpiece *Huckleberry Finn* can recall that Huck's rebellion against the slavocracy is foreshadowed early in the novel by Huck's resistance to corrections of his Pike County Missouri dialect. What linguist Donald Lloyd has labeled the "national mania for correctness" stems from a long-standing tradition of elitism in American life and language matters. Let us take a brief look at this tradition in hopes of clarifying some popular misconceptions about American English, Black English, and language in general.

Though Americans preach individualism and class mobility, they practice conformity and class stasis. The individual pioneer spirit is held in check by the need to keep up with the Joneses. Any number of American social critics — among them Norman Mailer, James Baldwin, Vance Packard — have dealt extensively with the rather schizophrenic nature of the American social sensibility. Paralleling this social class consciousness is the class anxiety that is reflected in the area of language, as is evident by sur-

veying the American schoolroom grammar tradition which had
its beginnings in England.

Language conventions and the English grammar handbooks
— which anyone who passes through the American educational
system is exposed to — are based on a preoccupation with the
all-engrossing question "What is correct English?" Not: What is
dynamic and vivid language? Not: What is contextually appropriate language? Not even: What is truthful language? But simply: What is "correct" language? Such uptight language attitudes, which are fostered in the schools, are grounded in the
"doctrine of correctness" that emerged during the eighteenth
century. The correctness obsession was a logical consequence of
the coming to power of the "primitive" middle classes and the
decline of the "refined" aristocracy in post-Middle Ages Europe.
Whereas Latin had enjoyed centuries of prestigious use and admiration, the Roman Empire had, after all, declined, and practical considerations dictated the necessity for British children to
be instructed in their own vernacular, the Anglo-Saxon tongue.
Richard Mulcaster, in his educational writings of the sixteenth
century, had decided to write in English because "though I appeal to the learned who understand Latin, I wish to reach also
the unlearned, who understand only English, and whose interests are to be the more considered that they have fewer chances
of information." The problem with the vernacular of the "unlearned," however, was that it was not in accord with Latin
grammatical rules and considered quite disorderly. As Mulcaster
himself had said, "our Sparta must be spunged, [there is a need
to bring] our tung to Art and form of disapline."

Pushed into prominence by the Industrial Revolution and ex-
panding technology, the newly risen middle class posed a potentially powerful threat to the declining aristocracy. The fears,
though, were unfounded because the new group wanted only to
ape and be accepted by their "betters," and they wanted neither
themselves nor their children to reflect any kinship with those
they had left behind. Instead, they wanted rules of conduct, linguistic and social, so as not to belie their rural or lower-class ori-
gins. (The eighteenth century also saw the rise of Emily Post–type
social etiquette books.) From our contemporary vantage point in

history, the imitational behavior of these fresh-from-the-bottom speakers of the "barbaric" tongue is especially ironic. After all, it had been the aristocracy, the feudal lords, that had oppressed their forefathers, and it had been the immoral greed of this power elite that had led to wars over land and property (as well as initiated the slave trade). Nonetheless, England was becoming an important world power, London the center of commercial life, and the middle-class rush was on. Certainly it was to the advantage of the elite to have their manners and speech adopted by these new social hordes. It would help to civilize them into the established values of the fallen monarchs and secure for that aristocratic set a permanent place in the upper ranks of the social order. Imitation is not only the highest form of flattery but a well-traveled road to sociopolitical co-optation.

The early grammarians who envisioned their task as one of "regularizing" and "purifying" common speech unwittingly became part of the grand design to perpetuate the centuries-old class system. One popular text, the Port Royal grammarians' *The Art of Speaking* translated from French into English in 1668, railed against the "depraved language of common people" and contended that

> the best Expressions grow low and degenerate, when profan'd by the populace, and applied to mean things. The use they make of them, infecting them with a mean and abject Idea, causes that we cannot use them without sullying and defiling those things, which are signified by them. But it is no hard matter to discern between the depraved Language of common People, and the noble refin'd expressions of the Gentry, whose condition and merits have advanced them above the other.

Bishop Robert Lowth's *Short Introduction to English Grammar* (1763) denigrated the "unruly, barbarous tongue of the Anglo-Saxons" and sought to give it "order and permanence" by superimposing upon it his own Latin-based standards. Even though in theory Lowth rejected the Latinate model, in actual practice, his *ipse dixit* rules and pronouncements for correct English usage came straight out of the Latin-Classical tradition. Not only did these self-appointed preservers and polishers of the national tongue find the language of everyday people at variance with Latinate and elitist norms, but even, according again to Lowth, the lingo of "the politest part of the nation . . . [and] writings of our most approved authors often offends against every part of Grammar." The English "doctrine of correctness" tradition was clearly undergirded by the belief that matters of English usage, like the divine right to rule, were decreed from on high.

Although Americans supposedly severed their colonial ties with the Mother Country in 1776, and although this country was founded in repudiation of the European class system, still the class-biased attitudes toward grammatical amenities came right on with the Mayflower. The American counterparts of British grammarians are strikingly exemplified in Goold Brown, in his *Grammar of English Grammars* (1851), and Lindley Murray in his *English Grammar* (1795). Murray, who even railed against contractions, wrote his grammar not simply to introduce the "proper" method of English usage among the young, but to inculcate in them all the morals and virtues commensurate with "proper" English. Dig Murray:

> The author of the following work wishes to promote the cause of virtue as well as of learning; and with this view, he has been studious, through the whole of the work, not only to avoid every example and illustration, which might have an improper effect on the minds of youth, but also to introduce on many occasions such as have a moral and religious tendency.

Thus Lindley Murray reiterated the English (and French) notion that there was something intrinsically virtuous and personally superior in those who used "correct" language forms. (Of course, on the face of it, there is nothing wrong with teaching moral and religious precepts. But what code of ethics could have any validity which excludes "correct" English examples about the evils of the slavocracy that was running rampant in a country which had just fought a war for liberty and justice? Like, everybody talkin bout Heaven ain goin there!)

Subsequent American English grammars tended merely to mirror these early elitist ones and to perpetuate the myth that language, like the Trinity, should never change. But it is not only that Latinate-prescriptive grammars helped to perpetuate a way of life built upon class discrimination and bias. This approach to the structure of English is linguistically invalid. Whereas the Latin-Classical model fits an inflected language, it cannot explain an uninflected language whose structure and meaning is dependent, in large part, on word position. For example, in English, *The boy loves the girl* is differentiated from *The girl loves the boy* by moving the elements of the sentence around, since certainly a different meaning is possible in the two sentences — after all, just cause he love her don't mean she love him! However, in Latin, *Puer puellam amat* is the same as *Puellam puer amat.* Despite reversed word order, the two mean the same, since in Latin, inflectional endings, not position, are keys to word meanings.

Or consider the rule that prepositions are not to be used to end sentences with. In Latin, this isn't possible, since Latin prepositions are not separable from the verb. For instance, Latin *voro,* "swallow," but *devoro* for "swallow down," in the sense of "put up with." (Sir Winston Churchill must be credited with the last word on this rule. When told not to end sentences with prepositions, he quipped: "This is the kind of nonsense up with which I will not put.")

The Latinate-prescriptive tradition enjoyed unchallenged longevity until the early years of the twentieth century and the rise of structural grammarians. Influenced by scientific-empirical thought, structuralists approached the study of English on the premise that language was in people, not in grammar handbooks. Emphasizing the primacy of spoken language, they argued that the linguist's task is to survey the social scene, collect representative samples of language in action, and *describe,* rather than *prescribe.* A grammar should be a description of the structure and operation of a language, not a list of social etiquette do's and don'ts. By codifying observable, empirical data, the structuralists insured that their descriptions were valid. Their analyses revealed numerous disparities between grammar-book dictates and the actual language practices of Americans. Departures from Latinate rules included such "errors" as ending sentences with prepositions and using objective case after copula (*It is me* for *It is I*). In their approach to the structure of English, the structuralists contributed a grammar describing the language in terms of its *own* signals and structural cues — use of word order, determiners, intonation patterns, and so on, to signal meaning. They demonstrated incontrovertibly that the Latinate model was inapplicable to an understanding of the structure of English.

In their attempt to free speakers from outmoded strictures and eighteenth-century norms, the structuralist-descriptivists induced the new "standard English" norms from the linguistic data of actual speakers. But the twentieth-century language pacesetters were invariably persons in upper- and middle-class positions. For example, in Charles C. Fries's *American English Grammar* (1940), he surveyed some 3,000 letters of veterans of varying class status and arrived at his Class I standard speakers on the basis of socioeconomic indices. Thus "standard English" became, as Fries defined it, the class dialect of the "socially acceptable . . . those who carry on the affairs of the country." The new standard thus didn't make thangs no better for common (and minority culture) folk. Instead of freeing speakers and writers from petty linguistic amenities, the immediate educational application of structuralist research was towards sociolinguistic conformity for the children whose parents had immigrated to this country in massive numbers around the turn of the century. (No broken English in this class, Antonio, and so on, like that). The melting pot has never been a reality, not even for whites. Black poet Haki Madhubuti has said it melted and we blacks burned. But so did a lot of other "divergent" languages and cultures, for the immigrants' kids became ashamed of they mommas and daddies who had sweated and toiled to bring they families to this country and then turned round and sweated some more to send they kids to school only to find them kids embarrassed bout them and they speech! Thus the descriptivist standard merely involved the substitution of one elitist norm for another — the white Anglo-Saxon Protestant group standard of America for the individualist "divinely inspired" Latinate standard of England. The contemporary emphasis on linguistic conformity to the dominant ethic of this new twentieth-century

American aristocracy has the same objective as the old: to make the rising plebeian outsiders talk and thereby think and act like the ruling-class insiders.

Despite the American ideal of equal opportunity for all, the oppressive "doctrine of correctness" still abounds. It is kept alive not only by popular misconceptions about "standard" English and "correct" speech, but also by persistent myths about languages in general. Perhaps one of the most prevalent myths is the notion that there are "primitive," "underdeveloped," or "inferior" languages. Another myth has to do with the belief that in any given country, some people are speaking "*the* language" while others are merely speaking "dialect" versions of "*the* language." Still another persistent myth is that the speech of certain persons in society is sloppy and unsystematic, while that of others is governed by rules and regulations. Through their study and knowledge of the various languages and cultures of the world, linguists have put the lie to all such myths, and have arrived at a number of "linguistic universals" underlying all languages. Unfortunately, much of this important work by linguists is framed in the jargon and concepts of modern linguistic science, with terminology that is confusing, technical, and often unintelligible to those outside the field of linguistics. Thus, despite linguistic truths now well over a century old, this vitally needed scientific information has not filtered down to precisely the place where it could have the greatest impact — the public school. For, as stated earlier, the public school is the main institution that continues to perpetuate myths and inaccuracies about language. In an effort to redress this situation, the following discussion of linguistic universals is offered in what I hope is clear, nontechnical language.

◆

First, we should note that all languages have variations which are properly called "dialects." Now in a popular sense, the term "dialect" suggests some form of speech that is substandard or inferior, but in a scientific, linguistic sense, a dialect is simply a variation of a language. Since everybody speaks a variation of "*the* language," everybody can be said to be speaking a dialect. The only way we can apprehend "*the* language" is through listening to, recording, or reading its many variations among the people who speak it. What is popularly termed the "real" language, then, exists only in the abstract. All we can point to or observe are the specific manifestations of the "real" English language in its multiplicity of speakers, all of whom represent varying and legitimate dialects of English.

This linguistic principle applied to English might be represented graphically as follows:

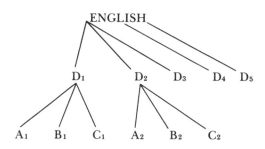

The D's in the diagram suggest the dialect groups comprising English throughout the English-speaking world — for example, Canadian English, American English, British English, and Australian English. Each of these different kinds of English has some forms of pronunciation, vocabulary, and idioms unique to the speakers in those countries. For example, in Canadian English, the *sch* of the word *schedule* is pronounced like the *sh* of *shoe*. In British English, a T.V. is a "telly." A speaker of Australian English refers to himself as an Austr*EYE*lian.

The ABC's in the diagram are used to suggest the various subgroups of a given dialect group of English. The number of dialects and subdialects varies, of course, depending on the language and the method of classification. For example, the American English dialect group might be broken down into geographical groupings representing the different regions of the United States, such as Southern American English dialect, Midwestern American English dialect, New England American English dialect, and so on. Or we might categorize American English dialects by social or ethnic groupings, such as Black English, white working-class English, upper-class Black and White English, and so forth. As with the larger groups of English speakers, each of these subgroups of American English speakers has some forms of pronunciation and idiomatic usage unique to its speakers. But I repeat: all these English dialect groups and subgroups represent varying and legitimate dialects of the English language; all the speakers can be said to be speaking the "real" English language. (As a matter of fact, one well-known linguist sigged: "Who's speaking *the* language and who's speaking only a dialect of *the* language depends on who has the army.")

The question arises: how do these different English dialect groups communicate with and understand one another? Here the modern linguistic concepts of "deep" and "surface" structure can help us.

All languages may be said to consist of deep and surface structures. The notion of deep structure is an abstract, intuitive concept that may be said to be like your gut-level understanding of what somebody says, and it is based on your understanding and knowledge of your native language. Though abstract, deep structure is where the true meaning of a given language resides. Through ordered linguistic rules, deep structures of a language are transformed into surface structures. These are the concrete manifestations of the deep structure, that is, what *actually* gets expressed in speech or writing. Although each speaker of a language has his or her unique way of talking, the speakers all share common deep structures; otherwise, they could not understand one another, and there would be no communication. For example, one American English speaker might say, *John hit the ball.* Another might say, *The ball was hit by John.* In the deep structure of English, these two sentences are really the same; thus despite being expressed in different ways, their meaning is clear to speakers of English. Similarly, one speaker might say, *He do know it.* And another might say, *He does know it.* Again, both statements are the same in the deep structure, and the two different versions are simply two ways of saying the same thing.

Shared deep structure is what helps us to understand one another even when surface structure doesn't indicate precisely what people mean. For instance, check out the following sentence, which was spoken by a highly educated American English speaker:

He told her he was going to Greece — which he went.

Or consider the following sentence, written by another highly educated American English speaker:

Dr. John Jones has been selected by President Smith to serve on the Advisory Committee to recommend a Dean for the College of Liberal Arts as a replacement for Clarence Johnson.

In both examples, despite the fact that the surface structure is confusingly worded, the statements are linguistically intelligible and we can understand the meaning because we share the deep structure of the speaker and writer.

Shared deep structures help in still other instances in communication. One example is the notion of "understood" meanings, as in the sentence: *Look out!* The listener is supposed to understand that the speaker means *You look out!* Such sentences are possible in American English because of shared deep structure. Another example concerns differences in vocabulary and pronunciation. For instance, in Boston's prestigious Beacon Hill area, one hears *pahk the cah*. In Grosse Pointe, home-of-Henry Ford, Michigan, it's *park the car*. Depending on the region of the country, carbonated beverages are *soda, tonic, soda pop*, or *pop*. In southern Indiana and Ohio you say *he took sick*. In California and the Midwest you say *he got sick*. Despite such differences in surface structures, all the speakers of these different states can understand one another, all are speaking the English language, and they can all communicate because the various dialects have the same source of meaning: English deep structure.

Since all languages consist of dialect variations, and since the "real" language is an abstraction, one may well ask: where does the notion of a national standard language come from? Although many people speak of the standard dialect in hallowed tones, there are *no* national standard languages which are decreed from on high. Rather, one particular dialect of a language may get to be elevated over other variations due to an arbitrary decision by the speakers of that language. Well, not truly "arbitrary," since the dialect that becomes the standard is generally the same dialect spoken by those with political and economic power. This, for instance, was the case with the many British dialects of Old and Middle English. In the years between 1150 and 1500 A.D., at least five different English dialects were spoken in the British Isles: Northern, West Midland, East Midland, Southern and Kentish. As mentioned earlier, by the eighteenth century, London had emerged as the commercial center of Britian, and thus, the dialect spoken there — a citified version of East Midland — evolved as the British national standard. It is that dialect which is the basis of present-day Received Standard British, that is, the British English speech of the universities, of the Crown and Parliament, of the BBC radio and television commentators, and of the "refined gentry" of England. In similar fashion, what has evolved as today's national standard American English dialect is the dialect of those Americans of economic and political power, namely the white, Anglo-Saxon, Protestant middle and upper classes.

Another important linguistic universal is the principle that every language is systematic and represents rule-governed behavior on the part of its speakers. Since dialects are the real, concrete reflection of the abstract language, it obviously follows that all dialect variations represent rules and patterned regularities of speakers. Related to this principle is the fact that all speakers, barring those with physiological defects, will acquire their native language and intuitive competence in its underlying principles without any formal, programmatic kind of instruction. Thus in America, small children quickly learn to go from "sentences" like "up" to "Pick me up." They learn principles of English word order like *The book is here,* not *Is here book the.* In Black America, speakers learn how to manipulate the rules for *be/non-be* without anybody telling them that *"be* is to express habitual conditions." (Because of these universal language behavior patterns, one school of modern linguists contends that language is a biological, creative human act, universally separating man from other animals.)

All native speakers of a language have an underlying competence in the forms of their language and thus can produce sentences they've never said before as well as understand those they've never heard before. Of course, we don't always perform at our maximum competence — not in any phase of life really, whether speech-making, music-making, or, for that matter, love-making. Still the potential ability is there, though oftentimes the linguistic computer of the mind is working faster than that of the mouth, as demonstrated in the sentences quoted earlier by those very highly educated and fluent speakers of American English. This principle is true for all speakers, regardless of how "quaint," "sloppy," "unpleasant" — or even "colored" — their speech sounds to someone else's ear.

Finally, a language reflects a people's culture and their world view, and thus each group's language is suited to the needs and habits of its users. The Eskimos have several words for and make verbal distinctions about various kinds of snow, whereas for English-speaking Americans, snow is snow. Obviously this does not make American English a "primitive" language — rather it's one in which the experience of snow is not an important reality. The Hopi Indians in the southwestern part of the United States are said to have a "timeless" language because Hopi verbs are not concerned with the time of any action (the tense), only with its truth or validity. And in some cultures, talking is not even valued at all: the Paliyans of South India communicate very little at all times and become almost silent by the age of forty — in their world, people who are verbal and communicative are regarded as abnormal and often as offensive. By the same token, despite the linguistic chauvinism of the literate West, oral and written language are of similar value and function to a culture, neither taking precedence over the other. Since all languages change, all are modified and modifiable according to the dictates, customs, and habits of their users; American English, for example, has added a multiplicity of words germane to the space age, such as "A-O.K."

Despite these important linguistic universals, studies of language attitudes show that people continue to make judgments — usually erroneous — about others, purely on the basis of their speech. As an example, Canadian researchers Lambert and

Tucker compared personality ratings of various American speakers. Black and white college students were asked to listen to voices on tape and to rank the speakers on the basis of intelligence, friendliness, faith in God, honesty, determination, and a whole host of other terms that Lambert and Tucker found people using to stereotype and categorize others. The speech of network newscasters was ranked higher than that of college-educated blacks or whites. That is, despite the fact that there is no correlation between one's style of speech and their intelligence or honesty, these newscasters were considered to be more friendly, intelligent, and honest simply because of the way they spoke! As to the speakers ranked the lowest, the black students judged the educated white Southern speakers least favorably, and the white students ranked the Southern black college student speakers the lowest. (In an earlier study, Lambert and Tucker found that speakers of Canadian English were ranked higher than the SAME voices speaking Canadian French, by both French and English Canadians — a striking demonstration of the correlation between language and politics.)

What is so deep about this matter of language attitudes is the unspoken rule especially pronounced among the power-holders, that those folks "over there" must do as I *say*, not necessarily as I *do*. Labov asked middle-class New Yorkers to rank the employability of other New Yorkers on the basis of speech samples. For any speaker they rejected, they were asked to indicate the feature of that person's speech that would cause him or her to get rejected. Yeah, y'all way ahead of me . . . Cause what Labov found was that they rejected the speaker for using forms of speech that they themselves used!

In a similar study, Robert Pooley surveyed the language of public school English teachers and college English professors speaking in quasi-formal situations, that is, during class sessions and in faculty meetings conducted by parliamentary procedure. Pooley found the English teachers and profs using many of the same forms of speech that they were attempting to drill their students out of in classroom composition and grammar assignments! Yeah, dig that.

An experience of mine brought out this attitude in stark clar-

by Ollie Harrington

"Doctor Jenkins, before you read us your paper on inter-stellar gravitational tensions in thermo-nuclear propulsion, would you sing us a good old spiritual?"

ity. I had approached the head of research at a large urban university where I was on the faculty. I was trying to solicit support for a study of attitudes of potential employers toward black speech. This white research man, in a salary range well above $30,000, contended that such a study would only prove the obvious since everybody knew that you had to speak the King's English to get ahead in America. With my research proposal thus dismissed, I started to leave. As I did so, the research division head turned to his assistant and said, "Listen, can you stay a few minutes? You and me have some work to do." Now, me bein me, I *had* to correct my man's "bad grammar." I said, "Hey, watch yo dialect — it's you and *I* have some work to do." He turned fifty shades o' red, and I split. Naturally, that siggin of mine had shonuff blowed the possibility of me gittin any grant money!

As America completes the Bicentennial and looks forward to moving toward the tricentennial, we find contemporary linguistic realities not much different from those of old. The "national mania for correctness" is, after all, a useful tool. The speech of blacks, the poor, and other powerless groups is used as a weapon to deny them access to full participation in the society. Teachers harp on the "bad" English of their students; potential employees are denied jobs because they don't talk "right"; future college graduates become force-outs because they write in "nonstandard" English. Yet what is "nonstandard" English is simply the language of "nonstandard" people. Their linguistic usage deviates from the collective dialect of the dominant culture — nothing more, as simple and yet as complex as that. For your language and the dialect in which it is actualized was acquired at around age two, pretty firmly fixed by about age five or six, and by adolescence your basic speech patterns have become a well-ingrained habit. Nearly impossible to change (except maybe over inordinately long periods of time — and then you have to be willing to surrender whole chunks of your identity to do so). What better weapon, then, with which to keep the outsiders out than the obstacle of speech?

From the viewpoint of Black Americans, it seems that White America's use of black speech as an economic impediment is, on the one hand, a new form of racism, a way to hinder blacks from gittin it on America, even if they acquire the education and skills; and on the other, a manifestation of White America's class bias. As James Baldwin has said, America is a country where everybody has status, and in a place where everybody has status, it is possible that *nobody* has status. Thus Americans in general, lacking a fixed place in the society, don't know where they be in terms of social class and personal identity. But, as Baldwin concludes, with nigguhs round, at least they always knows where the bottom bees.

7

Where Do We Go from Here? T.C.B.!

Social Policy and Educational Practice

FOLLOWING THE STYLE of the black preacher's sermon, uhma begin this last chapter by "taking a text." The work of Dr. Carter G. Woodson gon serve as my "Scriptural" reference. Read as follow:

> No systematic effort toward change has been possible, for, taught the same economics, history, philosophy, literature and religion which have established the present code of morals, the Negro's mind has been brought under the control of his oppressor. The problem of holding the Negro down, therefore, is easily solved. When you control a man's thinking you do not have to worry about his actions. You do not have to tell him not to stand here or go yonder. He will find his proper place and will stay in it. You do not need to send him to the back door. He will go without being told. In fact, if there is no back door, he will cut one for his special benefit. His education makes it necessary.

In 1916 Dr. Woodson founded the Association for the Study of Afro-American Life and History (then "*Negro* Life and History"). An esteemed historian, author, social critic, and giant intellectual among men, Dr. Woodson wrote numerous books and articles on the Afro-American experience. One of these was a baaaaaad little book of criticism about the education the Negro needed but had not gotten in America. Published in 1933, the book was appropriately titled *The Miseducation of the Negro*. Our theme here, then, will be "Black English and the miseducation of the Negro — again."

In the 1960s black students were suddenly bombarded with a plethora of language studies and remediation programs for the "disadvantaged" and "culturally deprived." These and other such "compensatory education" reforms had as their ultimate goal narrowing the disparity between black and white income. That is, it was argued that since education correlates with economic and social success in America, the way out of the black ghetto was through enhanced educational achievement. Hence programs such as Head Start, Upward Bound, Higher Horizons, High Potential, Project 300 (350, 500, etc., depending on the number of black students in these special programs) and other Great Society–type efforts. Just as Black Americans had come "up from slavery," they would now be brought "up from the ghetto." While a few remedial programs spoke of cognitive-linguistic "deficiency" in black students, most were politer and referred to cognitive-linguistic "differences." At bottom, though, both the deficit and the difference models are conceptualized within a framework of black pathology. As Henry Levin of Stanford University stated in the March 21, 1970, issue of *Saturday Review:*

> Inherent in [such] programs is the view that the urban minority child is somehow inferior to the middle-class child. The schools assume that his cultural differences represent inferiorities that must be eliminated . . . [There] is a total disregard for the cultures and experiences of Black and other minority children . . .

Eminent British sociologist Basil Bernstein takes compensatory education programs to task for having grossly misinterpreted and misapplied his concept of working-class "restricted code." In his "Critique of the Concept of Compensatory Education," in *Class, Codes and Control,* Dr. Bernstein states:

> Since the late 1950's there has been a steady outpouring of papers and books in the USA which are concerned with the education of children of low social class whose *material* circumstances are inadequate, or with the education of black children of low social class whose *material* circumstances are chronically inadequate . . . New educational categories were developed (the culturally deprived, the linguistically deprived, the socially disadvantaged) and the notion of compensatory education was introduced as a means of changing the status of those children in the above categories . . . I

find the term 'compensatory education' a curious one for a
number of reasons . . . the organization of schools creates delicate
overt and covert streaming [i.e., tracking] arrangements which
neatly lower the expectations and motivations of teachers and
taught . . . The concept "compensatory education" serves to direct
attention away from the internal organization and the educational
context of the school, and focus our attention upon the families
and children. The concept . . . implies that something is lacking in
the family, and so in the child. As a result the children are unable
to benefit from schools. It follows then that the school has to "com-
pensate" for the something which is missing in the family and the
children become little deficit systems. If only the parents were interested in the goodies we offer; if only they were like middle-class
parents, then we could do our job.

Course, Dr. Woodson told us all this way back in 1933 in discussing how a pathology approach was reflected in treatment and
attitudes toward Black English:

> In the study of language in school pupils were made to scoff at the
> Negro dialect as some peculiar possession of the Negro which they
> should despise rather than directed to study the background of
> this language as a broken down [i.e., linguistically polluted by En-
> glish] African tongue — in short to understand their own linguistic
> history, which is certainly more important for them than the study
> of French Phonetics or Historical Spanish Grammar.

In the final analysis, both difference and deficit language programs are concerned with sociolinguistic etiquette and the
norms of the white middle class. Such remedial efforts are not
designed to instill pride in Black Language and culture, nor to
teach black students critical thinking and analysis, nor, above all,
to give them tools to righteously examine the socioeconomic
workings of America. Quite clearly, the ideology of these programs is directed towards inculcating the values of the dominant
society and eliminating the cultural distinctiveness of Black
America.

One of the first government-financed language programs for
the black "disadvantaged" student was established in Detroit in
1959. It espoused the following ideology:

This specific language problem . . . involves criticism of an individual's language . . . It implies to many of our students that we were born into a different social, economic, and cultural level than they and that they must change if they wish to fit into the general cultural pattern of our particular area . . . It . . . must be acknowledged that standard language is a key that will open many doors, and conversely, many doors may be closed to those with nonstandard language . . . In other words, if they wish to progress in Northern and Midwestern urban communities, they must speak as we do . . . Negro students of a low socio-economic level in Detroit [must] change their patterns of speech . . .

Ten years later, in a supposedly more "enlightened" approach, an educator acknowledged that "nonstandard" dialect is just as good and communicative as "standard":

. . . such discussions remind both teachers and students that the presence or absence of standard forms in a peron's speech is not a moral or ethical issue. Among announcers, congressmen and movie stars there are some who are moral, honest, and upright and some who are not; yet both kinds are speakers of standard English . . . such discussions give the teacher an opportunity to grant that people who speak standard English do not always and invariably communicate any more clearly or forcefully than speakers of nonstandard dialects do . . . when a student says something like "I don't have no pencil" [it is a statement] whose import is perfectly clear, as the student well knows. The reason for learning to say "I don't have any pencil" has little to do with comprehensibility . . .

However, the value assigned to "nonstandard" speech only obtains so long as the "nonstandard" speech stays in its "place." For, as the same educator tells us, it is the "standard" — not the "nonstandard" — speaker who must be imitated if one is to get "ahead":

Undemocratic and unfair as it may seem, the fact is that standard English is "front door" English . . . The student needs to understand that a command of standard English is vital to any American (particularly any "minority-group" American) who aims to associate with speakers of the standard dialect on anything like an equal footing.

Thus, however liberal this type of pedagogy purports to be on the surface, its underlying insidious message is that though all dialects are equal, some are more equal than others.

Check out the deficit-difference ideologies in more detail. Consider first the "cognitive deficit" theorists. They brand blacks with "verbal deprivation" and attribute it to inferior intelligence (due to either genetic inheritance or environmental factors, but the result is the same). These crucial deficiencies in black speech (and thought) indicate language "retardation" and "impoverishment." Educators and psychologists holding this view advocate the total eradication of the "inferior" Black Dialect. For Black English is viewed as an "underdeveloped version of standard English," and a "non-logical mode of expressive behavior," lacking the "formal properties" necessary for the formulation of cognitive concepts. Some of the linguistic concepts found wanting in Black English, so we're told, are the concepts of negation and plurality. (Yeah, I know it doan make no kinda sense, but that's what they bees sayin, nonetheless!) Further, these deficit theorists contend that if students don't answer questions and make statements in complete sentences, they can't think whole, complete thoughts — or worse, can't think, period! Yet, as linguists have shown, *ain't none* is a negation concept, just as *isn't any* is, and the *three* of *three book* shows plurality just the same as *three books*. As for so-called "fragmentary" statements, they can be shown to be simply manifestations of whole statements transformed. The "complete thought" exists in the deep structure, and what the speaker feels is unnecessary wording or something that can be understood in context is simply deleted by the time the statement gets to the surface, that is, by the time the statement is spoken. For instance, just as in a standard White English context, *Come here* is "understood" to mean *You come here,* so the expression *He tired* in a Black English context is "understood" to mean *He tired now.* Similarly, the question *Where's my book?* can be answered with *on the desk,* which is a transformed surface representation of *The book is on the desk,* with *the book is* deleted.

Despite such obvious linguistically logical realities, the deficit-based programs use teaching strategies whose implicit message is that the black "culture of poverty" student can't talk and must be drilled in the use of oral language. In a typical classroom exercise, for instance, the teacher would hold up a variety of objects (chalk, books, pencils) and say after each one: *This is a book, This is a pencil, This is a piece of chalk,* and so on. Students would repeat each sentence after the teacher. Then the teacher might proceed to ask questions about each object, thus: (holding up a pencil, for instance) *Boys and girls, what is this?* The kids would have to say *That is a pencil.* They could not simply say *A pencil.* (Remember, kiddies, whole sentences equal whole thoughts!) So much for the deficit group and their particular kind of "miseducation of the Negro."

Another larger group of educators, psychologists, and some linguists purportedly see black language and culture not as deficient, but simply different. Somehow, though, the differences do not come out as equal and valid, but as inferior and insufficient, as deviances from the norm. Sometimes the origin of the differences is located in poverty and the harsh realities of coping with the black ghetto environment; occasionally the differences are viewed as archaic, rural Southernisms, impeding black progress in our modern, technological society. (Few are the educators who see black linguistic-cultural differences as legitimate African survivals whose retention is to be preserved and sustained.) At any rate, whatever the source of the black differences, black children's world must be "culturally enriched," for they are viewed as "culturally deprived." As one sociological theorist put it, "In considering the problems of the culturally deprived child, one cannot help but wonder what would happen if such a child were transferred to a culturally enriched home."

When it comes to the specific area of the language of the "culturally deprived" black child, the difference theorists, unlike the deficit folks, at least pay lip service acceptance to ghetto speech. Such linguists and educators argue that Black Dialect is linguistically systematic, its speakers perform according to regularized rules, and black "culturally disadvantaged" speakers are highly verbal in their own communities. But — Catch 22 — the social world "out there" (presumably beyond the ghetto, where all blacks aspire to, right?) demands linguistic conformity of blacks. Thus black students will need to master "correct" White English speech in order to git ovuh in the white world, hence they must learn to be switch hitters, dropping their Africanized English speech for White English as social situations warrant it. These linguists and educators are pushing a so-called bi-dialectal model, which, in effect, says that since the white middle class either cannot or will not accept the dialect of blacks, then blacks must accept and learn to use the dialect of the white middle class.

Like the deficit theorists, bi-dialectal theorists either ignore or incorrectly conceptualize the interaction between language, school, and the larger political reality. Schools, curricula, language teaching policies, and classroom practice are not autonomous entities, nor do they exist in a sociocultural vacuum. Rather, they are interrelated with and governed by the pervasive political and economic ideology of America. Talking about Black English, listing its features and suggesting ways of changing *or* adding to it, without commensurately advocating changes in the sociopolitical system in which black people struggle is not only short-sighted, it amounts to so much pure academic talk, and ultimately, is an implicit acknowledgement that the system is good and valid, and all that need be done is to alter the people to fit into it. Yet the history of black people has shown what continues to be true today: speaking White English is no guarantee to economic advancement. For educators, linguists, and anybody else to push that notion off on kids is to deal them a gross lie. (In fact, one could also argue that having a college degree, even with White English speech is no guarantee of economic mobility, as can be witnessed by the high number of college graduates — black as well as white — who are unemployed.) Meaningful and successful education for black kids can only proceed with concomitant changes in broader educational policy and in social and economic policy.

Although the difference–bi-dialectal theorists proceed from a linguistically sound and seemingly more humane premise than deficit theorists, they are unable to reconcile the obvious paradox in pedagogy which speaks to the regularized, functional quality of black speech, at the same time that it exhorts mastery of a set of "prestige" language norms in order to "succeed" in the "larger" society. (Some program designers use what they think are more careful, less judgmental terms, such as "college dialect" vs. "community dialect," the "language of work" vs. the "language of play," "home talk" vs. "school talk," but black "disadvantaged" students who done gone through these programs rightly contend that it all bees the same thang!) Thus blacks quickly perceive that Black Dialect must not be all that systematic or beautiful, for after all, they is gon to have to give it up when they bees moving on up in "higher" social and economic groups. And, to add insult to injury, we all know that there ain no cultural enrichment or "language programs for the disadvantaged" in white, middle-class schools. That is, it is only upon blacks that the virtues and greatness of bi-dialectalism are inflicted. As Baratz and Baratz explain:

> From social science's ethnocentric position, and without an adequate conception of black culture, the profession has tended to view behavioral differences such as non-standard black English not as signs of a different cultural system but as defects and deviances from our falsely hypothesized pan-cultural norm.

Thus the difference–bi-dialectal model ultimately comes to mean deficiency model, since the implication is that Black English is still unacceptable to the "larger" society. Again, the victims become culpable for the crime, for though poverty and racism created and sustained the economically impoverished position of blacks, still it is blacks who must surrender the "socially stigmatized" cultural and linguistic forms which are intolerable to the white mainstream. In short, the underlying ideology implies that it is blacks who must change, adapt, and tighten up the "cultural lag," not whites. In an acid attack on this position, one sociologist put it this way:

> . . . 350 years have left their mark and it shows itself in a lifestyle that is essentially maladaptive to the wider society . . . [the black man's] culture, then, is marvelously adaptive to the realities of his unhappy life situation, but serves to work against him now that the democratic processes are beginning to operate in his favor.
>
> The solution then is one of uplift. The black man must first have opportunity, but in order to avail himself of opportunity, he must "get with it."

There is thus a network of programs and institutions providing rehabilitative, educational remediation, and therapeutic services — all having as their goal the "uplift of the Negro."

Now, it ain nothin wrong with being "uplifted," but the miseducation comes in when we attempt to answer the questions: uplifted *from* what? *to* what? In the language area, teaching strategies which seek only to put white middle-class English into the mouths of black speakers ain did nothin to inculcate the black perspective necessary to address the crises in the black community. We have, rather, a case of black people crying for bread and White America sayin "let 'em eat cake." Let us consult Carter Woodson again:

> The educational system, as it has developed both in Europe and America, is an antiquated process which does not hit the mark even in the case of the needs of the white man himself . . . even if the Negroes do successfully imitate the white, nothing new has thereby been accomplished. You simply have a larger number of persons doing what others have been doing.

The linguistic pedagogy which emanates from the difference–bi-dialectalist concept generally reflects the power elite's perceived insignificance and hence rejection of Afro-American language and culture. And it has as its fundamental (albeit unarticulated) objective using blacks to sustain the status quo. With this goal in mind the cognitive input of language remediation programs has of necessity to be educationally patronizing and linguistically stultifying. Since it ain bout the acquisition of real knowledge at all — which gives people power, both to change themselves and their society — most of the instructional content in both difference and deficit programs don't do nothin more than present language drills based on the "national mania for correctness." For example, teachers lead their students in daily written and oral exercises by presenting a "model" sentence, such as *John works every day,* and having students repeat the sentence with different third person subjects (*Susan works every day, My mother works every day*). Some "teaching technologies" even suggest that teachers use language lab methods and have their students practice saying such sentences on tape. In still other curriculum handbooks, students are told to practice by juxtaposing the "standard" version of a sentence with the "nonstandard" version, thus: "In home talk, we say *John work every day*. In school talk, we say *John works every day*." Here is a typical exercise in detail:

> *Repetition Drills*. This illustrative drill and the others that follow are at the level of lower-grade pupils in the intermediate school, but they may readily be adapted to higher grades.
>
> Aim: To seek automatic response in the standard use of the verb *to be* in the present tense
>
> Procedure: The following assumes the use of the tape recorder — although the teacher may himself provide the model, if preferred. Ask the class to listen carefully to the tape. Replay the tape and ask the pupils to repeat the pattern in unison. Then ask one or two rows to repeat the pattern; call on several pupils to repeat it. The voice on the tape says each of the following sentences, and the pupils repeat it immediately afterward:
>
> > We're in the English class.
> > They're in the front of the room.
> > I'm in my seat.
> > The teacher is near the desk.
> > You're anxious to learn.
> > John's in the back of the room.
> > He's a tall boy.

A narrow conception of "standard English" is revealed in this kind of language instruction, for what is stressed is pure propriety, and then in the higher grades, verbosity and pretentiousness, rather than life, vigor, and truth. Indicting the university structure that forces him to teach "students to speak and write in ways that make me throw up," linguist James Sledd speaks to this point:

> Last spring I struggled through a depressing paper on education by a well-known young linguist and language-planner. "It is time," he wrote in his peroration, "that we stop asking whether or not it is to be recommended that the UNESCO recommendation on vernacular language education is to be recommended and to begin asking to what extent it can realistically be recommended."
>
> The quotation is verbatim.
>
> A few months later, I got a memorandum from the Vice-

President for Research at UT Austin: "Effective today," the world was informed, "the Office of the Vice-President for Research has been moved."

That was the first and last intimation I have ever had that that office (His Nibs capitalized it) was, is, or has been effective.

I abominate such abuses of the only language that I really know. That language-planner cannot think; our Vice-President for Research is contented with whatever pieces of bureaucratic jargon he finds lying about the corridors of the Main Building.

Over thirty years ago, George Orwell also rapped about bureaucratic jargon and what has now come to be called "public doublespeak." These are serious misuses of the language which cloud meaning and can be used to deceive others. In his well-known essay "Politics and the English Language," Orwell gave us the following "translation" of a verse from Ecclesiastes:

> Objective considerations of contemporary phenomena compel the conclusion that success or failure in competitive activities exhibits no tendency to be commensurate with innate capacity, but that a considerable element of the unpredictable must invariably be taken into account.

The Biblical version of the above is:

> I returned, and saw under the sun, that the race is not to the swift, nor the battle to the strong, neither yet bread to the wise, nor yet riches to men of understanding, nor yet favor to men of skill; but time and chance happeneth to them all.

Let us be very clear on what is being run down here. In the public schools, in the universities and in the popular mind, much of what passes for "correct" English is nothing more than bombastic, convoluted, and jargon-filled language. Classroom exercises and drills of the sort quoted earlier exemplify the unarticulated indoctrination of students with the notion that speech that conforms to white, middle class standards of etiquette is better and more logical than Africanized English (or any forms of non-middle-class speech, for that matter). To illustrate this point, linguist William Labov did a detailed comparison of the verbal responses of Larry, a black teen-ager from the street, with Charles, an upper class, black collegian. Both Bloods were rapping on questions relating to the nature of man and the universe — more precisely, the topic of life after death; the issue of the existence of God and the subject of witchcraft. Labov did a logical and linguistic analysis of their taped responses and contended that Larry, who spoke in what Labov terms "Negro Non-standard English," is a skilled speaker with great verbal presence of mind who puts forth a clear, effectively formulated and complex argument. Charles, on the other hand, comes off as something less than a "first-rate thinker," full of verbosity and anxious to avoid any misstatements or overstatements. From his analysis, Labov concluded:

> The initial impression of him [Charles] as a good speaker is simply our long-conditioned reaction to middle-class verbosity: we know that people who use these stylistic devices are educated people, and we are inclined to credit them with saying something intelligent. Our reactions are accurate in one sense: Charles M. is more educated than Larry. But is he more rational, more logical, or more intelligent? Is he any better at thinking out a problem to its solution? Does he deal more easily with abstractions? There is no reason to think so. Charles M. succeeds in letting us know that he is educated, but in the end we do not know what he is trying to say, and neither does he.

Another example of such linguistic miseducation is provided by the characteristic composition instruction in English classrooms. Namely, the red-penciled approach that stresses only "good" grammar, rather than good sense; neatness, correctness, and lifeless "objective" language, rather than rhetorical power and the language of social and political consciousness. (Jonathan Kozol calls this approach the "politics of syntax.") An example is the following theme written by a college freshman in a "special" minorities academic program. The assignment was: "Take a position on the war in Viet Nam and present arguments to defend your position."

> I think the war in Viet Nam bad. Because we don't have no business over there. My brother friend been in the war, and he say it's

hard and mean. I do not like war because it's bad. And so I don't
think we have no business there. The reason the war in China is
bad is that American boys is dying over there.

The paper was returned to the student with only one comment:
"Correct your grammar and resubmit." The problem with such
writing "instruction" is that it fails to deal with the basic problems of *most* student writers, be they black or white. Namely,
weaknesses in organization, content, logic, coherence, use of
supporting details, and communicative power.

On the other hand, if the writing is strong in organization,
content and rhetorical power, but written in the black, the writer
is severely penalized for Black English "errors" and typically re-
ceives a low or no-pass grade. Mis-instruction of this nature reinforces the erroneous notion that one need only be correct in
grammar, spelling, punctuation, and other mechanics to git
ovuh in the communication process. As one student put it, "You
ain got to write *good*, just correctly." As an example, the following theme by a black freshman was rejected by several composition instructors because it is sprinkled throughout with Black
English forms. Yet it exemplifies a creative response to the assignment, effective use of supporting details, coherence, and
overall communicative effectiveness. The assignment was: "Describe a person that you dislike and explain why."

My hatred for Roger Mason will last all my life. He the manager
at the club where I work. The one reason we can't get alone is he's
prejudice, and I can't stand no one who prejudice. He tries to treat
me like a dog but I put him in his place. If he had the power to fire
me he would. He's the Scrooge of Chicago, stingy as hell and evil
and wicked. Roger is a grey head man in his middle-fifties. With a
small hunch in his upper-back. Roll face with wrinkles everywhere.
I even think he had wrinkles on his nose. His nose is about a foot
long with a bubble on the end. He alway where one of those brown
1920 suits or either a grey one. When I'm on my break he follow
me watching me and cussing. I think the old man crazy. He's very
short, come's to my shoulders, so you can see how small he is. As a
matter of fact he look just like Scrooge. I think he eats Cottage
Chesse three time a day, Mason just loves Cottage Chesse cover with

pepper. They say he married, but I feel sorry for his wife. Got about
ten strands of hair and is always combing them. If you ever meet Mr.
Roger Mason don't shake hand he'll bite off your fingers.

My point is not only that black student-writers such as this are
penalized for superficial reasons, but what is worse, and more
miseducating is that they are not being helped! Due to the over-
emphasis on use of language forms that conform to Warriner's
or the Har-Brace handbook, the potential in such students is not
being harnessed and developed into greater expressive power
and linguistic fluency.

Similar kinds of language "teaching" . . . Black English and the
. . . can be found on all levels, wherever black students be, from
kindergarten through college . . . miseducation of the Negro —
again. These seemingly well-intentioned programs were and are
not designed at all to increase the black student's rappin and
verbal ability, but to freeze him or her into a mold of mediocrity,
precluding concerns for cognitive analysis, social sense, ethical
perspective, and above all, the political power of written and oral
communication. Dictating only that the rote, mechanical addition of s's and ed's be in the "right place," these programs are
gross misuses of important educational time, for the goals involve only lateral moves. Yet black folk need (upward) vertical
moves. That what we mean when we bees singin with Curtis
Mayfield, "We movin on up." *UP*, not sideways.

In another circumstance and time, such teaching calls to mind
the aims of the Abolitionists, do-gooder liberal whites of the ilk
of William Lloyd Garrison who wished to define the direction of
the Black Freedom struggle. Thus Abolitionists cautioned that
magnificent black rapper, Frederick Douglass, to go slow with
his raps in Abolitionist meetings. He was beginning to sound too
"radical," too rhetorically powerful and not at all like a mechanical White English speaker with a black face. Not only did the
Abolitionists want Douglass to confirm their and the audience's
notions of what a slave was like, they above all did not want him
to venture into new areas of thought, nor to suggest courses of
actions and implications beyond which the Abolitionists themselves were willing to go.

I was generally introduced as a chattel — a thing — a piece of southern property — the chairman assuring the audience that it could speak . . . During the first three or four months my speeches were almost exclusively made up of narrations of my own personal experience as a slave. Let us have the facts, said the people. So also said Friend George Foster, who always wished to pin me down to a simple narrative. Give us the facts, said Collins, we will take care of the philosophy. Just here arose some embarrassment. It was impossible for me to repeat the same old story month after month and keep up my interest in it. It was new to the people, it is true, but it was an old story to me, and to go through with it night after night was a task altogether too mechanical for my nature. Tell your story, Frederick, would whisper my revered friend, Mr. Garrison, as I stepped upon the platform. I could not always follow the injunction, for I was now reading and thinking. New views of the subject were being presented to my mind. It did not entirely satisfy me to narrate wrongs — I felt like denouncing them. I could not always curb my moral indignation for the perpetrators of slaveholding villainy long enough for a circumstantial statement of the facts which I felt almost sure everybody must know. Besides, I was growing and needed truth

◆

In the last decade or so, many eminent educators have come forth with critical attacks on the American educational system. Scholars like John Holt, Neal Postman, Charles Silberman and others have expounded upon the devastating psychological onslaughts and long range negative effects of a miseducation system. As a result of these recent critiques on American education, it is finally being recognized that the school plays a tremendous role in shaping the values and attitudes of tomorrow's adults. (Like, everybody and they momma pass through school even if they don't stay too long, right?) Schools have potentially strong influence upon their captive audiences. Traditionally, they have used that influencing energy to give sustenance to an unjust, dehumanizing system. Students of the sixties — white as well as black — peered behind the mask of "liberty and justice for all" and gazed on the awesome monster of privilege and advancement for a few. Many of these same students helped to strip away that mask for all the world to see. And some of them, using a protest borrowed from the black liberation struggle, even tried to transform the hideous creature into something of beauty and value.

Building on the insight and momentum provided by the students of the sixties, schools should begin to employ their power and influence judiciously and humanely to guide black students of the seventies and eighties. For if it is true that the schools do not properly serve white middle-class students of the contemporary world, they do a great *disservice* to black students. For the American school, with all its defects (as the great Dr. Carter Woodson would say), continues to be basically oriented toward and supportive of a lifestyle that coincides with that of the dominant culture. The message conveyed by this white middle-class orientation is that the black child has nothing of value and thus he or she must be uplifted and properly socialized by the school. The question becomes: how can schools instructing black students begin to T.C.B. — Take Care of Business?

Notwithstanding all that has been said about the overwhelming power of the school as an *institutional* entity, I contend that it is still *individual* teachers in their *individual* settings that are the single most important factor in the educational process. The individual teacher has a tremendous impact on, and responsibility for, how, what, and how much students learn. I am not referring here to something as simplistic as that rather silly concept of teacher "warmth" that abounds in discussions about black education. Many educators emphasize the importance of teachers being friendly and warm with their students, believing that this will increase the students' educational output. Certainly nobody can quibble with the notion that it's a lot hipper to be in a classroom where the teacher is pleasant and warm rather than evil and cold. But the fact is that human warmth alone, in and of itself, is not sufficient to raise the achievement level of black students. A recent study of black students in the San Francisco high schools revealed that "warmth only slightly increased student effort." What is needed to prevent further miseducation of black kids is a change in teacher attitude and behavior, a complete reordering of thought about the educational process and the place of black students in that process. The belief sets, the philosophy, the world view, and the pedagogical ideology of the teacher are all intertwined and interrelated. Those ideas and underlying assumptions are revealed in the behavior and practice of the teacher in the classroom. Check out a couple of specific instances of how a teacher's attitude toward black language belies the teacher's outward appearance of "warmth."

A sixth-grade math teacher was quite disturbed because his students referred to the concept of lowest common denominator as "breaking it down more smaller." The students obviously understood the concept and demonstrated, both on the board and in class and homework papers, that they could apply the concept to solve math problems. However, the teacher kept correcting them because his perception was that "these kids obviously don't know how to arrive at lowest common denominators." When I queried this seemingly warm and friendly teacher as to how, then, they were able to do problems involving the concept, his explanation was that "you can't do anything if you don't know the right word for it." (I guess he never heard of the semantic principle that the word is not the thing!) At any rate, that teacher's solution was to waste the next few days drilling his students on the spelling and textbook terminology of various mathematical operations that they already knew how to perform! This example is all the more ludicrous and sad when we consider that here is a classic case of students effectively interpreting and "translating" a mathematical concept represented in standard textbook English, into words that were more meaningful to them. Ain no way they could have managed this translation process if they didn't fully understand the standard textbook English words "lowest common denominator"! These students were, in effect, saying: "Oh yeah, I dig that, *lowest common denominator* means that I got to do something to *break it down more smaller.*"

Another example of the negative effect of teacher attitude toward black communicative style is represented by the following interaction which occurred in a primary unit classroom.

Student (excitedly):   Miz Jones, you remember that show you tole us bout? Well, me and my momma 'nem —

Teacher (interrupting with a "warm" smile):   Bernadette, start again, I'm sorry, but I can't understand you.

Student (confused):   Well, it was that show, me and my momma —

Teacher (interrupting again, still with that "warm" smile):   Sorry, I still can't understand you.

(Student, now silent, even more confused than ever, looks at floor, says nothing.)

Teacher: Now, Bernadette, first of all, it's *Mrs*. Jones, not *Miz* Jones. And you know it was an *exhibit*, not a *show*. Now, haven't I explained to the class over and over again that you always put yourself last when you are talking about a group of people and yourself doing something? So, therefore, you should say what?

Student: My momma and me —

Teacher (exasperated):   No! My mother and I. Now, start again, this time right.

Student: Aw, that's okay, it wasn't nothin.

What can be said about the communication and language of this interaction — or should I say lack of interaction? First, the teacher comprehended the dialect of the student full well; otherwise, how could she have translated the student's Black English into Standard White English and corrected her? And the student *knows* the teacher understood her and is therefore legitimately confused. Furthermore, the student's reference to *Mrs. Jones* as *Miz Jones* is perfect Black (as well as Southern) Dialect making a sound like *Miz/Miss*. (In fact, the recent feminist move toward *Ms.* as a blanket designation for all females, whether married or not, has been good Black English speaking practice all along.) The teacher knows that the student recognizes the marital status distinction between *Miss* and *Mrs.* from previous classroom interaction with her students. However, the teacher's concern, as she explained to me, was that the students should learn the "correct way to pronounce words." Also, the student understands the difference between a "show" as a movie and a "show" as an exhibit. (Feigning ignorance, I asked the student what the show was about and who were the movie stars playing in it. She replied, "Naw, not that kinda show. It was, you know, pictures and dolls and different stuff you could look at.") The teacher knows full well that an exhibit is in fact, semantically speaking, a "show" — a "showing" of a certain type. Further, the teacher knows that the student knows this too. But again, as she emphasized, she wants them to "know and use the correct words to express things."

If the masses of black kids are ever going to catch up with their white counterparts, such negative attitudes and behavior must be replaced by a genuine kind of teacher warmth. One that sincerly accepts the inherent legitimacy of the many varieties of English. One that honestly respects the power of both written and oral communicative styles. One that recognizes the connection between language and oppression and thus motivates the teacher to work to sever that connection. Ultimately, *both black and white students must be prepared for life in a multilinguistic, transnational world. This requires teachers able to cultivate in students a sense of respect for, perhaps even celebration of, linguistic-cultural differences — balanced by the recognition that, on the universal, "deep structure" level, the world is but one community.

We turn now to some recommendations for classroom policy and practice on the part of teachers of black students.

◆

At the many educational workshops and teaching seminars I have conducted, teachers often ask: "Are you saying we should teach the kids Black Dialect?" To answer a question with a question, why teach them something they already know? Rather, the real concern, and question, should be: How can I use what the kids *already* know to move them to what they *need* to know? This question presumes that you genuinely accept as viable the language and culture the child has acquired by the time he or she comes to school. This being the case, it follows that you allow the child to use that language to express himself or herself, not only to interact with their peers in the classroom, but with you, the teachers, as well.

For example, the call-response dynamic is integral to the communication system of Black English (as y'all now know, right?). Since black communication works in this interactive way, then maybe it means that black students who are passively listening aren't really learning. Teachers can capitalize on this dynamic by recognizing that they should expect — indeed, be desirous of — some "noisy" behavior from black kids. It means they diggin on what you sayin.

Just as blacks aren't passive communicators or listeners, they aren't passive learners. Another way to apply call-response to classroom teaching is to build on the principle of "each one teach one." Since blacks communicate best by interacting with one another, they can also *learn* best by interacting with one another. Thus students might be paired or grouped and allowed to talk and move about freely as they learn new information and practice educational skills. Further, students more advanced in a given class or subject can teach those less advanced. This will have a twofold benefit: the less advanced student improves his or her command of material in a nonthreatening and familiar form of educational exchange (learning from a peer who speaks his or her lingo); the more advanced student tightens up and enhances his or her knowledge of the same subject (you really find out how little you know about a subject when you have to teach it to someone else).

As another example, consider the feature of tonal semantics in Black English. Skillful teachers can employ it as a learning device. Using rhymes and rhyming patterns, an integral part of black communicative style, you can coordinate sound and learning activity. If you want students to remember a certain concept or principle, put it in the form of a rhyme. Combining call-response, tonal semantics, and black literature, one curriculum specialist, Winona Humphrey of the Highland Park Public Schools, demonstrated an exciting example of creative teaching. In a fifth grade class, she used Paul Laurence Dunbar's poem "A Black Love Song," which contains the response refrain, "jump back, honey, jump back," after each poetic line of the "call." First, the students recited the original version of the poem, the boys doing the calling, the girls the responding, then the girls calling, the boys responding. They then discussed the poem, its meaning, and the ways in which poems are similar to songs. In the next learning sequence, the students had a reading lesson based on the sounds of the poem. For example, Ms. Humphrey elicited from them several words that rhymed with *jump*, such as *hump, bump, pump, lump*. These words were then put on the blackboard as the "ump family," each defined, used in a sentence, and made available for language-experience reading lessons that were used periodically in the class. In still another learning sequence, Ms. Humphrey worked on creative written expression with the students, using the Dunbar poem as a kind of literary model. Each student wrote his or her own poetic lines and read them to the class, which formed itself into a kind of chorus, responding to each line with "jump back, honey, jump back." Finally, the class chose the best poetic lines and put them together into a class poem and tape-recorded the poem twice, first with half the class calling, the other half responding, then the second time around with callers and responders switching roles.

Now, admittedly, the kinds of activities described here will require skillful classroom management to be sure that the kids are T.C.B.-in and not S & J-in (shuckin and jivin). But the payoff will be well worth the extra effort.

In all school subjects and on all grade levels, then, we're talking about teaching students cognitive competencies, intellectual processes, and ways of seeking knowledge using whatever dialect the students possess. Especially in the early grades it is important to allow for free-flowing classroom interaction in the child's dialect. For one thing, the child will be experiencing enough difficulty adjusting to the institutional norm of the school itself. Then too there are important fundamental skills to be mastered at this stage of schooling. Because of misguided — or just plain poor — teaching and negative educational experiences, many black kids get stuck right here at this early level of school and never get beyond, say, reading at the third grade level. Now, the teacher does not have to be able to *speak* Black Dialect (though all the better if she or he can), but the teacher must be able to understand it, and, further, accept it as a legitimate form of human communication. The dialect thus becomes an educational code for transmitting knowledge. In this kind of classroom climate, students will not be stifled or inhibited in expressing themselves, nor will students be held back from advancement in educational skills until they learn all the "right" names and pronunciations for these skills. In point of fact, students of the New World (be they black or white) need to know that the label or word is not the same as the concept or process, that linguistic designations are arbitary, and that in all fields of human knowledge, language and terms for conceptual processes are subject to change (because of new discoveries in a field, or new ways of looking at accumulated human knowledge). As pointed out earlier, language change comes from people; it is not decreed from on high and there is nothing sacred about a given language.

◆

The educational literature and research on black students is shot through with statistical information on the reading disabilities of black youth. Though "reading problems of the disadvantaged" is now something of a cliché in educational circles, no one can deny the excruciating reality of the problem. Why are so many black students today coming out of school functionally illiterate? A major part of the answer relates to the blackening of American cities. As urban areas, and subsequently their schools, became blacker, whites fled to the suburbs. Though the teachers continued to work in city schools, they no longer lived in the same environment. (I remember in particular my days in a lower east side Detroit school in the late 1940s when several of my teachers lived within a ten-to-twelve block radius of our school. No more.) Thus a whole generation of whites grew up vastly alienated from black culture and black lifestyle. When members of this generation returned to these schools to teach, obviously they didn't know what was goin down with black language, never (or at least rarely) having heard it spoken.

Now picture the situation when black kids under this kind of teacher read a sentence like this: *The boy needs more money* (read as) *De boy need mo money*. The teacher's not sure such kids can read. But if she or he knew (as y'all now know, right?) that blacks delete final *r*'s, delete *s* in third person, and substitute *d* for initial *th* — if the teacher knew all this — then she or he would realize that the kid did not have a perceptual-vision problem nor a coding-decoding linguistic one — the child is simply rendering the sentence in good Black English. Or suppose the kids read: *They talkin bout it now* (for *They are talking about it now*). If the teacher is hip to Black English usage and phonology, she recognizes that the kids are simply reading the sentence in their own dialect. As a matter of fact, according to the research and conclusions of reading specialist Kenneth Goodman, the good readers always read by "translating" what's on the printed page into their own rap patterns. This translation process often produces homophones: *more* becomes *mow*, *during* becomes *doing* (because of loss of *r*), or *sing* becomes *sang* (as *thing* is pronounced *thang*). The point to be made here is that there are homophones in white middle-class dialect which readers have to learn to distinguish also, such as *their/there/they're* and *hear/here*. It is simply that Black English speakers have some additional and different sets of homophones. Again, it is vital that teachers know and understand the black sound.

Coupled with knowledge of the Black English system, as it relates to or conflicts with Standard White English written material, must be the teachers' commitment to the development and enhancement of their students' reading skills. That is, since reading is involved in every school subject, all teachers must learn to be teachers of reading. You can't just say, "Well, I teach science, reading's not my job," or "Why should I, a math teacher, have to be bothered with teaching reading?" If students are going to be able to master the subject matter of math or science, they have to be able to read the material. Even sewing and cooking teachers must grapple with this problem as they find students who can't read pattern instructions or cookbooks. Or, in driver's training, there are students who can't read the manual or pass the driver's license test.

Reading involves, of course, not simply "barking out the print," but the ability to decode, interpret, analyze, and see relationships derived from a given form of reading material. Though I recognize that not all teachers are trained to teach reading — I, for one, unfortunately was not — still a good deal can be gained by simply having oral in-class reading assignments. Here the teacher functions to guide, question, raise points and examples, as individual class members or the teacher read aloud a given lesson. Further, with emphasis on reading coming from all teachers in a school, pressure can be brought to bear for in-service programs to train all teachers to teach reading. I see this as an especially crucial and necessary move on the elementary school level.

On the secondary level, where the problem is more one of remedial than beginning reading, there are several kinds of educational kits, such as SRA (Science Research Associates), which contain material that is interesting to adolescents but carefully structured for reduced difficulty. By far, the most exciting and creative approach I have seen is the reading series called *Bridge,* which is geared toward adolescent black students reading at approximately 2.0 grade level. The stories in this reading program are either based on the black experience or adapted from black folklore (such as the Toasts "Shine" and "Stag-O-Lee"). The workbook exercises accompanying each story focus on reading, language, and communication skills. Tapping the orality of the black cultural experience and the interactive, tonal dynamics of black communication, stories and exercises are written in the verbal, imagistic style of good Black English rappers. The series combines this approach with tape-recorded readings of the stories and group exercises involving the students' audio-oral skills. The story "Shine," written in what the *Bridge* authors refer to as "Black Vernacular," is typical of the series.

SHINE

A Story in Black Vernacular

1.	*Titanic*	6.	stoker
2.	superbad	7.	survivors
3.	iceberg	8.	furnace
4.	unsinkable	9.	mercy
5.	shoveling	10.	squeezing

This story come from Black Folklore, you understand. Black folklore is stories that Black folk have told and sung for a whole lot of years. This here story is all about Shine, a strong Black man!

Maybe you heard other stories about Shine. Now come here and check out mine.

You ever hear of the Titanic? Yeah, that's right. It was one of them big ships. The kind they call a ocean liner. Now this here ship was the biggest and the baddest ship ever to sail the sea. You understand? It was suppose to be unsinkable. Wind, storm, iceberg — nothing could get next to it. It was a superbad ship, the meanest thing on the water. It could move like four Bloods in tennis shoes. It was out of sight!

But you know what? The very first time this here ship put out to sea, it got sunk. Can you get ready for that? On its first trip, this here bad, superbad ship got sunk. Now ain't that something.

Well anyway, this here bad, superbad ship went under. Word was, there was very few survivors. Just about everybody got drown. But quiet as it's kept, they say that the one dude who got away was a Blood. Yeah, can you get ready for that? He was a big, Black, strong Brother by the name of Shine.

Shine was a stoker on the Titanic. The Brother, he shovel coal into the ship furnace to make the engines go. Now dig. Check what went down on the day the Titanic sunk. Shine kept on going up to the captain of the ship. He kept on telling the captain that the ship was leaking.

Shine run on up to the captain and say, "Captain, Captain, I was down in the hole looking for something to eat. And you know what? The water rose above my feet."

The captain say, "Shine, Shine, boy, have no doubt. We got ninety-nine pumps to pump the water out. Now boy, get on back down in the hole and start shoveling some more coal."

Shine went on back down in the hole. He start to shoveling coal, singing, "Lord, Lord, please have mercy on my soul." As Shine was singing "Lord, Lord, please," the water, it rose above his knees.

Shine split back up on deck and say, "Captain, Captain, I was down in the hole. I was shoveling coal and singing 'Lord, Lord, please.' And you know what? The water, it rose above my knees."

The captain told Shine that all was cool. He say, "Shine, Shine, I done told you to have no doubt. Boy, we got ninety-nine pumps to pump that water out. Now get on back down in the hole and just keep shoveling coal."

Shine went on back down in the hole. He kept on shoveling coal. He stop to wipe the sweat off his face. That's when the water rose above his waist.

Shine run back up on deck. He say, "Captain, Captain, I was down in the hole just a shoveling coal. And when I stop to wipe the sweat off my face, the water, it rose above my waist!"

The captain say, "Shine, Shine, boy, now how many time do I have to tell you to have no doubt? If I done told you once, I done told you a hundred times. We got ninety-nine pumps to pump the water out. Now, boy, don't you trust your captain? I don't want to see you on deck again. You hear?"

Shine went on back down in the hole. He kept on shoveling coal. He start to eat a piece of bread. That's when the water rose above the Brother's head.

Shine split back up on deck. "Captain, Captain, you speak well, and your words, they sound true. But this time, Captain, your words they won't do. This here ship is sinking! Little fishes, big fishes, whales and sharks too, get out of my way, 'cause I'm coming through."

Shine yanked off his clothes in a flash. He jumped on in the water and started to splash.

The captain saw the water rise out of the hole and he start thinking, "That boy is right. This here ship is sinking." He call out to Shine, "Shine, Mr. Shine, please save me! I'll make you master of the sea!"

Shine say, "Master on land, master on sea. If you want to live, Captain, you better jump in here and swim like me."

The captain's wife ran out on deck in her nightgown, with her fine, fine self. She call out to Shine, "Shine, Shine, please save poor me! I'll give you more loving than you ever did see."

Shine say, "Loving ain't nothing but hugging and squeezing. Sometime it be tiring. Sometime it be pleasing. I can swim, but I ain't no fish. I like loving, but not like this."

An old fat banker come up on deck carrying his money bags. He called out to Shine, "Shine, Shine, please save me! I'll make you richer than any man could be."

Shine say, "Money's good on land, but it's weight in the sea. If you want to live, fatty, you better jump in here and swim like me."

Shine took one stroke and shot on off through the water like a motorboat. He met up with this here shark. The shark say, "Shine, Shine, you swim so fine. But if you miss one stroke, your butt is mine."

Shine say, "I swims the ocean. I swims the sea. There just ain't no shark that can outswim me." Shine outswimmed the shark.

"IF MEMORY SERVES ME CORRECTLY, YOU NEVER ASKED ME TO YOUR TABLE."

by permission of the artist

After a while, Shine met up with this here whale. The whale say, "I'm king of the ocean. I'm king of the sea."

Shine say, "You may be king of the ocean. And you just may be king of the sea, but you got to be about a swimming sucker to outswim me." Shine outswimmed the whale.

Now dig this. When the news reach land that the "Great *Titanic*" had sunk, Shine was down on the corner, half-way drunk.

With such an approach as revealed in "Shine," the question inevitably posed is: how effective can dialect readers be? Don't students need to learn how to read the functional dialect of newspapers and street signs, that is, the White English dialect which is the written medium of most everything students will need to read in order to survive in society? The answer is an obvious "yes." The solution, not always obvious to those who question the use of dialect readers, is to use black language as the medium of reading instruction whereby the teacher can teach comprehension ability and reading skills, all of which are intellectual competencies that can be taught in any dialect or language. Once students have mastered these basic skills in material both familiar and relevant to their own cultural experience, teachers can move on to expose them to materials written in other forms and reflecting other cultures. Here is where *Bridge* deserves special recognition for its innovative and effective approach. Though not a basal reading program, *Bridge* offers a solution to the reading–Black Dialect controversy that basal reading specialists could well adopt. Consider first that in some of the typical basal reading programs using Black Dialect the student is taken through two versions of the same simplistic Dick-and-Jane variety of stories. One story, for instance, will have the sentence "My momma work every day," and its counterpart will have the same sentence with merely a minute difference in surface representation, thus: "My momma works every day." Not only does it bore the poor kid to have to read the same story twice, his or her reading is not advanced, for the standard English versions introduce no new words or concepts to be mastered. By contrast, the *Bridge* series offers two other kinds of stories, a "transitional" set and a "standard English" set. Each set, however, represents different stories with different words and concepts to be mastered. Thus students gradually move from one stage to another. Further, if a given group of students reflects a varied range of reading abilities, the *Bridge* approach enables the teacher to have some students reading stories of one type, others reading another type.

◆

Finally, there is the emphasis on communicative competence. Communicative competence, quite simply, refers to the ability to communicate effectively. At this point, however, all simplicity ends. For to be able to speak or write with power is a very complex business, involving a universe of linguistic choices and alternatives. Such a speaker or writer must use language that is appropriate to the situation and the audience. He or she must be able to answer such questions as: who can say what to whom, under what conditions? who is my audience? what assumptions can I make about that audience? what are its interests, concerns, range of knowledge? in a given act of speaking or writing, what examples and details will fit best and where? I am here talking about aspects of communication such as content and message, style, choice of words, logical development, analysis and arrangement, originality of thought and expression, and so forth. Such are the real components of language power, and they cannot be measured or mastered by narrow conceptions of "correct grammar." While teachers frequently correct student language on the basis of such misguided conceptions, saying something correctly, and saying it well, are two entirely different Thangs.

Consider, for example, the following paragraph, which tries to pass itself off as an analysis of Imamu Amiri Baraka's play *Dutchman*. The assignment was to write a brief essay discussing the significance of the work and its suitability for the classroom.

> The play *Dutchman* is very intriguing. However, I would not use it in the classroom. The characters are also intriguing; yet the significance of the play is doubtful. High School students would certainly dislike it. Furthermore, though intriguing I can't accept the idea that a man would be murdered in front of a whole group of people. This novel is too far removed from reality, and thus I would not use it in the classroom.

Would you believe this was written by a white suburban college junior who was preparing to teach high school English (where he presumably *is* teaching now)? I told this student, as kindly as I could, that his "essay" was weak in content and repetitious, and that it did not demonstrate command of the literary critical tools that teachers of literature are supposed to possess, *plus it didn't really say nothing*! He lambasted me with "What's wrong with it? The spelling's correct, it's punctuated properly, and the subjects and verbs agree. You're just prejudiced, that's all!" I forgave him because he too is a product of the "national mania for correctness."

As another example, consider a paper written by a black ninth grader whose teacher gave it a "B" grade with only a few grammatical points corrected, and no other comments of analysis or suggestions for improvement. Though this theme reflects nothing in the way of distinct Black English forms, it certainly does not measure up to standards of communicative competence that I would set for a ninth grade class, black or white. Here is the theme, numbered and italicized for comments, showing how I would have corrected the paper. The subject was: If everybody knew what war was like, would we still have war?

No! Some people just don't understand the *hardship* of (1) a war. *Some* say lets keep fighting and we still are fighting. (2) *More people are being killed and the poor are starving to death.* (3) To me war is a terrible thing to happen in any country. *The causes of a war maybe very simple, one side* will disagree on a sub- (4) ject that is brought up. Like the poor should have money or better conditions to live in. The people should put in money for the poor. *The other side* may not agree. (5) Instead they think *the government should do the work. This may* (6)(7) *cause a war. Little things* like this and more can destroy the (8) world.

1. What kind or type of hardship?
2. "Some say . . ." Who is "some"?
3. "More people are being killed . . ." This should follow the next statement because it tells why war is a terrible thing.
4. "The causes of a war . . ." Explain how this fits here because it sounds to me like it's starting up on another subject.
5. Exactly who are the two sides you're talking about here? What category of people? Name them and tell something about them.
6. ". . . the government . . ." Aren't the people the government? What difference do you see between the people and the government?
7. Give me an example showing when and how such a disagreement leads to war.
8. "Little things . . ." Little??????? If it's gon destroy the world, it ain "little."

The following two papers on the theme of loneliness were done by black seventh grade students, one showing distinct Black English forms, the other relatively devoid of Black English.

THEME I

Loneliness is when you are in a house all alone and wish someone was there with you. When you are with a lot of people and they act like you aren't even there. When you start thinking of something and it seems like you are in another world and when you come back into the world people act like you don't exist. Being lonely is being rejected, ignored, or left out of things. Loneliness is when you wish someone special is with you that can not be and you think they forgot you. And all the time they wish the same about you. Loneliness is when you think nobody cares about you, but somewhere, someplace, someone is always thinking of you so don't ever think you are alone.

THEME II

Loneliness is when a person is sad or don't have no one to talk to. It means when a person tries to talk to somebody and that person don't understand. I be lonely all the time. It's a hurtin feeling to be lonely. It hurts a lot to be lonely.

I'm a lonely person. I'm the only one in my family. Sometimes I just sit and watch T V and play records. Sometimes I go upstairs in my bedroom and cry because I'm lonely. I have no one to talk to. No one understands me.

Now, it ain no question in my mind that the "blacker" theme reflects the greater degree of communicative competence. Its short, syntactic units more effectively convey the mood of a lonely individual, and the more colloquial idiom reflects a truer sense of the writer's feelings. All of this is in contrast to the rather artificial, formalized language and stilted tone of Theme I, which sounds like a speech memorized from a book in the public library.

Related to this matter of communicative competence in writing is another kind of necessary ability which involves both reading and writing skills. I have in mind here the language and structure of what I call "social negotiation forms" — marks of this highly bureaucratic society we live in, such as forms for health insurance, job applications, voter registration, social security, driver's license applications, college entrance forms, Medicare applications, and so forth. Such forms require an ability not only to read and decode the information asked for, but the ability to respond with the appropriate and appropriately worded information. On the secondary level, especially, teachers could devote some time to teaching students how to negotiate and interpret these forms and their accompanying bureaucratic structures because much of survival in contemporary America is dependent upon such competence.

While I have thus far concentrated on written communication, the competence being referred to here is obviously not limited to writing. In fact, in a lifetime, we will all do more speaking than writing, which would suggest that a good deal more classroom time should be spent on developing oral communication skills. I am not talking about just the language arts, but science, math, social studies, and all school subjects. Examples of such skills are: ability to answer and ask questions on a given subject; ability to express verbally knowledge of a certain principle or procedure; ability to explain how something works; ability to talk to a stranger without being nervous; ability to conduct oneself appropriately in a job interview (how much to talk, what kinds of responses are appropriate, maybe even knowing when to sit down); ability to give and interpret directions; ability to listen, not only for "courtesy" but to understand what's been said; ability to persuade another person to one's point of view; knowing what forms of address are appropriate.

It is a matter of oral communicative competence to know, for instance, that if someone says, "May I ask who's calling, please?" you can't answer simply with "yes." In fact, this "question" is not really a question at all, but a polite, standard English language convention that is actually a command. It means: tell me your name. I have encountered black students who gave only "yes" as the response to this question, then paused, waiting for the voice on the other end of the telephone to speak further (perhaps to ask, "What is your name?"). On the opposite side of the coin, there are whites who frequently use "uh," or lengthy pauses, when trying to get their thoughts together. This may be interpreted — in fact, blacks do interpret this — as a sign of slow-wittedness and ignorance of the topic being discussed. The black hesitation strategy, which I think is more functional, is to repeat a previous phrase or recycle back to the beginning of the statement.

Finally, students need communicative competence in the use and understanding of audio-oral-visual channels, that is, radio, television, film, videotape. Students should not only learn how to be encoders of such processes, but, more importantly, how to be efficient decoders. Being constantly bombarded with persuasive advertising devices and manipulation techniques in multimedia America, people need plenty of help in developing critical skills to examine these media. They should be taught, for instance, how visual arrangement, selection of material, style of presentation, and the like, all help to color our perceptions of reality and convey hidden messages. (For example, until recently, black ad models, even in black magazines, were all high-yellows with straight hair. In point of fact, the media does a job on all consumers: women are typically portrayed as Edith Bunker types, old people become gardening putterers with regularity problems, and men henpecked fools or macho beer-guzzlers.) Thus teachers must help students — who are consumers as well as adults-in-the-making — evaluate and develop standards of excellence for television programs and films. And beyond that, they should be taught the political mechanisms of recourse to make sure their voice and choices can be heard — for instance, Federal Communications Commission licensing regulations.

Lest there be some misunderstanding bout where uhm comin from here, let me run it down again. Communicative compe tence, in all the communication skills areas, has to do with linguistic and semantic appropriateness, and with the ability to employ rhetorical strategies to create a desired mood or effect in your audience and to move that audience in the direction you desire. Linguistic versatility and rhetorical competence of this caliber cannot be equated with the usual overly simplified conception of standard English as having to do with *s*'s, *ed*'s, and correct spelling. While I'm talking about something much deeper and more expansive than these superfluous norms, I shonuff ain talkin bout that off-the-deep-end permissiveness of letting the kids get away with anything! Too much of that already goes down in black education. Teachers must set standards of performance and criteria of excellence for black students and then use all their concern, warmth, and pedagogical energies to drive these students to achieve these standards. Dig on this: it is a fundamental communications principle that if you know what you doin, both the pen and the voice can be mightier than the Molotov cocktail. Can I get a witness?

◆

I have suggested that teachers should be bout the serious business of educating young black minds to deal with (and, if necessary, on) a society of power politics and incredible complexity. That dealing will require academic skills and intellectual competencies such as I have touched upon here. If schools are to be the leaders that they should be, rather than the followers that they have been, the task has to begin with the individual teacher in his or her individual setting. The teacher can definitely be an agent of social change. But it is not enough to work in the classroom alone. That is a necessary but not sufficient task. Inasmuch as teachers form part of the institutional fabric of the school, they help to shape the character and style of that institution. Certainly there are institutional forces that impinge upon the teachers themselves — such as administrative and state-wide accountability systems — but teachers can, in fact, turn a school completely around. For instance, the force of their collective energy has made teacher unions very powerful in some school districts. All of this is by way of stressing that teachers are *not* powerless cogs in a bureaucratic institutional machine. Not only do teachers themselves affect the educational environment right in their own classrooms, they have the capability of modifying the total educational climate in a given school, and even beyond that, in a given school district. There are, then, matters of educational policy that teachers can and should be shaping.

◆

One of the most far-reaching educational changes in recent years has been the restructuring of the curriculum to include black (and other ethnic) studies in the curriculum. This movement was especially strong in schools having predominately black, Latino, Asian, and Native American students. To limit multi-ethnic studies to such students is a short-sighted move on two counts. First, such students need to study white mainstream culture as well as their own to prevent their obtaining a distorted picture of the real world of the U.S.A. On the opposite side, white mainstream students need to know about nonmainstream cultures to prevent a similar distortion. (In fact, they very badly need black and other ethnic studies since whites are a numerical minority in the world.) The point is that as a matter of curriculum design and policy, all school districts should reflect America's diverse cultural heritage and the multicultural, multilinguistic character of our world. This goes for both nonwhite and white students. Why? Because, as the late and great Dr. Martin Luther King, Jr., said, we must all learn to live together or we shall all die together. The terms, conditions, and possibilities of our survival are right now being worked out in places like Angola, the Arab countries, South Africa, Portugal, China, and so on.

Note that I am not talking here about black studies purely for the sake of black pride or as cultural enrichment for white folks. There are, rather, some fundamental cultural and linguistic differences that must be understood if blacks and whites are to be able to communicate and exist in America. Throughout this book I have pointed out a number of cross-cultural communication interferences. I *strongly* recommend that white students learn the fundamentals of black communication. Such a learning experience, if properly organized, will not only teach them to be able to understand and communicate with blacks, but in the process they will be turned on to other linguistic-cultural minorities within America. Such a perspective will go a long way toward retarding linguistic-cultural chauvinism, which is surely the greatest impediment to world citizenship.

But to get back on the case of black education. The American school does not place nearly enough emphasis on other languages and cultures of the world. Consequently, black (and white) students have neither understanding nor respect for those who don't talk as they do. The French language and its people, though "witty and lyrical," are "quaint and archaic"; the

Germans, "guttural and crude"; Latin a "dead" but "prestigious" language, taken by the "smart" kids. The Chinese talk, as well as look, "funny," and Spanish "don't count" since only "dirty Mexicans" speak it. This myopic perception has been strikingly brought home in the continuing oil crisis, where black (as well as white) students have been heard to say that "those dirty Arabs better give us *our* oil" (emphasis mine). Thus black students, because they participate in mainstream culture — albeit based outside of it — share in its prejudices. In addition to the examples already given, this can be witnessed by the many black students who root for the white cowboys in "cowboy-Indian" movies. Multicultural education in black schools would enlarge the black experience to include the development of a humanistic understanding of those who are different from blacks. Further, it would broaden black students' political perception of those who are different in tongue, but similar in the oppression they have experienced.

Generally, the framers of the recent multicultural approach focus on history, literature, folklore, and culture as the content of the curriculum. They tend to forget the most fundamental fact of a people's culture: their language. Thus language study should be an integral dimension of the multicultural curriculum design in black schools.

◆

When is the last time you went to a cobbler? Well, that's one of the test words on the Peabody Picture Vocabulary Test administered to elementary school children. As a matter of traditional educational policy, a number of tests are administered and, unfortunately, relied upon in the public schools. Some of the tests, well-known to teachers, are the Peabody Picture Vocabulary; Iowa Basic Skills; Wechsler Intelligence; California Mental Maturities; Stanford Achievement, and so on, ad nauseam. It would behoove teachers to find out as much as possible about the contradictions and inadequacies of standardized tests and then devise their own measures of student performance and ability, based on *their* interaction and experience with their students.

At least three points should be noted about standardized tests.

1. They do not, *cannot*, measure intelligence, that is, "the broad range of experience encompassed by all intellectual functions." According to psychologist Dean Robert Green, "the test is no more than a measure of some of one's past experience at the time it is taken. The score reflects the opportunities and the disadvantages that have been a part of a person's past . . . IQ, or intelligence quotient, [is] simply . . . a numerical score earned on a test."

2. Not only are the tests biased against the experiences of minority people, they are also biased against the poor, of whatever hue. For example, a typical IQ test question for seven- and eight-year-olds is the following: "You are inside a large airport when you find a letter, already sealed and addressed with a stamp on it. You a) put the letter in a nearby mailbox; b) give the letter to a man in a uniform standing behind a desk; c) open the envelope to see if there is money inside." The student who answers this question gets three points for answer "a," two points for answer "b," and no points for answer "c." Now, anybody who's poor, providing they would even be in an airport in the first place, *has* to choose "c." Thus the test is only assessing how well a child subscribes to middle-class values. Dr. Green says this is because IQ tests are constructed by "middle and upper-income Ph.D's . . . with culturally narrow life experiences."

3. Test scores cannot predict the future of any individual test-taker, black or white. That is, a student may score low on tests in elementary school and then sail through high school with all A's. Or an entering law student may score low on the Law School Aptitude Test and then be in the top 10 percent of her class. Such examples are not hypothetical, but are based on actual experiences of students trying to negotiate the American educational system. Perhaps the classic case is that of Dr. Robert Williams, a well-known black psychologist and one of the founders of the Association of Black Psychologists. When he was fifteen years old, he scored 82 on an IQ test, just missing being placed in a special education track by three points. Dr. Williams's high school counselor advised him to take up masonry, but instead he went on to earn three degrees: a B.A., an M.A., and a Ph.D.

Because of the demonstrated cultural and linguistic biases of standardized tests, all tools of national educational assessment should be carefully screened and even then only used with the greatest amount of caution and discretion. These tests completely disregard the experience and culture of minority persons. Such tests after all, which are invalid in the first place, serve only to track ("trap" is a better word for it) students forever into a fixed slot in the school and later in the social world. I would here recommend that teachers follow the lead of a number of black and other concerned professionals who have called for a national moratorium on all testing until valid measurements are devised and policies instituted to prevent misuse of tests. For example, here is the statement adopted by the Association of Black Psychologists:

> The Association of Black Psychologists fully supports those parents who have chosen to defend their rights by refusing to allow their children and themselves to be subjected to achievement, intelligence, aptitude and performance tests which have been used to a) label Black people as uneducable; b) place Black children in 'special' classes and schools; c) perpetuate inferior education in Blacks; d) assign Black children to educational tracks; e) deny Black students higher educational opportunities; and f) destroy positive growth and development of Black people.

Another professional organization which supports this position and philosophy is the National Education Association. This group has called for a ten-year moratorium on the National Teacher's Examination on the grounds that the exam is culturally biased against minorities and permits itself to be misused in the selection of teachers.

Two prominent leaders who have called for an end to obligatory IQ testing are Benjamin Fine, former education editor for the *New York Times,* and Paul Houts, editor of *The National Elementary Principal.*

While the whole testing controversy is a complex issue, involving questions of methodology, sampling, and statistical apparatus, in another sense it's very simple. The tests exist because of politics and the multimillion-dollar testing industry, monopolistically controlled by the Educational Testing Service. Chuck Stone, former director of minority affairs for ETS, calls it the "godfather" of the corporate "testing Mafia."

◆

The whole issue of testing extends beyond educational institutions into all sectors of American life. Nearly all jobs require some form of testing — police and fire departments, clerical jobs, all civil service jobs, street sweeping, and so forth. These tests too are biased against minority people. But that's not surprising since the same industry produces the employment tests too. Not only are these tests culturally and linguistically biased, most do not even remotely measure skills related to the job. In a major breakthrough in this area, the U.S. Supreme Court ruled in a 1971 decision that employment tests must be job-related. Yet, according to Chuck Stone, "80 percent of all employment tests, especially those in public employment, have no relevance to the particular job responsibilities. Public agencies and private corporations are, in effect, violating Federal law and a Supreme Court decision."

Since teachers are not only educators but members of the citizenry, they should take the lead in helping to establish national public policies regarding both testing and language. The moratorium on tests could, for instance, be extended into public sectors of American life. Employers could be pressured to hire speakers of Black English since the dialect is no indicator of intelligence nor a hindrance to job capability. (There is evidence that some employers have already deduced this for themselves: many Bell telephone operators in urban areas are clearly identifiable as black.) Teachers could also push for educational resolutions and policy statements reaffirming the "students' right to their own language." The Conference on College Composition and Communication, a group of educators concerned with English and communication instruction in the first two years of college, recently adopted such a policy statement at its national session. Finally, an ultimate goal would be for teachers to struggle for a national public policy on language which would reassert the legitimacy of languages other than English, and American dialects other than standard. If these goals seem far-fetched, teachers have only to reflect on the tremendous power potential of their teacher unions and professional educational organizations — such structures could form the massive political units needed to extend the concept of linguistic-cultural diversity and legitimacy beyond the classroom.

Admittedly, T.C.B.-in in the constellation of tasks outside the safe confines of the classroom is a hard task. Certainly, it is easier to work on fitting people into the mainstream than to try to change the *course* of the stream. Yet the lesson of contemporary history is that the people didn't fit, and the course of the stream began to change anyway. After the various calls to power of blacks and other oppressed minorities, this country will never be the same again. (Of course, there is always the very frightening possibility that it will become worse. But one thing is certain: it will never be the same.) As agents of change, teachers can work to help mold American society into a humane and pluralistic social universe. Effectuating changes in language attitudes and policies, in the classroom and beyond, is a major step in this direction. What teachers would be doing, then, amounts to a social and political act, which, like charity, begins at home. Can I get a witness?

Afterword

ALTHOUGH I GREW UP speaking Black English, I did not become conscious of the disparity between my native tongue and the language of America's majority culture until I was forced to take a speech correction class to qualify for a teaching certificate in the State of Michigan. While that memory lingered throughout my years of teaching high-school English and Latin, it was the clarion call of the Black Power Movement of the 1960s that propelled me to view my personal encounter with linguistic imperialism as a lesson in Black Life and, finally, to articulate that vision in *Talkin and Testifyin*.

To understand how this came to pass, reflect on the events of the past generation, circa 1955, when Rosa Parks' historic refusal to give up her seat to Whites and move to the back of the bus charted a new course for Black-White relations in our time. For Black America, struggling to free itself not only of debilitating political and economic forces but also of the cultural and linguistic tyranny of Americanism, the call for Black Power was a bold call for new directions and strategies. The hope of a people struggling for community and identity was that research and study of Blackness would link AfroAmerica to Africa, forever lay to rest notions of Black inferiority, and lead to liberation on all levels of Black Life.

Moved by this spirit, *Talkin and Testifyin* began to take shape. Conceived from the dual vantage point of my baptism in the linguistic fire of Black Folk and my Eurocentric training in research and analysis, the book was intended to celebrate the community which gave me birth and to educate those in that community charged with molding the next generation. It was intended to be entertaining but scholarly, technical yet readable. It would seek to blend the intellectual tradition of DuBois, Woodson, and Turner with the wisdom and wit of testifiers and toast-tellers. Amidst the voluminous works on Black American speech by Whites since the 1960s, the book would stand alone as a major contribution to the subject by a *Black* scholar.

At the time of its publication in 1977, I anticipated that most readers of *Talkin and Testifyin* would be teachers and others involved in the educational enterprise. However, within a week after the book was put on sale, I found myself, to my astonishment, discussing the language of Black America on NBC's *Today* program! This turned out to be only the first of a succession of national and local media appearances and interviews—Phil Donahue, Dick Cavett, *People* magazine, *The New York Times*, and so on. From that point on, I became "the author."

Even more unexpected was my central role in what became internationally known as the Ann Arbor "Black English Case." Shortly after the book was published, Detroit attorney Kenneth Lewis, in a rare moment of television watching, heard me discussing the linguistic tyranny of American education and its negative effects on Black students. Although he and Attorney Gabe Kaimowitz, both at that time with Michigan Legal Services, had filed suit against the Ann Arbor School District for failing to educate some of its Black students, the language aspect had seemed to offer the least fruitful possibility for litigation until that propitious media appearance of "the author." From then until July 12, 1979, when Federal Judge Charles Joiner issued a ruling in favor of the children, I served as consultant and chief expert witness on an advocacy team for fifteen of the Black children attending the Martin Luther King Junior Elementary School in Ann Arbor, Michigan. Our work in *King* v. *Ann Arbor* focused on what had been the central educational thesis of *Talkin and Testifyin*: schools must teach speakers of Black English literacy in the language of the school, the professions, and the marketplace, while simultaneously recognizing and "taking into account"—as Judge Joiner would later put it in his lengthy opinion—the legitimacy of the language of Black America.*

Talkin and Testifyin and its role in *King* v. *Ann Arbor* gave broader public exposure to the issue of the legitimacy of Black American speech, not only in the United States but in Europe, Africa, and the Caribbean. A subject which before had only been discussed in ivied halls became of intense interest to institutions and community organizations, here and abroad, which solicited not only White scholars but the emerging cadre of Black linguists to research, speak, and write on Black English. For instance, in my case alone, over 350 institutions have invited "the author" to "talk and testify." It is rare that the labors of a scholar toiling in the vineyards of social change can bear such fruit—especially in her lifetime. In thus taking the subject of Black Language off the library shelves and out of ivory and ebony towers into the public domain, this celebration of Black Language has influenced popular discussion and debate about Black English and the role of language in the formation of positive identity and self-esteem.

Geneva Smitherman
September, 1985

*For more on the court case, see Geneva Smitherman, ed., *Black English and the Education of Black Children and Youth* (Wayne State University Center for Black Studies, 1981).

Appendix A

Some Well-Known Black Proverbs and Sayings

1. You never miss yo water till yo well run dry.

2. Grits ain't groceries, eggs ain't poultry, and Mona Lisa was a man. (I must be telling the truth since grits *are* groceries, eggs *are* poultry and Mona Lisa sure wasn't a man!)

3. You ain't got a pot to piss in or a window to throw it out of. (you are in poor financial straits)

4. If I'm lying, I'm flying. (proving truth: I must not be lying, if I were, I'd be flying)

5. You so dumb you can't throw rain water out of a boot, and the directions say how.

6. The blacker the berry, the sweeter the juice. (he or she must be fine, he or she is so ripe and sweet; also suggestive of sexuality and sensual power)

7. What goes around comes around. (you reap what you sow)

8. If I tell you a hen dip snuff, look under its wing and find a whole box. (proving truth and claim of infallibility by speaker)

9. Study long, you study wrong. (listen to first impulses, because lengthy deliberations are liable to be inaccurate)

10. The eagle flies on Friday. (eagle, symbolizing money; statement commemorates payday)

11. Let the door hit you where the good Lord split you. (nasty command to leave, euphemism of "split you" avoiding profanity)

12. A hard head make a soft behind. (being stubborn, refusing to listen can make you pay a stiff price)

13. If you make yo bed hard, you gon have to lie in it.

14. It was so quiet you could hear a rat piss on cotton.

15. Pretty is as pretty does. (you are known by your actions)

16. Action speak louder than words. (same as above, this proverb is more common among younger blacks today)

17. You don't believe fat meat is greasy. (signifyin on fools who insist on adhering to certain beliefs or opinions in the face of logical evidence to the contrary)

18. Tight as Dick's hatband. (financially stingy, refusing to share or give)

For an outstanding collection and analysis of proverbs, see Jack L. Daniel, "Towards an Ethnography of Afro American Proverbial Usage," *Black Lines*, Winter 1972, pp. 3–12.

Appendix B

*Get Down Exercises on Black English
Sounds and Structure*

To "get down" is to do something vigorously, such as dance, sing, work, talk, or do exercises like these. The following should help you to "check yo'self" to see if you have an understanding of the sounds and grammatical patterns of Black Dialect.

I. Get Down on *Pronunciation*. Pronounce the words below in correct Black English. Indicate the rule from Chapter Two that governs the pronunciation. Get down!

   1. tooth
   2. sore
   3. desks
   4. this
   5. dead
   6. self
   7. insurance
   8. king
   9. rest
   10. torc

II. Get Down on *be/non-be*. Supply the correct form of *be, non-be,* or *do + be*. Indicate *non-be* with the symbol ⌀.

   1. The principal _____ in his office now.
   2. He alway _____ messing with me.
   3. They ain't left, _____ they?
   4. Where _____ they _____ _____ at every day?

5. Speaker A: He _____ blind, but now he see.

Speaker B: That's okay, he _____ blind again tomorrow when it come to her.

III. Get Down on *been*. Convert White English forms into the correct Black English equivalents. Change only the underlined phrases. Caution: Some forms might not need to be changed.

1. If you *had been* there, you would really have seen something.

2. Wow! She *has been gone a long time*.

3. Her folks *was* down South last year.

4. Tony *has been looking* at her an hour.

5. If you *haven't been telling* the truth, don't even speak to me anymore.

IV. Get Down on *done*. Using the rules for *done*, write the appropriate Black English sentence for each speaker, according to the description given.

1. Speaker A is telling Speaker B that the refrigerator has gone on the blink. A says: _____.

B replies that the refrigerator will be repaired before A even gets home from work the next day. B says: _____.

2. Speaker A is reprimanding Speaker B about incomplete class work and says, "You have done no work today at all." Speaker B contradicts with emphasis. B says: _____.

3. Speaker A is trying to convince Speaker B that B's Afro comb is nowhere to be found. A says: _____.

Speaker B proceeds to tell A all the places that A has not looked. B says: _____.

4. In the following dialogue, both speakers are using *incorrect* Black English forms of *done* in combination with another verb. Change the speakers' usage to correct Black English.

Speaker A: "I did done that twenty-five time."

Speaker B: "Quit lyin! If you had done done that twenty-five time, it wouldn't still be looking like that."

5. Speaker A tells Speaker B about somebody who has not been seen in five years. A says: _____.

B has faith that the person in question will contact them soon before they even know it. B says: _____.

V. Get Down on Marking Structure by Context. Express the following sentences in correct Black English.

1. My mother looks young.

2. He failed me last semester.

3. Mr. Smith's dog was killed.

4. Scientists are inventing many things.

5. That same boy gets kicked out of school every day.

VI. Get Down on Noun and Pronoun Forms, Adverbs and Negatives. Decide if the statements are correct or incorrect according to rules for Black English structure. Correct those that are incorrect.

1. Only a few people want nice things these days.

2. There's five kids in my family.

3. Dis dude, see, he was jes waitin round

4. Duh ownuh, he always leave early.

5. Here go duh pencil I los.

6. Is there a new one?

7. Look lak everybody and their momma was dere.

8. Now it's jes duh two of us — he and I.

9. Everybody wants dis car

10. Nobody wants dis car.

KEY TO GET DOWN EXERCISES

I. *PRONUNCIATION*
1. toof — rule 2, page 17
2. so — rule 3, page 17
3. desses — rule 5, page 18
4. dis — rule 1, page 17
5. dea — rule 5, page 18
6. sef — rule 4, page 17
7. in-SHO-ance — rules 3 and 8, pages 17–18
8. kang — rule 6, page 18

9. res — rule 5, page 18
10. toe — rule 3, page 17

II. *BE/NON-BE*
    1. ∅
    2. be
    3. is
    4. do . . . be
    5. was; be

III. *BEEN*
    1. If you been there . . .
    2. Wow! She BEEN gone!
    3. no change, correct Black English as is.
    4. Tony been lookin . . .
    5. . . . you ain been tellin . . .

IV. *DONE*
    1. A: Duh frigerator *done broke.*
       B: It *be done got fix* foe you git home from work tomorrow.
    2. B: I *DID do* my work today!
    3. A: Yo Afro comb *done been los* somewhere round here.
       B: You jes *ain done look* for it everywhere (or: You jes *done haf look* for it).
    4. A: I *done did* that . . .
       B: . . . If you *done done* that . . .
    5. A: I *ain seen* _____ in five year.
       B: _____ *be done show* up here foe you know it.

V. *CONTEXT*
    1. My momma look young.
    2. He fail me las semester.
    3. Mr. Smif dog was kill.
    4. Scientist inventin many thang.
    5. Dat same boy git kick out of school eveyday.

VI. *NOUN/PRONOUNS, ADVERBS AND NEGATIVES*
    1. Incorrect. Doan but a few peoples want nice thang dese day.
    2. Incorrect. It's five kid in my family.
    3. Correct.
    4. Incorrect. Duh ownuh, he alway leave early.
    5. Correct.
    6. Incorrect. Is it a new one?
    7. Incorrect. Look lak everybody and they momma was dere.
    8. Incorrect. Now it's jes duh two of us — him and me.
    9. Incorrect. Eveybody want dis car.
    10. Incorrect. Doan nobody want dis car (or: Ain nobody want dis car).

Appendix C

Black Semantics — A Selected Glossary

I. Terms for Blacks (used only by blacks)

Afro-American, pages 42–43, 62.*

black, pages 35–43, 62.

blood, highly positive term, for males and females; obvious reference to genetic kinship of blacks who all share the same racial blood line.

boojy, an adjective, derived from *bourgeoisie*, referring to elitist blacks whose money and position make them think they're white

boot, neutral to positive term, depending on user; obvious reference to blackness of boots; possible allusion, via whites, to "bootblack," since shoeshine "boys" stereotypically are blacks.

bright, adjective designating a light-skinned black person; a more neutral term than *high-yelluh*, but still with some shading of ambivalence.

color struck, adjective denoting one who prefers light-skinned blacks; also high-yellows "stuck" on themselves because of their color.

elites, pronounced *e-lights*, same meaning as *boojy*.

hankerchief head, same as *Tom*.

head, neutral term, possibly derived from reference to hair, typically of major importance to blacks.

jitterbug, a superhip, streetified black, often used with just a touch of scorn; originally from a fast dance done in the thirties.

member, club member, positive term, stressing racial bond and togetherness.

Negro, pages 35–43.

nigger, pages 36, 62.

*Page numbers refer to terms explained elsewhere in the book.

oreo, like the cookie, black on the outside, white on the inside; a more modern version of a Tom.

Sam, negative term, possibly from Sambo in *Little Black Sambo*.

Sapphire, page 68.

Shine, negative term, possible racial designation due to shiny appearance of ebony black skin. The central protagonist of the Toast "Shine and the Sinking of the Titanic" is given this name.

Sister, Brother, Soul Brother, page 57.

spliv, splib, spli, a positive to neutral term for males and females; shonuff black speakers would not distinctly articulate either of the final consonant sounds.

spook, historically a racial epithet used by whites and assigned positive to neutral value by blacks.

that's mighty white of you, sarcastic expression used to refer to patronizing action characterized by putting on airs; sometimes used in pure jest.

Tom, Dr. Thomas, Uncle Thomas, Aunt Thomasina, Aunt Jane, highly negative references to black male and female sell-outs, those abandoning black culture for whiteness, as well as those who shuffle before The Man. The Tom combinations are all obvious references to Harriet Beecher Stowe's character in *Uncle Tom's Cabin*. A *Dr. Tom* is a cap on educated Uncle Toms. *Aunt* and *Uncle* are a throwback to the customary Southern white practice of addressing all blacks as *aunt or aunty and uncle*, a practice always resented by black people though few revealed it openly.

yellow, high-yellow, pronounced in soul talk as *yelluh*; refers to very light-skinned blacks; ambivalent term. Since whiteness was valued, those closest to white were viewed in a somewhat positive sense; on the other hand, they were also envied and distrusted since their skin color suggested an uncomfortably close association to the "enemy"; further, in black folklore, there are many stories suggesting that high-yelluhs are evil devils; unattractive high-yelluhs are often described as a "whole lotta yelluh wasted."

II. Terms for Whites

blue-eyed soul, extension of soul brother concept to include together whites; see page 57.

Charley, Charles, Chuck, derogatory references to white male.

cracker, negative term for whites, especially those who are extremely racist; possibly derived from association with whiteness of soda crackers, but also possibly linked to whites of certain regions of Georgia who survived off a diet of cracked corn, and thus were called (by whites themselves) "crackers."

devil, very negative term for whites, equating them with sinister quality of Satan; possibly from the Black Muslim belief that evil was introduced into black paradise through the unwise creation of the black scientist, Yakub, who took his knowledge and scientific inventive curiosity too far and produced a monster devil — the white man.*

gray, by now a fairly neutral term; possible origin from association with whiteness of gray hair; also possibly from gray of Confederacy; if so, originally must have referred to racist, supremacist whites.

honky, derisive term for whites, introduced in recent times by black activists Rap Brown and Stokely Carmichael; original term, *hunky*, seems to have come from whites, who used it to refer derisively to Hungarians; by association, blacks came to use it to refer to any "broken English"–speaking foreign whites and then to all whites; note black phonological shift in pronunciation, producing *honky*, similar to black pronunciation of *hunk*, which would be *honk*, and *hungry*, which would be *hongry*; obviously, *Hungary* is *Hongary*.

Miss Ann, page 68.

ofay, fay, now neutral, originally negative, see p. 47.

patty, paddy, by now a fairly neutral reference to whites, origin unknown: in true Black English pronunciation, /d/ and /t/ sounds can be used interchangeably.

peckerwood, peck, wood, Southern-derived term, derisively referring to poor whites; reference possibly to prevalence of red-colored birds in the South, known as "woodpeckers," which blacks associated with whites (due to redness of skin). Nowadays used to refer negatively to any whites, rich or poor.

pink toes, page 68.

The Man, page 68.

whitey, negative term for whites, now on its way to becoming neutralized; origin obvious.

III. Terms Blacks Find Offensive, but Often Used by Whites

boy. Resentment against *boy* is so extreme among black males that they even recoil at its apparently innocent use, as in the case of the white gym

---

*For a complete treatment of the Black Muslims from an inside perspective, see E. U. Essien-Udom, *Black Nationalism*, New York: Dell Publishing Co., 1964. The Yakub story is given in detail on pp. 145–151.

teacher who thought he was paying the highest compliment to the black basketball star when he shouted: "Attaboy! Way to go!"

coloreds or blackie, no explanation needed.

first names to address blacks when the white person is not acquainted with them on a friendly, intimate basis. By contrast, in today's white corporate world, first name usage upon immediately being introduced to another corporate white is an immediate acknowledgment that the individual is in the club of power elites. This cross-cultural communication problem created adjustment difficulties for black "firsts" in executive positions in equal opportunity employment institutions: "If all the white execs are addressing each other by first name, does it not appear absurd for me, the lone black exec, to insist upon last name, but then does the 'Bob' that is addressed to me mean the same as the 'Bob' addressed to the white Robert, or is this that old-timey racist stuff of not giving blacks respect by reducing them to a familiar, first-name entity?"

gal, used by white males to refer to females, black or white; black women take offense at this term, as a possible throwback to white denial of black adult womanhood, and see it as nearly synonymous with *girl.* By contrast, older white women seem not to take offense when white males refer to them as *gal;* younger white women or those more feminism-oriented appear uncomfortable with the term.

girl, especially when used to refer to older black women; black domestics, regardless of age, are characteristically referred to by white women as "my girl."

nigger, surely obvious, but what may not be so obvious is black people's resentment of various derivatives, such as *nigger-toes,* referring to type of nut; also "playful" rhymes, such as "eenie, meenie, minie, moe/catch a nigger by his toe/if he hollers, let him go/eenie, meenie, minie, moe." (This rhyme has a pre–Civil War runaway slave origin.)

punk, in Black Semantics, a homosexual, though the white usage may merely indicate a man who is engaging in behavior the speaker dislikes intensely, as in "Those young, tough punks." (Other Black Semantic synonyms for homosexual include: *sissy, sweet, homo* for the male homosexuals, and *bulldagger* for lesbians.)

you people, you folks (this one should need no explanation at this late date in the history of race relations).

you're good as we are, or similar versions, such as "why, there's no difference between us." Blacks view such a lame *apologia pro vita sua* as a guilt-ridden attempt at talking away racial differences and white racism.

IV. Terms Blacks Use That Whites Find Offensive

mess around, meaning to blacks to do nothing but just be hanging around, chewing the fat, or lounging; however, to many whites, "mess around" connotes sexual activity.

muthafucka, see pages 61–62; of all the "obscenities" used by blacks, this one, no matter what context it's used in, never fails to offend many whites. Incest is not a big problem in Black America, and blacks tend to view white rejection of this term as so much "methinks thou dost protest too much."

nigger, see page 62; possibly due to white misperception about the many positive values blacks assign to this term; nevertheless it bothers many whites when blacks use the word in their presence.

V. Forms of Address Between Blacks

Many of the terms that blacks use to refer to blacks are also used in addressing one another; for example, "How you doin, Sister?", "Hey, Blood, what's happening?", "Say Bro, what's yo name?", or "Hey, baby, where you been, ain seen you since Hector was a pup." The following are terms of address only.

girl, used between black women, as in "Girl, let me tell you bout this."

man or woman, used by males and females to address one another, as well as those of the same sex; however, *woman* is more characteristically limited to men addressing women, as in the Brother's admonition, "Woman, don't tell me no mess like dat!" Few black women will address each other as *woman.* It is more usual to hear *girl* or *momma.*

Miss (plus first name or last name), term of address regardless of whether the female is married or not, usually pronounced *Miz,* as in "Miz Johnson [who is actually a Mrs. Johnson] called me today." The new feminist preference for *Ms.* (which is also pronounced *Miz*) is thus no big thang for Black English speakers.

momma, both males and females use this term to address black women; generally limited to younger or stomp-down shonuff-into-a-Black-Thang women.

sweety (occasionally also *sugar*), generally used by males to address females, does not necessarily convey intimacy.

VI. Terms Referring to Music and Dance.
This is a list that could go on and on; only a few will be cited here.

blow, a jazz musical performance, by extension any artistic excellence in one's work; also to lose something, as in "He blew his woman."

boogie, any kind of dance activity, originally from boogie-woogie, a form of dancing popular in the thirties.

bop, from *bebop*, a jazz form combining African and European rhythms, associated with the music of Charlie Parker, Dizzy Gillespie, and Thelonious Monk; by association, a type of walk, as in "bopping down the street," walking with musical rhythm and coolness; also a form of dance that has now spanned at least two generations of Black Americans: despite new dances coming and going, everybody's still doing some form of the bop.

gittin down, see Appendix B.

jam, from the musician, to play music enthusiastically; thus, by extension, *jams* are records, and by further extension, *to jam* is *to dance*, to *party*.

Also there are the names of most popular dances, from roughly 1950 to the present: *applejack; chicken; boogaloo; soul cha-cha; twist; locomotion; football; rocking charlie; charge; emancipation; fly; monkey; alligator; watergate; bump; hustle.*

VII. Terms Referring to Food and Drink

brew, beer.

chitlins, chitterlings, the insides of the pig, originally thrown away by the slavemaster and considered fit only for the slaves; Big Mommas took this "waste" and, by careful cleaning and cooking, turned it into a delicacy. Today expensively priced by whites who capitalized upon their value among blacks, now many blacks can't afford them. Big Momma's traditional tender loving care was definitely exhibited in the preparation of chitlins, which often took hours to clean and required long, slow cooking. She added special "secret" ingredients to keep down the unpleasant smell during cooking.

grits, food in general.

hog maws, stomach of pig, also eaten as a delicacy, today not as expensive as chitlins, but pretty high nonetheless.

pluck, wine; possibly derived from the plucking of grapes from which wine is made.

Q, barbecue, ribs only.

taste, liquor or wine, but not beer.

VIII. Terms Referring to Clothes and Dress

clean, dressed up.

gators, alligator shoes, very popular as a symbol of success among black men.

laid, same as *clean*; also refers to being high on alcohol or drugs.

rags, fine clothes.

strides, kicks, shoes in general.

threads, same as *rags*.

vine, man's suit, so named because when they're really fitting, they "hang."

IX. Church Terms

A & B, Gospel soul reference to singing of two songs by a group on a musical program, "giving an A & B."

Amen Corner, place in church where the older members sit, especially the church "mothers," perceived as the "watch dogs of Christ": by extension, any section of church especially responsive to preacher's call.

bear witness, synonymous with *testify*, but localized to church, whereas *testify* is not.

dead, referring to absence of emotion in church service, as in "Dem sho was some dead folks over at dat church."

show some sign, to manifest the power and spirit of God by verbal behavior, such as moaning or shouting.

to take a text, ritual of preacher, announcing Scriptural reference and message of sermon (see Chapter Four); by extension, in secular usage, *taking a text* on somebody is to *read* them, to tell them off in no uncertain terms.

X. Terms for Clandestine and Underworld Activities

boosters, shoplifters.

boy, heroin.

game, a series of shrewd maneuvers, a "story" for obtaining what one wants; also, by extension, a style of carrying and expressing oneself that enables someone to manipulate people and achieve a desired end.

girl, cocaine.

hustlers, usually males, who survive by deviousness and *game* involving a wide variety of activities, such as con game, numbers, fencing (purchasing and selling stolen goods from boosters). By extension, a *hustle* is any method (legal or not) of earning extra money.

Jones, addiction to drugs; also reference to male sex organ.

nod, state of semiconsciousness induced by injection of heroin.

numbers man, numbers lady, person who accepts bets on numbers; such persons are said to be *backing numbers* (in this sense, blacks have been playing the lottery all the time). The winning combination of digits is said to have *fell out*; thus, "My name fell out yesterday" means the number that stands for the person's name was the winner for that day; a *numbers dream book* contains the numerical symbols for a variety of human events, including personal names. Charlatan preachers who "sell blessings" are often selling numbers in disguise. A person who collects the bets in the community is a *pick-up man* (or *lady*); *single action* refers to playing to hit only one digit of the winning number combination, thus the *single action lady* (or *man,* but more usually a lady) is the one who goes in and out of the community collecting bets on what the next digit of the winning combination is going to be. While dope pushers, pimps, and other hustlers characteristically are condemned in the community, numbers men and the numbers game are pretty positively viewed.

pimp, male who lives off earnings of female prostitutes; by extension, any black man being supported by a black woman (even though she is not a prostitute) is said to be *pimping.*

strung out, to be addicted to drugs; also reference to state of being hung up on any person or activity, as in "My man is strung out behind this new lady he just copped."

weed, smoke, marijuana.

XI. General

all she wrote, the end of something, as after finishing a huge serving of chitlins, the Sister said, "Well, that's all she wrote!"

bag, one's specialty, as in "What's your bag?" meaning "What are you into now?"; also reference to dope activity, a *bag man* is a *dope man.*

bear, booger bear, pronounced *booguh bear,* ugly female.

call yo'self, to assume to be doing something, to intend to do a thing, as in "I call myself having this dinner ready on time," or "Girl, what you call yo'self doing?"

cat faces, wrinkles in clothes when ironing them, as in "Chile, you call yo'self done iron this, with all these cat faces in it?"

down home, any place south of the Mason-Dixon line; conceptually, suggests place of psychological peace and nitty-gritty blackness; *down home* began to be particularly longed for after the vast urban migration of blacks to the "promised lands" of Northern Black Bottoms.

dues, the rough spots in life, hardships; *to pay dues* is to have it hard, in the sense of "paying" for your smooth spots.

fine, referring to beautiful female or male.

fox, stallion, star, beautiful female.

front street, being out front, vulnerable to attack, either verbally or otherwise.

jive, deceptive, putting somebody on.

later, goodbye, the end

like to, to almost do something; as in "Momma like to drop the baby."

max, maximum, to the hilt, the height of something.

may like, to pretend, to "make like" something is true when it isn't, as in "She may like she was sick."

mother wit, common sense.

on "E," financially broke.

on full, plenty of money.

on time, on T., doing or saying something at the appropriate psychological moment, regardless of "clock" time, possibly from the black church, popular saying associated with the story of Job: "He [God] may not come when you want Him, but He's right on time."

psych-out, to fool, to fake out through mental power.

put the ig on, also simply, *to ig,* to ignore somebody, act like you don't know them when you do.

read, to tell somebody off; synonymous with *taking a text.*

shuckin and jivin, just talking for the sake of talk; saying you are going to do something, but not really intending to do it; bullshitting.

steppin, struttin, stridin, soulful walk.

swear, to curse, as in "You better stop using those swear words."

T.C.B., taking care of business, seriously doing something, "on the case."

T.I. Is, telling it like it 'tis, as in, "She was jes tellin it like it T.I. Is."

T.L.C., tender, loving care.

up on it, hip to something, informed.

waste, to spill, as in "James wasted all the milk, now we ain got none."

Notes

Chapter 1

A *pidgin* is a mixture of two languages, with a simplified structure, to facilitate communication. As a result of the slave trade, various African-European pidgins evolved — for instance, Dutch Pidgin, Portuguese Pidgin, English Pidgin. A *pidgin* becomes a *creole* when it is in widespread use and is the first and only language of a speech community, as was the case of the plantation English Creole used in slave communities in America. Some linguists maintain that a creole represents a more fully developed and sophisticated stage of the language mixture. For a more thorough listing and discussion of West African language rules and some comparisons with Gullah English Creole, see Turner (1949). Turner, along with Skinner (1972), gives sample texts from the Gullah dialect. Speech samples from Carolina and Georgia ex-slaves, some of whom are undoubtedly of Geechee origin, can be found in Botkin (1945). For more samples of newspaper advertisements for runaway slaves, see Read (1939). Most of the samples of early Black English are from Dillard (1972). See his Chapters 3 and 4 for an exhaustive treatment of the history of Black English as well as examples of whites speaking Africanized Pidgin English.

Chapter 2

The material on Detroit dialects can be found in Shuy (1966–1968) and Wolfram (1969). Analysis of the Black English of junior high students in Detroit appears in Smitherman (1969). Other important studies of contemporary Black English sound and structure are cited in the bibliography. The "grammar and goodness" quote is from Hughes (1957).

Chapter 3

For an interesting, concise discussion of the controversy over "Negro" and "black," see Bennett (1967). *Ebony* magazine discusses the results of a national survey on the question of racial designation in its photo-editorial, "What's in a Name?", June 1968. Almost any standard dictionary of Americanisms attests to the historical synonymity between "negro" and "nigger." See, for instance, *A Dictionary of Americanisms on Historical Principles*, Mitford Mathews, ed. (Chicago: University of Chicago Press, 1950). An earlier view of Black American attitudes toward terms of race can be found in the exchange of letters and editorials in DuBois (1928; 1930). Turner's major work has been referred to in the notes to Chapter One above; for a summary article, see Turner (1958) and Garrett (1966). Dalby's *New York Times* articles appear in Dalby (1969a; 1970). The *Times* Editorial Sections for 1970 and 1971 should also prove enlightening. Longer and more heavily documented treatments of Dalby's work appear in Dalby (1969b; 1972). Consult Dillard (1972), pp. 245–257, for a historical survey of Fine Talk and references to its use in Caribbean culture. Thomas Wentworth Higginson is generally credited with being the first to collect and record the Negro spirituals, beginning in approximately 1861 and continuing through 1867. See Allen (1867); Krehbiel (1914); and Courlander (1963). DuBois (1924) gives a short but powerful treatment of this music. I am indebted to my good friend Edward Boyer, reporter for *Time* magazine, for reminding me of stylin and profilin on the golf course. He is reponsible for the short piece on "Soul Golf" in *Time*, June 16, 1975; for a really dynamite treatment, done in Boyer's inimitable style, see his 1975 article cited in the bibliography. The Malcolm X material is from *The Autobiography of Malcolm X* (Evergreen Black Cat Book, pp. 52–54 and 122–23).

Chapter 4

The material from Thompson (1974) is found on pp. 5–45; that from Forde (1954) on p. x. Sowande (1974) and Mbiti (1969) are other excellent sources of information on the cosmology of traditional Africa. Jahn (1961), a useful study of African orality, provided the quote on Nommo, pp. 125–133. A *griot* (pronounced *greeo*) is one who, by memory alone, preserves and teaches the tradition and history of the tribe. In some traditional African societies, this master of "historical oratory" is an important sacred figure — akin to a story-teller, minstrel, jester, herald, annalist, troubadour, gleeman, and poet all rolled into one. The legend of Sundiata was told to D. T. Niane by an "obscure griot" from a village in Guinea and was translated by Pickett (1965). Mitchell (1970) presents a thorough analysis of black preaching style. Mitchell (1975) explores the relationship between the black church, black values, and African heritage. Daniel and Smitherman (1976) is a more concise treatment of the same. Washington (1973) is good on background and description of black religious cults. The quote from C. Eric Lincoln is from the Foreword in Barrett (1974), p. viii. On August 21, 1831, preacher Nat Turner led the greatest slave rebellion in history, killing some sixty whites in Southampton County, Virginia, and sending the entire South into a state of panic. He was captured on October 30 and hanged in Jerusalem, the county seat, twelve days later. For more rhymes, toasts and choice quotes from Muhammad Ali, see Cottrell (1967) and Olson (1967).

Chapter 5

Wright's 1960 essay, reprinted in Wright (1964), is a concise, informative overview of Black American literature in the United States. The Jackson quote is found in the Preface to *Kuntu Drama*, Paul Harrison, ed. (New York: Grove, 1974), pp. ix–xiii. The brief quote on African communication is from Doob (1961); Thompson's work was cited earlier; see Notes, Chapter Four. Brewer (1972) contains the folk material cited here. For more on tone in African languages, see Turner (1949). The introduction to *Sundiata* in Pickett (1965) discusses the African story-telling tradition; also Mutwa (1966). The reference to Akan culture and African elders comes from Abrahams (1969), whose work should be added to those mentioned above in connection with African philosophical thought. In addition to Brewer, examples of folk stories and "tall" tales can be found in Hughes and Bontemps (1958) and Hurston (1935). Chesnutt's story appears in most standard anthologies of Black American literature, such as *Cavalcade*, Davis and Redding, eds. (Boston: Houghton Mifflin, 1971). The "Malitis" story is found in Botkin (1945), pp. 4–5. The excerpt from Henry Alsup's poem "mean" is in *Get It Up Set It Out* (Detroit: Ink & Soul, 1973), p. 27. Collections of Toasts are Abrahams (1964) and Jackson (1974). Labov (1972; 1973) gives a brilliant analysis of the aesthetic, versification, and metrical style of the Toasts as well as a critical evaluation and comparison of the verbal abilities of various Toast-tellers.

Chapter 6

The opening quote is from Langston Hughes's play "Simply Heavenly," in *Five Plays*. J. Mitchell Morse (1973) is responsible for the article on the "shuffling speech of slavery"; Green (1963) for the one on the "last barrier to integration"; Sledd (1969; 1972) for discussions of the "linguistics of white supremacy." For the 1968 study, see Smitherman (1969). Baraka's reference to black language appears in Baraka (1966); Fanon's discussion of Caribbean language attitudes in Fanon (1967). Rodgers (1969) provides the quote on the new black poetry. The sociological essay referred to is that of Gerald McWorter (1969) who also takes up the matter of language concepts in the same essay. Haki Madhubuti (1969) provides the guide to black writers. The Larry Neal quote is from the Afterword to *Black Fire* (New York: William Morrow, 1968), pp. 654–655. Lambert and Tucker (1969) and Lambert et al. (1960) provide the Canadian material on language attitudes; Labov (1966) the New York data; and Pooley (1969) that on English teachers.

Chapter 7

The 1959 study referred to is that of Golden (1960). The later study is that of Allen (1969). For the more racist and glaringly erroneous of the "cognitive deficit" charges against Black English, see Martin P. Deutsch, "The Disadvantaged Child and the Learning Process," in *Education in Depressed Areas* (New York: Columbia University Press, 1963), pp. 163–179; also Fred Hechinger, ed., *Pre-School Education Today* (New York: Doubleday, 1966). For an excellent rebuttal, see Labov (1970; 1972). Examples of "difference" language programs can be found in Lin (1965); Jewett et al. (1964); *Language Programs for the Disadvantaged* (1965); *On the Dialects of Children* (1968); and in *Nonstandard Dialect* (1968), which is also the source of the language exercise quoted on p. 211. The quote on cultural enrichment is found in Schenck (1969); the Baratz reference is from Kochman (1972); the attack from the sociologist in Miller (1969). Sledd is well-known for his caustic commentaries on the "national mania for correctness." The material quoted here is from Sledd (1976). Orwell's essay has been widely reprinted in a number of collections dealing with language and literature. For this essay and more of Orwellian thought, see Orwell and Angus (1970). Labov's analysis is from his essay "The Logic of Non-Standard English" (1969). For a British perspective on the subject of language and social class, see Rosen (1972). The "politics of syntax" is discussed at length in Kozol (1975). The material from Frederick Douglass appears in his *Life and Times* (Collier Books, 1962), pp. 217–218. The Baratzes (1970) discuss concepts of "warmth" in the classroom, and the San Francisco high school study referred to can be found in Massey et al. (1975). For more on reading and dialect, see any of the following publications by Goodman: *Miscue Analysis: Application to Reading Instruction; Linguistics and the Teaching of Reading; The Psycholinguistic Nature of the Reading Process; Theoretically Based Studies of Patterns of Miscues in Oral Reading Performance*. The *Bridge* series is the work of Simpkins et al. (1976). Both Green (1975) and Stone (1975) are excellent articles on the testing controversy.

Bibliography

Abrahams, Roger. *Deep Down in the Jungle*. Chicago: Aldine Publishing Co., 1970 (originally published in Hatboro, Pennsylvania, 1964).

Abrahams, W. E. *The African Mind*. Chicago: University of Chicago Press, 1969.

Achebe, Chinua. *Things Fall Apart*. New York: Fawcett, 1959.

———. *No Longer at Ease*. New York: Fawcett, 1960.

Adoff, Arnold, ed. *Black on Black*. New York: Macmillan, 1968.

Alatis, James, E., ed. *Linguistics and the Teaching of Standard English to Speakers of Other Languages or Dialects*. Washington: Georgetown University Press, 1969.

———, ed. *Bilingualism and Language Contact: Anthropological, Linguistic, Psychological and Sociological Aspects*. Washington: Georgetown University Press, 1970.

Alexandre, Pierre. *Languages and Language in Black Africa*. Evanston: Northwestern University Press, 1972.

Allen, Virginia. "Teaching Standard English as a Second Dialect," *Florida Foreign Language Reporter*, Spring/Summer 1969, pp. 123–29.

Allen, W. F., et al. *Slave Songs of the United States*. New York: Oak Publications, 1965 (originally published in 1867).

Alsup, Henry. *Get It Up Set It Out*. Detroit: Ink & Soul, 1973.

Anastasi, A., and D'Angelo, P. "A Comparison of Negro and White Pre-School Children in Language Development and Goodenough Draw-A-Man I.Q.," *Journal of Genetical Psychology*, vol. LXXXI, 1952, pp. 1947–65.

Angelou, Maya. *Just Give Me a Cool Drink of Water 'fore I Diiie*. New York: Random House, 1971.

Bailey, Beryl. *Jamaican Creole Syntax*. Cambridge: Cambridge University Press, 1966.

———. "Toward A New Perspective in Negro English Dialectology," *American Speech*, vol. XL, no. 3, 1965, pp. 171–77.

———. "Some Arguments against the Use of Dialect Readers in the Teaching of Initial Reading," *Florida Foreign Language Reporter*, Spring/Fall 1970, pp. 8ff.

Baraka, Imamu. *Blues People*. New York: William Morrow, 1963.

_____. *Dutchman and the Slave.* New York: William Morrow, 1964.

_____. *Home.* New York: William Morrow, 1966.

_____. *It's Nation Time.* Chicago: Third World Press, 1970.

Baratz, Joan C. "Ain't ain't no error," *Florida Foreign Language Reporter,* Spring/Fall 1971, pp. 9ff.

_____. "Who Should Do What to Whom . . . and Why?" *Florida Foreign Language Reporter,* Spring/Summer 1969, pp. 75ff.

Baratz, Joan and Steven. "Black Culture on Black Terms: A Rejection of the Social Pathology Model," in Thomas Kochman, *Rappin and Stylin Out,* 1972.

Baratz, Joan and Steven. "Early Childhood Intervention: The Social Science Basis of Institutional Racism," *Harvard Educational Review,* vol. 40, Winter 1970, pp. 29–50.

Barrett, Leonard E. *Soul-Force.* New York: Anchor Books, 1974.

Bennett, Lerone. "What's in a Name?" *Ebony,* November 1967, pp. 46–54.

Bernstein, Basil. *Class, Codes and Control.* New York: Schocken Books, 1971.

_____. "Social Class and Linguistic Development: A Theory of Social Learning," in *Education, Economy, and Society,* A. H. Halsey, ed., Glencoe: *The Free Press,* 1961, pp. 288–314.

Bentley, Robert H., and Crawford, Samuel D. *Black Language Reader.* Glenview, Ill.: Scott, Foresman and Co., 1973.

"Black Language and Culture: Implications for Education." Special Issue of the *Florida Foreign Language Reporter,* Spring/Fall 1971.

Board of Education of the City of New York and the National Council of Teachers of English. *Nonstandard Dialect.* Urbana: National Council of Teachers of English, 1968.

Bosmajian, Haig A. "The Language of White Racism." *College English,* January 1970, pp. 263–272.

Botkin, B. A., ed. *Lay My Burden Down: A Folk History of Slavery.* Chicago: University of Chicago Press, 1945.

Boyer, Edward. "Soul Golf." *Time Magazine,* June 16, 1975.

_____. "Teeing off Down Home Style: Black Golfers." *The Detroit Free Press* (Sunday Magazine), August 17, 1975, pp. 10–16.

Brawley, Benjamin, ed. *Early Negro American Writers.* New York: Dover, 1970 (originally published in 1935).

Brewer, J. Mason. *American Negro Folklore.* Chicago: Quadrangle Books, 1972.

Brown, Claude. *Manchild in the Promised Land.* New York: Signet, 1965.

_____. "The Language of Soul." *Esquire Magazine,* April 1968, pp. 88–89.

Brown, Goold. *Grammar of English Grammars.* New York: W. Wood, 1851.

Brown, Hubert Rap. *"Die Nigger Die!"* New York: Dial Press, 1969.

Brown, William Wells. *Clotel.* New York: Arno Press Edition, 1969 (originally published in London, 1853).

Burgest, David R. "The Racist Use of the English Language," *Black Scholar,* September 1973, pp. 37–45.

Charters, Samuel. *The Poetry of the Blues.* New York: Avon Books, 1970.

Chesnutt, Charles Wadell, "The Goopherd Grapevine," in *Cavalcade,* Davis and Redding, eds., Boston: Houghton Mifflin, 1971, pp. 169–79.

Chomsky, Noam. *Language and Mind.* New York: Harcourt, Brace (Enlarged Edition), 1972.

Claerbaut, David. *Black Jargon in White America.* Grand Rapids: William B. Ferdmans Publishing Co., 1972.

Cottrell, John. *Muhammad Ali: The Man of Destiny, Formerly Cassius Clay.* New York: Muller, 1967.

Courlander, Harold. *Negro Folk Music, U.S.A.* New York: Columbia University Press, 1963.

Cullinan, Bernice, ed. *Black Dialects & Reading.* Urbana: Eric Clearinghouse on Reading and Communication Skills, 1974.

Dalby, David. (a) "Americanisms That May Once Have Been Africanisms," *The New York Times,* July 19, 1969.

――――. (b) *Black Through White: Patterns of Communication in Africa and the New World.* Bloomington: Indiana University Press, 1969.

――――. "Jazz, Jitter and Jam," *The New York Times,* November 10, 1970.

――――. "The African Element in American English." in Kochman, 1972. pp. 170–86.

Daniel, Jack L., ed. *Black Communication: Dimensions of Research and Instruction.* New York: Speech Communication Association, 1974.

――――. "Towards an Ethnography of AfroAmerican Proverbial Usage." *Black Lines,* Winter 1972, pp. 3–12.

―――― and Smitherman, Geneva. " 'How I Got Over': Communication Dynamics in the Black Community," *Quarterly Journal of Speech,* February 1976, pp. 26–39.

Davis, A. L., ed. *On the Dialects of Children.* Urbana: National Council of Teachers of English, 1968.

Davis, Arthur P., and Redding, Saunders, eds. *Cavalcade.* Boston: Houghton Mifflin, 1971.

DeStefano, Johanna. "Productive Language Differences in Fifth Grade, Black Students' Syntactic Forms." *Elementary English,* vol. XLIX, April 1972, pp. 522–58.

――――. "Black Attitudes toward Black English: A Pilot Study," *Florida Foreign Language Reporter,* Spring/Fall 1971, pp. 9ff.

Deutsch, Martin. "The Disadvantaged Child and the Learning Process." *Education in Depressed Areas.* New York: Columbia University Press, 1963.

Dillard, J. L. *Black English.* New York: Random House, 1972.

Doob, Leonard. *Communication in Africa.* New Haven: Yale University Press, 1961.

Douglass, Frederick. *Life and Times*. New York: Collier Books Edition, 1962 (originally published in 1881).

⸺. *My Bondage and My Freedom*. New York: Arno Press and New York Times, 1969 (originally published in 1855).

⸺. *Narrative of the Life of Frederick Douglass, an American Slave*. New York: Signet Edition, 1968 (originally published in 1845).

DuBois, William E. B. *Black Folk, Then and Now: An Essay in the History and Sociology of the Negro Race*. New York: Octagon Books, 1970.

⸺. *Black Reconstruction in America*. 1860–1880. New York: Harcourt Brace & Company, 1935.

⸺. "Postscript." *The Crisis*, February & May, 1930, pp. 63, 172.

⸺. "Postscript." *The Crisis*, March 1928, pp. 96–97.

⸺. *Souls of Black Folk*. New York: Fawcett Edition, 1961 (originally published in 1903).

The Gift of Black Folk. New York. Washington Square Press edition, 1970 (originally published in 1924).

Dundes, Alan. *Mother Wit from the Laughing Barrel*. New Jersey: Prentice-Hall, 1973.

Elder, Lonnie. *Ceremonies in Dark Old Men*. New York: Farrar, Straus and Giroux, 1965.

Ellison, Ralph. *Invisible Man*. New York: Random House, 1952.

⸺. "Mister Toussan," in *Black American Literature*, Darwin Turner, ed. Columbus: Charles E. Merrill, pp. 96–102.

Emanuel, James A. *Langston Hughes*. New York: Twayne Publishers, 1967.

Erickson, Frederick David. " 'F' Get You Honky!': A New Look at Black Dialect and the School," *Elementary English*, April 1969, pp. 495–99.

Evertts, Eldonna L., ed. *Dimensions of Dialect*. Champaign: National Council of Teachers of English, 1967.

Fanon, Frantz. "The Negro and Language," *Black Skin, White Masks*. New York: Grove Press Inc., 1967.

Fasold, Ralph W. and Shuy, Roger W. *Teaching Standard English in the Inner City*. Washington, D. C.: Center for Applied Linguistics, 1970.

Fickett, Joan G. "Tense and Aspect In Black English." *Journal of English Linguistics*, vol. VI, 1972, pp. 17–19.

Fishman, Joshua A. "Sociolinguistics," *Florida Foreign Language Reporter*, Spring/Fall 1970, pp. 40ff.

Forde, Daryll, ed. *African Worlds: Studies in the Cosmological Ideas and Social Values of African Peoples*. New York: Oxford University Press, 1954.

France, Kenneth. "Effects of 'White' and of 'Black' Examiner Voices on IQ Scores of Children," *Developmental Psychology*, 1973, pp. 144ff.

Franklin, John Hope. *From Slavery to Freedom*. New York: Random House, 1969 (originally published in 1947).

Fries, Charles. *American English Grammar*. New York: Appleton-Century, 1940.

Garland, Phyl. *The Sound of Soul.* New York: Pocket Books, 1971.

Garrett, Romeo B. "African Survivals in American Culture," *The Journal of Negro History,* vol. LI, October 1966, pp. 239–45.

Giglioli, Pier Paoli, ed. *Language and Social Context: Selected Readings.* Baltimore: Penguin Books, 1972.

Golden, James L. and Rieke, Richard. *The Rhetoric of Black Americans.* Columbus: Charles E. Merrill, 1971.

Golden, Ruth I. *Improving Patterns of Language Usage.* Detroit: Wayne State University Press, 1960.

Gonzales, Ambrose. *Black Border.* Columbia, S. C.: The State Co., 1922.

Goodman, Kenneth. *Linguistics and the Teaching of Reading.* Newark: International Reading Association, 1967.

———. *Miscue Analysis: Application to Reading Instruction.* Urbana: National Council of Teachers of English, 1973.

———. *The Psycholinguistic Nature of the Reading Process.* Detroit: Wayne State University Press, 1968.

———. *Theoretically Based Studies of Patterns of Miscues in Oral Reading Performance.* USOE Project No. 9-0375. Washington: Office of Education, 1973.

Green, Gordon C. "Negro Dialect, the Last Barrier to Integration," *The Journal of Negro Education,* vol. XXXII, Winter 1963, pp. 81–83.

Green, Robert L. "Tips on Educational Testing: What Teachers & Parents Should Know," *Phi Delta Kappan,* October 1975, pp. 89–93.

Hall, Robert A. *Pidgin and Creole Languages.* Ithaca: Cornell University Press, 1966.

Harris, Middleton. *The Black Book.* New York: Random House, 1974.

Harrison, James A. "Negro English," *Anglia,* vol. VII, 1884, pp. 232–79.

Harrison, Paul, ed. *Kuntu Drama.* New York: Grove Press, 1974.

Hayes, Alfred S. and Taylor, Orlando L. "A Summary of the Center's 'BALA' Project," *The Linguistic Reporter,* vol. XIII, Fall 1971, pp. 1–4.

Hechinger, Fred, ed. *Pre-School Education Today.* New York: Doubleday, 1966.

Herskovits, Melville. *Myth of the Negro Past.* Boston: Beacon Press, 1941.

Himes, Chester. *Hot Day, Hot Night.* New York: Dell, 1969.

Hodges, Frenchy. *Piece De Way Home.* Detroit: Tibi Productions, 1975.

Hughes, Langston. *Ask Your Mama: 12 Moods for Jazz.* New York: Knopf, 1961.

———. *Best of Simple.* New York: Hill & Wang, 1961.

———. *Selected Poems.* New York: Knopf, 1970.

———. *Simple Stakes a Claim.* New York: Rinehart, 1957.

———. "Simply Heavenly," in *Five Plays,* Webster Smalley, ed., Bloomington: Indiana University Press, 1968.

——— and Bontemps, Arna. *The Book of Negro Folklore.* New York: Dodd, Mead, 1958.

Hurston, Zora Neale. *Mules and Men.* Philadelphia: J. B. Lippincott, 1935.

Hymes, Dell. *Foundations in Sociolinguistics.* Philadelphia: University of Pennsylvania Press, 1974.

———, ed. *Pidginization and Creolization of Languages.* Cambridge: Cambridge University Press, 1971.

Institute of the Black World, ed. *Education and Black Struggle: Notes from the Colonized World.* Cambridge: Harvard Educational Review, Monograph no. 2, 1974.

Isenbarger, Joan, and Smith, Veta. "How Would You Feel If You Had to Change 'Your' Dialect?" *English Journal,* vol. LXII, October 1973, pp. 994–97.

Jackson, Bruce. *"Get Your Ass in the Water and Swim Like Me."* Cambridge: Harvard University Press, 1974.

Jackson, Oliver, in Preface to *Kuntu Drama,* Paul Harrison, ed. New York: Grove Press, 1974, pp. IX-XIII.

Jahn, Janheinz. *Muntu.* London: Faber and Faber, 1961

Jensen, A. R. "How Much Can We Boost I.Q. and Scholastic Achievement." *Harvard Educational Review,* vol. XXXIX, Winter 1969, pp. 1–117.

Jewett, Arno, et al. *Improving English Skills of Culturally Different Youth in Large Cities.* Washington: U.S. Department of Health, Education and Welfare, 1964.

Johnson, Kenneth R. "Black Kinesics — Some Nonverbal Communication Patterns in the Black Culture," *Florida Foreign Language Reporter,* Spring/Fall 1971, pp. 17ff

Jordan, June. "Black English: The Politics of Translation," *School Library Journal,* May 15, 1973, pp. 21–24.

Kochman, Thomas. *Rappin' and Stylin' Out: Communication in Urban Black America.* Chicago: University of Illinois Press, 1972.

Kozol, Jonathan. "The Politics of Syntax," *English Journal,* December 1975, pp. 22–27.

Knight, Etheridge. *Poems from Prison.* Detroit: Broadside Press, 1968.

Krapp, George. "The English of the Negro," *The American Mercury,* vol. II, May–August 1924, pp. 190–195.

Krehbiel, H. E. *Afro-American Folksongs.* New York: G. Schirmer, 1914.

Kurath, Hans. "The Linguistic Atlas of the United States and Canada." *Proceedings of the Second International Congress of Phonetic Sciences* (Daniel Jones and D. B. Fry, eds.) Cambridge: Cambridge University Press, 1936.

Labov, William. *Language in the Inner City.* Philadelphia: University of Pennsylvania Press, 1972.

———. *Sociolinguistic Patterns.* Philadelphia: University of Pennsylvania Press, 1972.

———. *The Study of Nonstandard English.* Champaign: National Council of Teachers of English, 1970.

———. "Toasts," in Alan Dundes, ed., *Mother Wit from the Laughing Barrel.* New Jersey: Prentice-Hall, 1973.

_____. *The Social Stratification of English in New York City*. Washington, D.C.: Center for Applied Linguistics, 1966.

_____. "The Logic of Non-Standard English," *Linguistic-Cultural Differences and American Education*. Special Edition of the *Florida Foreign Language Reporter*, Spring/Summer 1969, pp. 60–74, 169.

Lambert, W. E., et al. "Evaluational Reactions to Spoken Language," *Journal of Abnormal and Social Psychology*, vol. LX, January 1960, pp. 44–51.

_____ and Tucker, G. R. "White and Negro Listeners' Reaction to Various American-English Dialects," *Social Forces*, vol. XLVII, June 1969, pp. 463–68.

Language Programs for the Disadvantaged. Urbana: National Council of Teachers of English, 1965.

Larkin, Rochelle. *Soul Music*. New York: Lancer Books, 1970.

Leonard, Sterling Andrus. *The Doctrine of Correctness in English Usage, 1700–1800*. New York: Russell & Russell, 1962.

Lester, Julius. *Black Folktales*. New York: Grove Press, 1969.

Lin, San-Su C. *Pattern Practices in the Teaching of Standard English to Students with a Non-Standard Dialect*. Washington, D. C.: United States Office of Education, 1965.

Locke, Alain, ed. *The New Negro*. New York: Arno Press, 1968 (originally published in 1925).

McDavid, Raven. "American Social Dialects." *College English*, Oct.–May 1964–1965, pp. 254–60.

_____. "Historical, Regional and Social Variation." *Journal of English Linguistics*, March 1967, pp. 39ff.

_____ and McDavid, Virginia. "The Relationship of the Speech of American Negroes to the Speech of Whites." *American Speech*, vol. XXVI, February 1951, pp. 3–17.

McDowell, Tremaine. "Notes on Negro Dialect in the American Novel to 1821." *American Speech*, vol. 5, October–August 1929–30, pp. 291–96.

McWorter, Gerald. "Ideology of a Black Social Science," *Black Scholar*, December 1969, pp. 28–35.

Madhubuti, Haki (Don Lee). "Directions for Black Writers," *Black Scholar*, December 1969, pp. 53–57.

_____. *Don't Cry, Scream*. Detroit: Broadside Press, 1969.

Major, Clarence. *Dictionary of Afro-American Slang*. New York: International Publishers, 1970.

Mbiti, John S. *African Religions and Philosophies*. New York: Doubleday, 1969.

Malcolm X. *Malcolm X Speaks*. New York: Grove Press, 1965.

_____. *The Autobiography of Malcolm X*. New York: Grove Press, 1965.

Massey, Grace Carroll, et al. "Racism Without Racists: Institutional Racism in Urban Schools," *Black Scholar*, vol. VIII, November 1975, pp. 10–19.

Mathews, Mitford, ed. *A Dictionary of Americanisms on Historical Principles.* Chicago: University of Chicago Press, 1950.

Miller, Henry. "Social Work in the Black Ghetto: the New Colonialism," *Social Work,* July 1969, pp. 65–76.

Mitchell, Henry. *Black Belief.* New York: Harper and Row, 1975.

_____. *Black Preaching.* Philadelphia: J. B. Lippincott, 1970.

Morse, J. Mitchell. "The Shuffling Speech of Slavery: Black English." *College English,* March 1973, pp. 834–43.

Murray, Lindley. *English Grammar.* New York: Collins & Company, 1819 (originally published, 1795).

Mutwa, Vusamazulu Credo. *Indaba My Children.* London: Blue Crane Books, 1966.

Neal, Larry. "Afterword," in *Black Fire,* Imamu Baraka and Larry Neal, eds. New York: Morrow, 1968, pp. 654–55.

New York Times, Editorial Section, November 10, 1970; December 4, 1970; December 14, 1970, December 19, 1970; January 8, 1971; January 20, 1971.

Nicholas, A. X. *The Poetry of Soul.* New York: Bantam Books, 1971.

Olson, Jack. *Black Is Best.* New York: Putnam, 1967.

O'Neil, Wayne. "The Politics of Bidialectalism," *College English,* vol. XXXIII, January 1972, pp. 433–38.

Orwell, Sonia, and Angus, Ian, eds. *The Collected Essays and Letters of George Orwell,* vol. IV. London: Penguin Books, 1970

Pharr, Robert, *Book of Numbers.* Garden City, New York: Doubleday, 1969.

Pickett, G. D., ed. and trans. *Sundiata: An epic of old Mali.* London: Longman Group Ltd. Edition, 1965.

Pooley, Robert C. "The Oral Usage of English Teachers," in Virginia McDavid, ed., *Language and Teaching.* Chicago: Chicago State College, 1969, pp. 55–61.

Read, Allen Walker. "Bilingualism in the Middle Colonies, 1725–1775." *American Speech,* April 1937, pp. 93–99.

_____. "British Recognition of American Speech in the Eighteenth Century." *Dialect Notes,* vol. VI, Part VI, 1933, pp. 313–34.

_____. "The Speech of Negroes in Colonial America," *Journal of Negro History,* vol. XXIV, July 1939, pp. 247–58.

Reed, Ishamel. *19 Necromancers from Now.* New York: Doubleday, 1970.

Rodgers, Carolyn. "Black Poetry — Where It's At," *Black World,* September 1969, pp. 7–16.

Rosen, Harold. *Language and Class.* Bristol, England: Falling Wall Press Ltd., 1972.

Ruddell, Robert B., and Graves, Barbara W. "Socio-ethnic Status and the Language Achievement of First-Grade Children," *Elementary English,* May 1968, pp. 635–42.

Sanchez, Sonia. *We A Badd DDD People.* Detroit: Broadside Press, 1970.

Schenck, Mary-Lou. "A Southern Negro Girl in a White Northern

Family: A Case Study," *Social Work*, July 1969, pp. 77–83.

Shuy, Roger, et al. *Detroit Dialect Study*. Washington, D. C.: Center for Applied Linguistics and National Institute of Mental Health, 1966–68.

————. *Discovering American Dialects*. Urbana: National Council of Teachers of English, 1967.

———— and Fasold, Ralph. *Teaching Standard English in the Inner City*. Washington, D. C.: Center for Applied Linguistics, 1970.

————, ed. *Social Dialects and Language Learning*. Urbana: National Council of Teachers of English, 1969.

Sidran, Ben. *Black Talk*. New York: Holt, Rinehart & Winston, 1971.

Simmons, Gloria, and Hutchinson, Helene, eds. *Black Culture: Reading and Writing Black*. New York: Holt, Rinehart and Winston, 1972.

Simpkins, Gary, et al. *Bridge*. Boston: Houghton Mifflin, 1976.

Skinner, Elliot P., ed. *Drums & Shadows*. New York: Anchor Books, 1972.

Slanger, William R. "Effecting Dialect Change Through Oral Drill," *English Journal*, November 1967, pp. 1166–76.

Sledd, James. "After Bidialectalism, What?" *English Journal*, no. 5, May 1973, pp. 770–73.

————. "Bi-Dialectalism: The Linguistics of White Supremacy," *English Journal*, December 1969, pp. 1307–29.

————. "Doublespeak: Dialectology in the Service of Big Brother," *College English*, January 1972, pp. 439–56.

————. "We Have Met the Enemy — and He Is Us." Paper given at the Modern Language Association Commission on Minorities, Symposium, "Minority Language and Literature: Retrospective and Perspective," in New York, November 4–6, 1976.

Smith, Arthur, ed. *Language, Communication and Rhetoric in Black America*. New York: Harper & Row, 1972.

————. *Rhetoric of Black Revolution*. Boston: Allyn and Bacon, 1969.

Smitherman, Geneva. *A Comparison of the Oral and Written Styles of a Group of Inner-City Black Students*, Ph.D. dissertation, University of Michigan, 1969.

————. *Black Language and Culture: Sounds of Soul*. New York: Harper & Row, 1975.

————. "Black Power Is Black Language." *Black Culture: Reading and Writing Black*, Simmons, ed. New York: Holt, Rinehart and Winston, 1972.

————. "Soul N' Style," *English Journal*, February–May 1974, September 1975, February 1976.

————. "The Power of the Rap: The Black Idiom and the New Black Poetry," *Twentieth Century Literature*, October 1973, pp. 259–74.

Sowande, Fela. "The Quest of an African World View: The Utilization of African Discourse," in Jack L. Daniel, ed., *Black Communication: Dimensions of Research and Instruction*. New York: Speech Communication Association, 1974.

Stephenson, Bobby L. *An Investigation of the Psycholinguistic Abilities of Negro and White Children from Four Socio-Economic Status Levels.* Washington, D. C.: U.S. Office of Education, no. 9-G-058, May 1970.

Stewart, William. "Sociolinguistic Factors in the History of American Negro Dialects," *Florida Foreign Language Reporter,* Spring 1967, pp. 2–4.

———, ed. *Non-Standard Speech and the Teaching of English.* Washington: Center for Applied Linguistics, 1964.

Stoller, Paul, ed. *Black American English.* New York: Dell, 1975.

Stone, Chuck. "A Black Paper; Standardized Tests: True or False," *The Black Collegian,* November/December, 1975, pp. 46–56.

"Students' Right to Their Own Language." *College Composition and Communication Journal,* Special Issue, Fall, 1974.

Talley, Thomas. *Negro Folk Rhymes.* Port Washington: Kennikat Press, 1968 (originally published in 1922).

Templin, Mildred C. "Relation of Speech and Language Development to Intelligence and Socio-economic Status." *Volta Review,* vol. LX, September 1968, pp. 331–34.

Thompson, Robert Farris. *African Art in Motion.* Los Angeles: University of California Press, 1974.

Toliver-Weddington, Gloria. "The Scope of Black English," *Journal of Black Studies,* vol. IV, December 1973, pp. 107–14.

Tucker, Beverly. *The Partisan Leader.* New York: Rudd & Carleton, 1841 (originally published in 1836).

Turner, Darwin, compiler. *Afro-American Writers* (Goldentree Bibliography of Afro-American Literature). New York: Appleton-Century-Crofts, 1970.

Turner, Lorenzo D. *Africanisms in the Gullah Dialect.* Chicago: University of Chicago Press, 1949.

———. "African Survivals in the New World with Special Emphasis on the Arts." *Presence Africaine,* Special edition, 1958. Reprinted by the American Society of African Culture, New York, December 1963, pp. 101–16.

Twain, Mark. *Huckleberry Finn.* Boston: Houghton Mifflin, 1958.

Walser, Richard. "Negro Dialect in Eighteenth-Century American Drama," *American Speech,* December 1955, pp. 269–76.

Washington, Joseph R. *Black Sects and Cults.* New York: Doubleday, 1973.

Whitten, Norman, and Szwed, John. *Afro-American Anthropology.* New York: Free Press, 1970.

Whorf, Benjamin. *Language, Thought and Reality,* John B. Carroll, ed. Cambridge: M.I.T. Press, 1956.

Williams, Frederick; Whitehead, Jack; and Miller, Leslie. "Attitudinal Correlates of Children's Speech Characteristics." Austin: Center for Communication Research, the University of Texas at Austin, March 1971.

276 TALKIN AND TESTIFYIN

_____, ed. *Language and Poverty: Perspectives on a Theme*. Chicago: Markham Publishing Co., 1972.

Williams, John A., and Harris, Charles, ed. *Amistad 2*. New York: Random House, 1971.

Williamson, Juanita, and Burke, Virginia. *A Various Language*. New York: Holt, Rinehart and Winston, 1971.

_____. *The Speech of Negro High School Students in Memphis*. Washington: United States Office of Education, no. 9-G-058, May 1970.

Williams, Robert L., ed. *Ebonics: The True Language of Black Folks*. St. Louis: Institute of Black Studies, 1975.

Wolfram, Walter. *A Sociolinguistic Description of Detroit Negro Speech*. Washington, D. C.: Center for Applied Linguistics, 1969.

_____, and Clarke, Nona H., eds. *Black-White Speech Relationships*. Washington, D. C.: Center for Applied Linguistics, 1971.

Woodson, Carter. *Miseducation of the Negro*. Washington, D. C.: Associated Publishers, 1933.

_____. *The African Background Outlined*. New York: New American Library, 1936.

Wright, Richard. *Black Boy*. New York: Harper & Row, 1966.

_____. *Lawd Today*. New York: Walker and Company, 1963.

_____. The Literature of the Negro in the United States," in *White Man, Listen!* New York: Anchor Books, 1964.

_____. *The Long Dream*. Garden City, N.Y.: Doubleday, 1958.

_____. *Uncle Tom's Children*. New York: Harper & Row, 1965.

Achebe, Chinua, 95; *No Longer at Ease*, 46–47; *Things Fall Apart*, 99
Adjective, placing of, after noun, 15
Adverbial demonstratives, 30
"African," use of term, for black Americans, 36, 37
African Lodge No. 459, 36
African (Methodist) Episcopal Church, 11, 36
"Afro-American," "African-American," recent use of terms, 41–42
Ali, Muhammad, 100, 147
Allen, Richard, 11
Amazing Grace, 93
American Colonization Society, 37
American Weekly Mercury, 13
Angelou, Maya, *Just Give Me a Cool Drink of Water 'fore I Diiie*, 182–83
Art of Speaking, The, 187
As God is my secret judge, 57
ashy, 67–68
Association of Black Psychologists, 238, 239
Association for the Study of Afro-American Life and History, 201

baby, different meanings of word, 62–64

bad, 44; two levels of meaning of word, 59–60
bad mouth, 45
Baldwin, James, 185, 200
Baraka, Imamu (LeRoi Jones), 93, 178; *Blues People*, 51; *Dutchman*, 54, 229; "The Nation Is Like Ourselves," 141; on unity of black language and black identity, 175
Baratz, Joan and Steven, 208
be, used to indicate recurring event or habitual condition, 3, 19–20; absence of forms of, 5–6, 8, 9–10, 21; patterns using, 19–23; used to convey sense of future time, 20; appearance of forms of, when needed for meaning, 20–21; used with *done* to render future perfect, 25–26
Beatles, 55
been: used to express recently completed past action, 21–23; used to show emphasis, 23; used in combination with *done*, 23–24
Bernstein, Basil, *Class, Codes and Control*, 202–3
Bi-dialectalism, 31, 173, 207–9
Big Momma, 68
"Black," shift from "Negro" to, as term of racial identification, 35, 40–41, 42
Black Arts Movement, 177–85

Black consciousness movement, 2, 41
Black Panthers, 1, 83
Black power, 2, 40, 177
Black Semantic(s): defined, 42–43; derived from West African language background, 43–44; derived from condition of servitude and oppression, 47–49; music and "cool talk" as source of, 50–54; influence of traditional black church on, 55–58; interpretation of White English words, 59–64; terms referring to Afro-American physical characteristics, 64–69; terms referring to black-white interactional conflict, 64, 68–69; concepts, entry of, into American cultural mainstream, 69; dynamism of, 70; viewed as metaphorical and imagistic, 70–72; fluid social and generational boundaries of, 72
bogue, 45
Bohannan, Laura, 109
Boyer, Edward, 58–59
Brewer, J. Mason, 102, 112; American Negro Folklore, 101–2
Bridge (reading series), 224–228
Brooks, Gwendolyn, "We Real Cool," 55
Brother, 57
Brown, Claude, Manchild in the Promised Land, 1, 63, 173–74
Brown, Goold, Grammar of English Grammars, 188
Brown, Hubert "Rap," 60, 176; Die Nigger Die!, 82
Brown, James, 93, 96, 134, 139; "Please, Please, Please," 141
Brown, Sterling, 179

Brown, William Wells, Clotel, 146
Bruce, Roscoe Conklin, 39
Bullins, Ed, 179

Caesar (Massachusetts Negro), 8
California Mental Maturities Test, 237
Call-response, 103, 118; described, 104–8; relationship between traditional African world view and, 108–10; relationship of, to black music, 110–13; examples of, in black literature, 113–18; application of, to classroom teaching, 220–21
Calques, see Loan-translations
capping, 119–20
Carmichael, Stokely, 40, 120, 134
changes, 53
Charles, Ray, 140–41
Chesnutt, Charles Waddell, "The Goophered Grapevine," 156
Chicago Defender, 32
Church, traditional black: influence on Black Semantics of, 55–58; importance of, to oral tradition, 87–94; hierarchy of, 109–10
Churchill, Sir Winston, 178, 189
Civil rights movement, 2
Clay, Henry, 37
Cleveland, Rev. James, 93
Clovers, 111
co-sign, 70
cold, 70
Cole, Nat King, 65
Colonization efforts, 37
"Colored": resurfacing of term, 38; pull away from term, 39; used among masses, 40
Coltrane, John, 141–42

Communicative competence,
233–34; written, 230–32; oral,
232; in use and understanding
of audio-oral-visual channels,
233
Composition writing, instruction
in, 212–14
Conference on College Composition and Communication, 240
Cooke, Sam, 93
cooking, 53
cool, 52, 69; defined, 53
"Correctness, doctrine of," 186,
188, 191
Creole, 5, 8, 10, 13
Crisis, The, 39
Crocker, Frankie, 147
Cuffe, Paul, 37
Cullen, Countee, 177
Curriculum: restructuring of, to
include black and other ethnic
studies, 234–35; multicultural,
235–37

Dalby, David, 44
Davis, Angela, 59
Davis, Sammy, 60
De-creolization process, 11, 15, 16
Delaney, Martin, *Blake*, 40
Dialects, 191–93; variations in,
193–95
dig, 69; defined, 45
do, do-rag, 65–67
doin it to death, 53
"Dolemite" (Toast), 158
done: used by itself and combined
with other verbs, 23–25; used
with *be* to render future perfect,
25–26
Douglass, Frederick, 13, 38,
48–49, 214–15

Dozens, 82 and n, 88, 96, 103,
128–34, 182–83
DuBois, W. E. B., 39, 40, 48, 176;
on "double consciousness," 11;
Souls of Black Folk, 49, 170; on
"Red Summer" of 1919, 178
Dunbar, Paul Laurence, 220–21

eagle-flyin day, 72
-ed, absence of, in past tense or
past participle, 26
Education: compensatory, 202–3;
critical attacks on American,
215–16. *See also* Teachers
Educational Testing Service
(ETS), 240
Elder (griot), role of, in African
tribal culture, 76, 148
Elder, Lonne, *Ceremonies in Dark
Old Men*, 30
Ellison, Ralph: *The Invisible Man*,
114, 131, 163–65; "Mister
Toussan," 114–18
Exercises and drills, classroom,
210, 212

Fanon, Frantz, 77, 171, 175–76
fat mouth, 45
Federal Communications Com-
mission, 233
Fine, Benjamin, 239
Folk stories, narrative, 155–56
Folklore, Black American, 101–3
Forde, Daryll, 74
Forum magazine, 40
"Frankie and Albert" (Toast), 158
Franklin, Aretha, 54, 58, 95, 142;
Amazing Grace, 93; technique of
talk-singing used by, 134, 139,
140–41

Franklin, Rev. C. L., 58; "The Eagle Stirreth Her Nest," 151–55
Frazier, E. Franklin, 176
Free African Society, 36
Fries, Charles C., *American English Grammar*, 190
funky, 53

Garland, Phyl, *The Sound of Soul*, 51
Garrison, William Lloyd, 214, 215
Geechee speech, *see* Gullah Creole
gig, 53
Giovanni, Nikki, 1; "Ego Tripping," 159–60
gittin down, 72
gittin happy, 72
gittin high, 72
gittin ovuh, 72, 73
gittin the spirit, 57
Golf, use of black lingo in game of, 58–59
Gonzales, Ambrose, 172
Good Ship Jesus, 5
Goodman, Kenneth, 223
Grammar handbooks, English and American, 186–90
Grammatical structure, 18–19
Great Society, 2, 202
Green, Dean Robert, 238
Gullah Creole, 14–15, 172

haincty, 68
Hair: terms referring to blacks', 64; straightening, 64–65, 66; attitude of blacks toward kinky, 65–67
Haki Madhubuti (Don Lee), 93, 181, 190; "In a Period of Growth," 35; "Don't Cry, Scream," 141–42; "Poem to

Complement Other Poems," 142; on taking black poetry to the masses, 179; his poetic tribute to Malcolm X, 182; "But he was cool: or he even stopped for green lights," 184
Hammon, Jupiter, 13
Hampton, Lionel, 67
Hampton Institute, folklore collection of, 83
Harlem Renaissance movement, 177–79
Harris, Joel Chandler, 155
hat up, 70
Hathorne, Justice, 5
Hausa, 5, 7
hawk, 67
Hayes, Isaac, 139
Head Start, 202
Henry, Patrick, 6
Herskovits, Melville, *The Myth of the Negro Past*, 135–36, 137
High Potential, 202
Higher Horizons, 202
Himes, Chester, *Hot Day, Hot Night*, 122–24
hip, 70; defined, 45; versus *hep*, 69
Hodges, Frenchy, *Piece De Way Home*, 148–49
Holiday, Billie, 54–55
Holt, John, 215
Homophones, 223
hot, 53
Hot comb, 64–65, 66–67
Houts, Paul, 239
Hughes, Langston, 10, 169; on "grammar and goodness," 32–34; *Ask Your Mama*, 131; and Harlem Renaissance movement, 177, 179
Humphrey, Winona, 220–21
Hypercorrection, process of, 9, 28

Ibo, 5, 7, 14, 44, 95
Image-making, used in raps, 97
Indirection, used in raps, 98–100
Inflated vocabulary (High Talk, Fine Talk), 45–47
Integration, 39
Intonational contouring, in tonal semantics, 145
Iowa Basic Skills Test, 237

Jackson, Jesse, 3, 60, 97, 120, 174; speaking style of, 134, 143, 176
Jackson, Oliver, 108
Jackson Five, 54
jazz, 69; defined, 53
Jensen, Arthur, 1
jive, 69
joaning, 119–20
Johnson, Jack, 158
Jones, Absalom, 11
Jordan, Mrs. Josie, 156–57

Killens, John Oliver, 179
King, B. B., 139
King, Martin Luther, Jr., 2, 94, 120, 143, 235; speaking style of, 134, 135, 176
King, Woodie, "The Game," 85
kitchen, 65
Knight, Etheridge, *Poems From Prison*, 183
Kozol, Jonathan, 212
Krapp, George Philip, *English Language in America*, 172–73

Labov, William, 197, 212
Lady Sings the Blues, 54–55
Lambert, W. E., 197
lames, 70–72
Language: as dimension of black speech, 3, 16; exaggerated, used in raps, 94–95

Language attitudes: black-white, 169–77 *passim*; long-standing tradition of elitist, 185–91
Language programs, difference and deficit, 202–9
Lester, Julius, *Black Folk Tales*, 160–61
Levin, Henry, 202
Lincoln, Abraham, 37, 123
Lincoln, C. Eric, 91
Linguistic universals, 191–96
Liston, Sonny, 147
Literature, black, 177; examples of call-response in, 113–18. *See also* Poets, black
Lloyd, Donald, 185
Loan-translations (calques), Black English, 44–45
Locke, Alain, 177–78
Lord ham mercy, Lord a mercy, 57
L'Ouverture, Toussaint, 115–18, 156
Lowth, Bishop Robert, *Short Introduction to English Grammar*, 187–88
lugging (dropping lugs), 119–20

McKay, Claude, 177, 178; "If We Must Die," 178
McKenzie, Reverend, 135
McWorter, Gerald, 176
Mailer, Norman, 1, 69, 185
Major, Clarence, *Dictionary of Afro-American Slang*, 51
Malcolm X, 60, 96, 97–9⁰ 120, 135; *Autobiography*, 66–67; speaking style of, 143–45, 146–47, 176; Haki Madhubuti's poetic tribute to, 182
Man, The, 68
Mandingo, 14, 44, 45, 52, 53
Mayfield, Curtis, 56, 214

Mbiti, John S., 74
Mead, Margaret, 76
mean, 70; defined, 45
Mimicry, used in raps, 94–95
Miss Ann, 66; defined, 68
Monroe, James, 37
Moore, Rudy Ray, 158
motherfucker, negative and positive use of word, 60
Mother's Day, 72
Mulcaster, Richard, 186
Murray, Lindley, *English Grammar*, 188
Music: and "cool talk," as source of Black Semantics, 50–55; soul, 55, 93–94, 111; relationship of call-response to black, 110–13; importance of, as cultural dynamic in Black America, 181
Mutwa, Credo, *Indaba My Children*, 137

NAACP (National Association for the Advancement of Colored People), 1, 39
Napoleon, Reverend, 100
nappy, 64
Narrative sequencing, 103, 147–50; in preaching and testifying, 150–55; in folk stories, 155–56; in "tall" tales, 156–57; and Toasts, 157–61; in rendering of abstractions and responses to events in real world, 161–66
National Black Political Assembly, 175
National Education Association, 239
National Elementary Principal, The, 239
National Teacher's Examination, 239

Neal, Larry, 179–80
Negation patterns, 30–31
Negro: shift to "black" from, as term of racial identification, 35, 40–41, 42; use of term, by blacks, 38–39; argument for capitalization of, 39–40
New York Evening Post, 12
New York Times, 39–40, 44, 239
Niagara Movement, 38
"Nigger": as racial epithet, 36, 42; different meanings of word, 62
Nommo, concept of, 78, 79
North-Carolina Gazette, 13

okay, 44; defined, 45
Oral tradition, Afro-American, 73–74, 76–79. *See also* Raps
Orwell, George, 211

Packard, Vance, 185
Parker, Charlie, 54
Parks, Rosa, 2
Peabody Picture Vocabulary Test, 237
Pennsylvania Augustine Society, 38
perm, permanent, 65
Pharr, Robert, *Book of Numbers*, 47
Pidgin English, 5, 6, 7–8
Pig Latin, 50
"Pimp and Bulldaggers' Ball, The" (Toast), 158
pink toes, 68
players, 72
Plurals, Black English, 8–9, 28
Poets, black, contributions of, to eradication of negative black attitudes toward Black English, 177–85
Poitier, Sidney, 67
Pooley, Robert, 197

Possession, concept of, 28
Postman, Neal, 215
Powell, Adam Clayton, 63–64
Preaching and testifying, narrative sequencing in, 150–55
process, 65
Profanity, 60–62
Project 300 (350, 500, etc.), 202
Pronoun system, personal, 29
Pronunciation system, of Black versus White English, 16–18
Proverbs, used in raps, 95
Pryor, Richard, 87, 92, 135
Punning, used in raps, 95–96
"Push-pull" syndrome, 10–12, 13–14, 170

Racial labeling process, history of, 35–36, 37–42
Randolph, John, 37
raps: definitions of, 69; kinds of, 79–80; street corner, 80–82; boastful, to devastate enemies, 82–83; love, 83–85; church (sermons), 87–90, 93; exaggerated language used in, 94–95; mimicry used in, 94–95; proverbs used in, 95; punning used in, 95–96; spontaneity used in, 96; image-making used in, 96–97; braggadocio used in, 97; indirection used in, 97–99; tonal semantics used in, 99–100
Rawls, Lou, 93
Reading disabilities of black youth, remedies for, 222–28
Redmond, Eugene, 3
Reed, Ishmael, 179; 19 *Necromancers from Now*, 177
Repetition and alliterative wordplay, in tonal semantics, 142–45

Rhyme, in tonal semantics, 145–47
Robinson, Jackie, 65
Robinson, Smokey, 97, 139
Rodgers, Carolyn, 176
Ross, Diana, 55

-s, omission of, 8, 28, 30
Sacred and secular style of black language, 88–90, 93–94, 103
saddity, 68
Sanchez, Sonia, *We A BaddDDD People*, 181
Sapphire, 68
Saturday Review, 202
Sea Islands, Geechee community of, 14
selling woof tickets, 83
Sermons, *see under raps*
Servitude and oppression, Black Semantics derived from condition of, 47–49
"Shine and the Sinking of the Titanic" (Toast), 158, 183, 224–27
Shockley, William, 1
shout, 57
Sidran, Ben, *Black Talk*, 57
Signification, 82, 103; defined, 82n, 118–19; examples of, 119–22; characteristics of, 120, 121; examples illustrating extended use of, 122–28; Dozens as form of, 128–34
"Signifying Monkey, The" (Toast), 158
Silberman, Charles, 215
silks, 68
Simone, Nina, 3, 93
Sister, 57
skin, 45

Skin, terms referring to black,
    67–68
Slang, concept of, 43
Slave Trade Act (1808), 12
Slavery, 5, 12
Sledd, James, 210–11
Smith, Bessie, 54
Social change movements (1960s),
    2
"Social negotiation forms,"
    231–32
soul clap, 57
soul shake, 57–58
sounding, 119–20
Southern Workman, 83
Sowande, Fela, 74
Spinners, 140
Spirituals, Negro, 48–49, 73
Spontaneity, used in raps, 96
SRA (Science Research As-
    sociates), 224
"Stag-O-Lee" (Toast), 52, 158,
    160–61, 224
Stagger Lee, 52
Stanford Achievement Test, 237
Staple Singers, 93
Stone, Chuck, 240
Stone, Sly, 93
Story-telling tradition, see Narra-
    tive sequencing
Structure(s), language: fitting
    words and sounds of new lan-
    guage into native, 6–7; deep
    and surface, 193; shared deep,
    194
Style, as dimension of black
    speech, 3, 16
Subject(s): repetition of noun,
    with pronoun, 6, 8, 15, 28–29;
    same verb form for all, 26–28
Supreme Court, U. S., 2, 240
Supremes, 54

Talk-singing, in tonal semantics,
    137–42
Teachers: importance of, in
    educational processes, 216–17;
    need for change in attitude and
    behavior of, 217–19; recom-
    mendations for classroom pol-
    icy and practice of, 219–22; as
    agents of social change, 234,
    241
Tell the truth!, 57
Temptations, 97
Tense, same verb form serving
    present and past, 26
testifyin, 58
Testifying and preaching, narra-
    tive sequencing in, 150–55
Tests: standardized, 237–40; issue
    of, beyond educational institu-
    tions, 240–41
Thirteens, 182–83
Thompson, Robert Farris, 74,
    108–9
Tituba (Barbadian slave), 5, 8
Toasts, 88, 103, 147, 157–61, 183
Toby (Barbadian slave), 8–9
together, 70
Tonal semantics, 103, 134–37;
    used in raps, 100; talk-singing
    in, 137–42; repetition and al-
    literative word-play in, 142–45;
    intonational contouring in, 145;
    rhyme in, 145–47; application
    of, to classroom teaching,
    220–21
Trial of Atticus Before Justice Beau,
    for a Rape, 8
Tubman, Harriet, 48
Tucker, Beverly, The Partisan
    Leader, 13
Tucker, G. R., 197
Turner, Lorenzo, 14–15, 43

Turner, Nat, 48, 90
Twain, Mark, *Huckleberry Finn*, 36, 185

Underground Railroad, symbolic, 48
Undisputed Truth, 95
United States Government Printing Office, 40
Universe, African view of, 75–76
uptight, 69
Upward Bound, 202

Vassa, Gustavus, 36

War (musical group), 113
Ward, Clara, 56
Warwick, Dionne, 93
Washington, Dinah, 93
Wechsler Intelligence Test, 237
Well, all right!, 57
Welsing, Frances, 36
West African language background, Black Semantics derived from, 43–47
Wheatley, Phillis, 13

White, Barry, 139
White English, black speakers of, 12–14
Williams, Robert, 238
Wilson, Flip, 87, 135
Wolof, 14, 44, 45
Women: attitude of black men toward black, 84–85; verbal aggressiveness from, 85
Wonder, Stevie, 113
Woodson, Carter G., 203, 209, 216; *The Miseducation of the Negro*, 201
woofin, 83
World view, African, 74–76, 103; relationship between call-response and, 108–10
Wright, Richard, 102–3; *Black Boy*, 80–82; *The Long Dream*, 113–14; *Lawd Today*, 121–22, 126–28, 131; "Big Boy Leaves Home," 132–33, 146

Yoruba, 5, 7, 14, 44
Young, Al, *Snakes*, 83–84

Geneva Smitherman is Professor of Speech Communication and Senior Research Associate at the Center for Black Studies, Wayne State University. She received her Ph.D. from the University of Michigan.

The book was originally published by Houghton Mifflin Company. The typeface for this reprint, text and display, is Baskerville, based on the original design by John Baskerville in the eighteenth century. The text is printed on 55-lb. Glatfelter text paper. The book is bound in Riegel's Carolina cover CIS.

Manufactured in the United States of America.